Communications in Computer and Information Science 2897

Rationale

The CCIS series is devoted to the publication of proceedings of computer science conferences. Its aim is to efficiently disseminate original research results in informatics in printed and electronic form. While the focus is on publication of peer-reviewed full papers presenting mature work, inclusion of reviewed short papers reporting on work in progress is welcome, too. Besides globally relevant meetings with internationally representative program committees guaranteeing a strict peer-reviewing and paper selection process, conferences run by societies or of high regional or national relevance are also considered for publication.

Topics

The topical scope of CCIS spans the entire spectrum of informatics ranging from foundational topics in the theory of computing to information and communications science and technology and a broad variety of interdisciplinary application fields.

Information for Volume Editors and Authors

Publication in CCIS is free of charge. No royalties are paid, however, we offer registered conference participants temporary free access to the online version of the conference proceedings on SpringerLink (http://link.springer.com) by means of an http referrer from the conference website and/or a number of complimentary printed copies, as specified in the official acceptance email of the event.

CCIS proceedings can be published in time for distribution at conferences or as post-proceedings, and delivered in the form of printed books and/or electronically as USBs and/or e-content licenses for accessing proceedings at SpringerLink. Furthermore, CCIS proceedings are included in the CCIS electronic book series hosted in the SpringerLink digital library at http://link.springer.com/bookseries/7899. Conferences publishing in CCIS are allowed to use our online conference service (Meteor) for managing the whole proceedings lifecycle (from submission and reviewing to preparing for publication) free of charge.

Publication process

The language of publication is exclusively English. Authors publishing in CCIS have to sign the Springer CCIS copyright transfer form, however, they are free to use their material published in CCIS for substantially changed, more elaborate subsequent publications elsewhere. For the preparation of the camera-ready papers/files, authors have to strictly adhere to the Springer CCIS Authors' Instructions and are strongly encouraged to use the CCIS LaTeX style files or templates.

Abstracting/Indexing

CCIS is abstracted/indexed in DBLP, Google Scholar, EI-Compendex, Mathematical Reviews, SCImago, Scopus. CCIS volumes are also submitted for the inclusion in ISI Proceedings.

How to start

To start the evaluation of your proposal for inclusion in the CCIS series, please send an e-mail to ccis@springer.com

Wenjuan Li · Sokratis Katsikas · Jun Shao
Editors

Emerging Information Security and Applications

6th International conference, EISA 2025
Hangzhou, China, December 12–13, 2025
Proceedings

Editors
Wenjuan Li
The Education University of Hong Kong
Tai Po, Hong Kong

Jun Shao
Zhejiang Gongshang University
Hangzhou, China

Sokratis Katsikas
Norwegian University of Science
and Technology
Gjøvik, Norway

ISSN 1865-0929 ISSN 1865-0937 (electronic)
Communications in Computer and Information Science
ISBN 978-3-032-21176-7 ISBN 978-3-032-21177-4 (eBook)
https://doi.org/10.1007/978-3-032-21177-4

This Springer imprint is published by the registered company Springer Nature Switzerland AG
The registered company address is: Gewerbestrasse 11, 6330 Cham, Switzerland

Preface

The 6th International Conference on Emerging Information Security and Applications (EISA 2025) was held on 12–13 December, in Hangzhou, China.

With recent evolution of adversarial techniques, intrusions have become more complex and may threaten the security of various assets regarding information and applications. In addition, coordinated intrusions such as worm outbreaks continue to be a major threat to information, system and network security in the near future. The popularity of the Internet may generate a large volume of different types of sensitive information. Therefore, there is a need for emerging techniques, theories and applications to protect information and practical security. This event aims to provide a platform for researchers and practitioners across the world to exchange their ideas. It seeks original submissions that discuss practical or theoretical solutions to enhance the information and application security in practice.

This year, EISA 2025 received 38 submissions, and each submission was reviewed by at least three reviewers, using a single-blind review process. Finally, 10 regular papers were accepted, giving an acceptance rate of 26.3%. For the conference program, we had two keynote speakers, namely Wenliang Du (Zhejiang University, China), and Huazhong Liu (Hainan University, China).

For the success of EISA 2025, we would like to thank the authors of all submissions and all the PC members for their great efforts in selecting the papers. We would like to thank our General Chairs, Rongxing Lu, Javier Lopez, Abderrahim Benslimane, and Weizhi Meng; Publicity Chair: Yunguo Guan, Xueqing Liang, and Long Meng; Publication Chairs: Wei-Yang Chiu; and Local Chairs: Xu Wu and Chi Zhang. We also thank all the external reviewers for assisting the reviewing process.

December 2025

Wenjuan Li
Sokratis Katsikas
Jun Shao

Organization

Organization

General Co-Chairs

Rongxing Lu	Queen's University, Canada
Javier Lopez	University of Málaga, Spain
Abderrahim Benslimane	Avignon University, France
Weizhi Meng	Lancaster University, UK

Program Co-Chairs

Wenjuan Li	Education University of Hong Kong, China
Sokratis K. Katsikas	Norwegian University of Science and Technology, Norway
Jun Shao	Zhejiang Gongshang University, China

Publicitys Chairs

Yunguo Guan	Eastern Michigan University, USA
Xueqing Liang	Xidian University, China
Long Meng	University of Surrey, UK

Publication Chair

Wei-Yang Chiu	Technical University of Denmark, Denmark

Technical Program Committee

Raja Naeem Akram	University of Aberdeen, UK
Yousef Al Hammadi	UAE University, United Arab Emirates
Francesco Buccafurri	Università Mediterranea di Reggio Calabria, Italy
Chen-Mou Cheng	BTQ Technologies Corp, Canada

Keting Jia	Tsinghua University, China
Saru Kumari	Chaudhary Charan Singh University, India
Albert Levi	Sabanci University, Turkey
Wenjuan Li	Education University of Hong Kong, China
Xueqin Liang	Xidian University, China
Xiaozhen Lu	Nanjing University of Aeronautics and Astronautics, China
Jun Shao	Zhejiang Gongshang University, China
Chunhua Su	University of Aizu, Japan
Je Sen The	Universiti Sains Malaysia, Malaysia
Yangguang Tian	University of Surrey, UK
Yalan Wang	University of Surrey, UK
Zhipeng Wang	University of Manchester, UK
Qianhong Wu	Beihang University, China
Zhe Xia	Wuhan University of Technology, China
Haiyang Xue	Singapore Management University, China
Wun-She Yap	Universiti Tunku Abdul Rahman, Malaysia
Yue Zhang	Shandong University, China
Shoichi Hirose	University of Fukui, Japan
Yicheng Zhang	University of California, Riverside, USA
Mingjun Wang	Xidian University, China
Beibei Li	Sichuan University, China
Giovanni Livraga	University of Milan, Italy
Yunhe Feng	University of North Texas, USA
Xin Jin	Ohio State University, USA
Steven Furnell	University of Nottingham, UK
Lei Wu	Shandong Normal University, China
Mahmoud Nabil	North Carolina A&T University, USA
Alessandro Brighente	University of Padua, Italy

Additional Reviewers

Hao Gao
Sachin Kumar
Tianyi Zhang

Steering Committee

Jiageng Chen	Central China Normal University, China
Liqun Chen	University of Surrey, UK
Steven Furnell	University of Nottingham, UK
Sokratis K. Katsikas	Norwegian University of Science and Technology, Norway
Javier Lopez	University of Málaga, Spain
Weizhi Meng	Lancaster University, UK

Contents

Volume-Hiding Forward and Backward Private Dynamic Searchable Symmetric Encryption for Conjunctive Queries 1
Cong Zuo, Manyue Hu, Qing Fan, Shi-Feng Sun, Josef Pieprzyk, Huaxiong Wang, and Liehuang Zhu

Privacy-Preserving Fine-Grained Similarity Queries for Aging in Place System 25
Zhuliang Jia, Suprio Ray, Rongxing Lu, and Mohammad Mamun

VulFocus: Interpret AI Models in Software Vulnerability Detection 40
Yuejun Guo, Zeming Dong, and Qiang Tang

Diffusion-Based Intrusion Detection: A Unified Comparison of Augmentation, Feature Extraction, and Purification with Bayesian Optimization 59
Zenghui Wang

Flower Gone? Exploring Insider Attacks and the Effects on Federated Learning 75
Adam Copeland and Weizhi Meng

Privacy Paradox in Health Monitoring: Towards Future Privacy Predictive Model Development 97
Luyi Sun and Bian Yang

Decoding Privacy Threats in Mobile Applications: A Multi-layer Analysis of Encrypted Traffic and Server Interactions 119
Ahmed Mohamed Saad Emam Saad

Efficient Deduplication over Encrypted Data Under Flexible Access Control ... 142
Xiaofeng Jia and Songnian Zhang

A 2D-ELSCM-Based Chaotic Image Encryption Scheme for Incomplete Fingerprints 163
Haoyu Sun, Tianran Dong, and Xinyu Zhou

A Blockchain-Based Dynamic Game Incentive Mechanism for Privacy-Preserving Computation 177
Sicheng Pan, Jiayi Tang, Youqi Li, Cong Zuo, Licheng Wang, Yanli Yuan, and Liehuang Zhu

Author Index 197

Volume-Hiding Forward and Backward Private Dynamic Searchable Symmetric Encryption for Conjunctive Queries

Cong Zuo[1], Manyue Hu[1], Qing Fan[2(✉)], Shi-Feng Sun[3], Josef Pieprzyk[4,5], Huaxiong Wang[6], and Liehuang Zhu[1,7]

[1] Beijing Institute of Technology, Beijing 100081, China
[2] North China Electric Power University, Beijing 102206, China
qingfan@ncepu.edu.cn
[3] Shanghai Jiao Tong University, Shanghai 200240, China
[4] Institute of Computer Science, Polish Academy of Sciences, Warsaw, Poland
[5] Data61, CSIRO, Eveleigh, Australia
[6] Nanyang Technological University, Singapore 639798, Singapore
[7] Shandong Raone Intelligent Technology Co., Ltd., Jinan, China

Abstract. Searchable symmetric encryption for conjunctive queries allows for locating encrypted files that contain multiple keywords while safeguarding query privacy. The update capability of dynamic searchable symmetric encryption (DSSE) for conjunctive queries further enhances its applicability in real-world scenarios. Unfortunately, leakage-abuse attacks and volumetric-injection attacks (Zhang et al., USENIX Security 2023) demonstrate update information can be leveraged to compromise query privacy. Although many DSSE schemes are proposed to resist existing attacks, none support conjunctive queries with volume-hiding, forward and backward privacy. To address this, we first present a scalable bitmap index and refines security definitions to support conjunctive queries. Then we introduce two new schemes with volume-hiding, forward and backward private DSSE for conjunctive queries: VFBDSSE-CQ and SVFBDSSE-CQ. VFBDSSE-CQ offers fast updates for frequently changing data, while SVFBDSSE-CQ lowers client storage at the cost of slower updates, fitting large keyword datasets. Both schemes are proven to meet volume-hiding, forward and backward privacy. Finally, experimental results demonstrate that VFBDSSE-CQ achieves up to 200× faster performance on Enron Email and 600× faster on Chicago Crime, while SVFBDSSE-CQ achieves up to 200× and 3000× faster performance, compared to ODXT (Patranabis et al., NDSS 2021).

Keywords: Dynamic searchable symmetric encryption · Volume-hiding · Forward and backward privacy · Conjunctive queries

1 Introduction

Searchable Symmetric Encryption (SSE) [27] enables data owners to outsource encrypted datasets to third-party cloud servers while supporting keyword search

W. Li et al. (Eds.): EISA 2025, CCIS 2897, pp. 1–24, 2026.
https://doi.org/10.1007/978-3-032-21177-4_1

and preserving privacy, ensuring data confidentiality and **query privacy**. However, complex physical factors in cloud environments influence SSE query privacy, including client-server interactions, data storage mechanisms, and access structures. With the wide adoption of privacy standards like the International Standard for Information Security (ISO/IEC 27001) and the General Data Protection Regulation (GDPR), strong security guarantees for query privacy are increasingly crucial in the SSE design.

In the context of practical SSE applications, conjunctive multi-keyword search has garnered significant attention. **conjunctive SSE** schemes address multi-keyword search challenges by using specialized data structures with cross-tags that span multiple keywords, reducing redundant file scans and information leakage [6] compared to repeatedly performing single-keyword searches and computing intersections. However, most existing conjunctive SSE schemes are static [6,21], lacking flexibility for dynamic file additions or deletions—a significant limitation in real-world scenarios where user data evolves continuously.

To address data updates, dynamic SSE (DSSE) introduces deletion arrays and free lists for file updates [19,22], but information leakage during updates can compromise query privacy [5,32] through leakage-abuse attacks. Forward and backward privacy [2,23] counter these risks: forward privacy prevents servers from determining if new files match previous queries, while backward privacy ensures servers cannot learn about files that were added then deleted. Three levels of backward privacy exist, from Type-I (strongest) to Type-III (weakest), but existing security definitions mainly apply to single-keyword queries. Although some **conjunctive DSSE** schemes provide **forward and backward privacy** [25,30], they either adopt single-keyword security definitions or provide structure-specific definitions. We introduce Type-C backward privacy for conjunctive DSSE, more accurately capturing information leakage from deletion.

Evolving attacks exploit result size leakage (volume patterns) to compromise query privacy—using response file counts, word frequencies, and leakage-abuse/reconstruction to recover keywords or keys. These attacks apply widely to query forms [20], often relying on prior knowledge or assumptions like uniform query distribution. Volume pattern leakage boosts attack recovery rates vs. search-pattern-only attacks [24]; volumetric-injection attacks reach up to 80% [31] query recovery in worst cases.

If we denote the properties of supporting **c**onjunctive keyword queries, **d**ynamic updates, and **v**olume-hiding as 'C', 'D', and 'V', respectively. Then there exist 'C+V' SSE schemes [17,37], 'D+V' SSE schemes [22,29], and 'C+D' schemes [16,34]. However, a comprehensive 'C+D+V' SSE scheme remains unexplored. This leads to a natural and important question:

*Could we design a **dynamic** searchable symmetric encryption scheme that supports **conjunctive queries** with **volume-hiding**, while also achieving forward and backward privacy?*

We provide a positive answer to the above question in this paper. To construct a volume-hiding dynamic searchable symmetric encryption scheme for conjunctive queries with forward and backward privacy: First, we set the number of

Table 1. Comparison of Results

Scheme	FP	BP	QT	VH	Client	Computation		Query-result Size
					Storage	**Search**	**Update**	(Communication)
FB-DSSE [36]	✓	Type-I$^-$	S	×	$O(\|\mathbf{W}\|)$	$O(u_w)$	$O(1)$	$O(\ell)$
$\mathtt{SD}_a$ [11]	✓	Type-II	S	×	$O(1)$	$O(u_w + \log N)$	$O(\log N)$ am.	$O(\|\mathtt{DB}(w)\|)\|f\|$
$\mathbf{2ch_{FB}}$ [1]	✓	Type-II	S	✓	$O(\|\mathbf{W}\|)$	$O(m \log\log N)$	$O(m)$	$O(m \log\log N)\|f\|$
$\mathbf{2ch^{s}_{FB}}$ [1]	✓	Type-II	S	✓	$\omega(\log N)$	$O(m \log\log N)$	$O(m \log N)$	$O(m \log\log N)\|f\|$
VH-DSSE [33]	✓	Type-I	S	✓	$O(1)$	$O(m + \log L)$	$O(\log L)$ am.	$O(\log L)\|f\|$
$\mathtt{VH\text{-}DSSE}^k$ [33]	✓	Type-I	S	✓	$O(1)$	$\lambda' O(m + \log L)$	$\lambda' O(\log L)$ am.	$\lambda' O(\log L)\|f\|$
VBTree [30]	✓	×	C	×	$O(\|\mathbf{W}\|)$	$O(x \log \ell)$	$O(\log \ell)$	$O(\|\mathtt{DB}(q)\|)\|f\|$
ODXT [25]	✓[a]	Type-II[b]	C	×	$O(\|\mathbf{W}\|)$	$O(x(\|q\|-1))$	$O(1)$	$O(\|\mathtt{DB}(q)\|)\|f\|$
VFBDSSE-CQ	✓	Type-C	C	✓	$O(\|\mathbf{W}\|)$	$O(\|q\|u_w)$	$O(1)$	$O(a\ell)$
SVFBDSSE-CQ	✓	Type-C	C	✓	$O(1)$	$O(\|q\|(u_w + \log N))$	$O(\log N)$ am.	$O(a\ell)$

FP (forward privacy), BP (backward privacy), QT (query type), VH (volume-hiding), S (single keyword queries), C (conjunctive queries). $|\mathbf{W}|$ denotes the number of distinct keywords. $|q|$ stands for the number of keywords in a conjunctive query q. $|\mathtt{DB}(w)|$ and $|\mathtt{DB}(q)|$ are the number of matching files for w (single) and q (conjunctive), respectively. $x = \min_{w \in q} |\mathtt{DB}(w)|$ denotes the minimum number of matching files among all keywords in q. $|f|$ is the bit length of file index f. ℓ is the maximum number of files, and a is the number of bits per file. $m = \max_{w \in \mathbf{W}} |\mathtt{DB}(w)|$ is the maximum volume, and N is the number of keyword/file pairs. ℓ_0 is the size of the initial database and u is the total number of update operations. $L = \ell_0 + u$ for brevity. u_w is the number of updates for keyword w. λ is the security parameter, and λ' denotes $\omega(\log \lambda)$. *am.* stands for amortized efficiency. [a] ODXT does not guarantee FP for particular forms of conjunctive queries. [b] Type-I, Type-II and Type-III are unsuitable for C, and we define Type-C for C. Nevertheless, the leakages of each keyword in our Type-C is similar to Type-I$^-$.

bits used to represent a file as the maximum admissible number of keywords for conjunctive queries. Second, we utilize modular homomorphic encryption to encrypt values, enabling dynamic updates and multi-keyword queries. Third, deletion and addition operations are performed directly on ciphertexts, effectively disconnecting the relationship between the update front and back.

Our Contributions. We propose the first volume-hiding forward and backward private DSSE for conjunctive queries (VFBDSSE-CQ) based on the scalable bitmap index, supporting efficient file addition/deletion. However, its client storage scales linearly with keyword count. To reduce this, we present a variant (SVFBDSSE-CQ) that achieves small client storage at the cost of update time. Table 1 compares our schemes with other related works. Our main contributions in this work are as follows:

- We present a scalable bitmap index structure that maps file identifiers to binary strings, inherently defining the acceptable maximum number of keywords for conjunctive queries. This design naturally supports volume-hiding and conjunctive keyword searches. Furthermore, the proposed bitmap index structure extends seamlessly to disjunctive keyword queries.

- We modify the existing security notions to handle both conjunctive queries $q = (w_1, \cdots, w_d)$ and single keyword queries ($d = 1$). Particularly, we initiate the study of volume-hiding DSSE for conjunctive queries and first propose two novel volume-hiding DSSE schemes that support conjunctive queries. Formal security analysis guarantees volume-hiding, forward and backward privacy of our schemes.
- We implement our proposed schemes (`VFBDSSE-CQ`, `SVFBDSSE-CQ`) and baselines (i.e., `ODXT` and `VBTree`) on Enron Email and Chicago Crime datasets. Comprehensive evaluation confirms our schemes' efficiency and competitive communication cost. Specifically, `VFBDSSE-CQ` is 200× (Enron) and 600× (Chicago) faster in search than `ODXT` [25], while `SVFBDSSE-CQ` achieves 200× and 3000× speedups respectively.

2 Related Work

Song et al. [27] have initiated research in searchable symmetric encryption. However, search time in their SSE scheme is linear with the total number of file/keyword pairs. To improve the search efficiency, Curtmola et al. [9] have given a new SSE with sublinear search time by deploying an inverted index data structure. Many SSE schemes with different designs have been proposed [6,9,14,19,26,35].

Early SSE schemes do not allow encrypted data to be updated. To support updates, researchers [19] introduced dynamic SSE (DSSE). Unfortunately, these schemes leak information during updates that can be exploited by adversaries [5,32], highlighting the need for forward and backward privacy. Bost [3] formally defined forward privacy, while Bost et al. [4] proposed three backward privacy definitions (Type-I, Type-II, and Type-III) with corresponding schemes: `MONETA` achieving Type-I using ORAM [15], and `FIDES` achieving Type-II. Subsequently, Sun et al. [28] improved efficiency with `Janas++` (Type-III), and Zuo et al. [36] introduced `FB-DSSE` achieving stronger Type-I$^-$ backward privacy. These schemes, however, support only single keyword queries.

To enable richer query functionalities, researchers extended DSSE to support range and conjunctive queries. For range queries, Zuo et al. [35] constructed forward/backward private schemes and Zuo et al. [38] built `FBDSSE-RQ` reducing communication rounds. For conjunctive queries, Wu et al. [30] developed forward private schemes based on the `OXT` [6] framework, while Patranabis et al. [25] proposed `ODXT` achieving both forward and backward privacy. However, it does not protect forward privacy against some forms of conjunctive queries.

Despite these advances, recent attacks have demonstrated vulnerabilities through volume pattern analysis. While volume-hiding techniques [18] address leakage via padding, significant challenges remain in dynamic settings with fine-grained updates. Another critical consideration is client storage efficiency. Although some schemes [4,7] achieve optimal client storage using ORAM, they are impractical for large databases. To balance efficiency and storage, Demertzis et al. [11] have designed an efficient DSSE that requires a small client storage (named $\mathtt{SD}_a$). However, it supports only single keyword queries.

3 Preliminaries

In this section, we present a scalable bitmap index, which is the main data structure used in our work. To securely operate the bitmaps, we introduce a simple symmetric encryption with homomorphic addition.

3.1 Symmetric Encryption with Homomorphic Addition

To efficiently and securely operate on bit strings, we need a simple symmetric encryption with homomorphic addition (see also [36,38]). Recall (Sect. 2.1 of [38]) that the encryption is defined by the following algorithms $\Pi = (\mathtt{Enc}, \mathtt{Dec}, \mathtt{Add})$, where

- $c \leftarrow \mathtt{Enc}(sk, m, n)$: For an input that consists of a message m $(0 \leq m < n)$, a random secret key sk $(0 \leq sk < n)$ and an integer n, it outputs a ciphertext $c = sk + m \bmod n$, where the secret key sk can be used only once and must be kept for decryption.
- $m \leftarrow \mathtt{Dec}(sk, c, n)$: For an input: a secret key sk, a ciphertext c and an integer n, it computes a message $m = c - sk \bmod n$.
- $\hat{c} \leftarrow \mathtt{Add}(c_0, c_1, n)$: For an input: two ciphertexts $(c_0,\ c_1)$ and an integer n, it generates $\hat{c} = c_0 + c_1 \bmod n$, where $c_0 \leftarrow \mathtt{Enc}(sk_0, m_0, n)$, $c_1 \leftarrow \mathtt{Enc}(sk_1, m_1, n)$ and $0 \leq sk_0, sk_1 < n$.

Homomorphic Addition. We claim that Π supports homomorphic addition, because anyone can compute $\hat{c} = c_0 + c_1 \bmod n$ with knowledge of the two ciphertexts $c_0 = m_0 + sk_0 \bmod n$ and $c_1 = m_1 + sk_1 \bmod n$. However, to decrypt $\hat{c}$, one needs to know $\hat{sk} = sk_0 + sk_1 \bmod n$. Its correctness can be checked as

$$\mathtt{Dec}(\hat{sk}, \hat{c}, n) = \hat{c} - \hat{sk} \bmod n = m_0 + m_1 \bmod n,$$

where $\hat{sk} = sk_0 + sk_1 \bmod n$.

Π is perfectly secure when secret keys are used only once. This holds because Π selects a new uniformly random secret key for each message, analogously to the one-time pad (OTP). The formal definition follows.

Perfect Security. We define that Π is perfectly secure if for any adversary $\mathcal{A}$, its advantage

$$\mathbf{Adv}^{\mathtt{ps}}_{\Pi,\mathcal{A}}(\lambda) = |\Pr[\mathcal{A}(\mathtt{Enc}(sk, m_0, n)) = 1] - \Pr[\mathcal{A}(\mathtt{Enc}(sk, m_1, n)) = 1]|$$

is negligible, where n is an integer, the key sk $(0 \leq sk < n)$ is kept secret and $\mathcal{A}$ chooses m_0, m_1 st. $0 \leq m_0, m_1 < n$.

3.2 Dynamic Searchable Symmetric Encryption

DSSE consists of a **Setup** algorithm and two interactive protocols executed between a client and a server (**Search** and **Update**). More formally,

- $(\texttt{EDB}, \sigma) \leftarrow$ **Setup**$(1^\lambda, \texttt{DB})$: On input a security parameter λ and DB, it returns a state σ and an encrypted database EDB. The state σ is secret and kept by the client and EDB is public and stored by the server.
- $(\mathcal{I}, \perp) \leftarrow$ **Search**$(q, \sigma; \texttt{EDB})$: On input a state σ and a query q, the client produces a search token and sends it to the server. The server retrieves EDB using the search token. Finally, it returns nothing and the client outputs matching file identifiers $\mathcal{I}$.
- $(\sigma', \texttt{EDB}') \leftarrow$ **Update**$(\sigma, op, in; \texttt{EDB})$: On input an operation $op \in \{add, del\}$, a state σ and a list of file-identifier/keyword-set pairs $in = (f, \mathbf{w})$, the client generates an update token and sends it to the server. Next, the server updates EDB with the update token. Finally, the server outputs an updated encrypted database EDB′ and the client gets an updated state σ'.

Remark. In SSE literature, servers typically adopt two approaches to handle query results: (1) output encrypted file IDs for client decryption (e.g., [6]); (2) return plaintext file IDs directly (e.g., [3]). Volume-hiding DSSE schemes [1,33] require the first approach, and our volume-hiding work also adopts this (server outputs encrypted file IDs to clients).

4 Formal Security Definitions

The section describes DSSE and its security model. In particular, we take the DSSE definition and its security model from Sects. 3 and 4.1 of [38]. We define $\texttt{DB} = (f_i, \mathbf{W}_i)_{i=0}^{y-1}$, where f_i is a file identifier, $\mathbf{W}_i$ is a set of keywords, and y is the number of all files in DB $(0 < y \leq \ell)$. $\mathbf{W} = \cup_{i=0}^{y-1} \mathbf{W}_i$ denotes all distinct keywords in DB, and its number is denoted by $|\mathbf{W}|$. DB(q) stands for files matching conjunctive query q. For DB, we first parse it into a scalable bitmap index. Conjunctive and update queries are denoted by $q = (w_1, \cdots, w_d)$ and $u = (op, (w, bs))$, respectively. Following prior works [1,6,33], we focus on index update/search—both involve manipulating bit strings representing f_i.

4.1 Security Model

To evaluate the security of DSSE, we give two worlds called REAL and IDEAL. The REAL world represents an original DSSE scheme and the IDEAL world is simulated by a simulator $\mathcal{S}$ with leakages of the original scheme. The leakages are formally defined by a function $\mathcal{L} = (\mathcal{L}^{Setup}, \mathcal{L}^{Search}, \mathcal{L}^{Update})$, which identifies the leakages due to execution of **Setup**, **Search**, and **Update**. Roughly speaking, if the advantage of $\mathcal{A}$ in distinguishing REAL from IDEAL is negligible, we can conclude that there is no extra leak apart from the leaks defined by $\mathcal{L}$.

Assume $\mathcal{A}$ interacts with a single world that can be either REAL or IDEAL. The goal of $\mathcal{A}$ is to guess the world. If its guess is REAL, $\mathcal{A}$ returns 0. Otherwise, it outputs 1. Formally, our security game is defined as follows:

- $\texttt{REAL}_{\mathcal{A}}(\lambda)$: $\mathcal{A}$ selects a database DB. For an input (a security parameter λ and a database DB), it returns an encrypted database EDB to $\mathcal{A}$ by running the **Setup**(λ, DB). $\mathcal{A}$ can interact with this real world by issuing queries (either search queries q or update queries (op, in)). Finally, $\mathcal{A}$ returns a bit z, where $z \in \{0, 1\}$.
- $\texttt{IDEAL}_{\mathcal{A},\mathcal{S}}(\lambda)$: The encrypted database EDB is simulated by a simulator $\mathcal{S}$ with setup leakage $\mathcal{L}^{Setup}(\lambda, \texttt{DB}))$. While handling queries (either search queries q or update queries (op, in)) issued by $\mathcal{A}$, the simulator $\mathcal{S}$ uses an appropriate leakage function, i.e. $\mathcal{L}^{Search}(q)$ for search queries or $\mathcal{L}^{Update}(op, in))$ for update queries. Finally, $\mathcal{A}$ returns a bit z, where $z \in \{0, 1\}$.

Definition 1. *We say that a DSSE scheme is $\mathcal{L}$-adaptively-secure if for every probabilistic polynomial time (PPT) adversary $\mathcal{A}$, there exists an efficient simulator $\mathcal{S}$ (with the input $\mathcal{L}$) such that,*

$$|\Pr[\mathit{REAL}_{\mathcal{A}}(\lambda) = 1] - \Pr[\mathit{IDEAL}_{\mathcal{A},\mathcal{S}}(\lambda) = 1]| \leq negl(\lambda).$$

4.2 Volume-Hiding

According to [18], for volume-hiding schemes, it is required that the size of the search result (i.e., volume pattern) should be the same for each query[1]. The volume of each query is hidden since they share the same volume pattern. In particular, we define the result length (rl) (i.e., volume pattern). Formally,

$$\texttt{rl}(q) = \{\{|bs|\}_{w \in q}\}_{q \in Q},$$

where Q is a collection of conjunctive queries, $|bs|$ is the length of the bit string bs, which is the same for all queries.

4.3 Forward Privacy

In practice, all interactions between a client and a server may be observed by an adversary $\mathcal{A}$. Forward privacy requires that the server (or the adversary $\mathcal{A}$) cannot match a new update operation with previously issued searches. Formally,

Definition 2. *(see [3]) An $\mathcal{L}$-adaptively-secure DSSE scheme is forward private if an update leakage function $\mathcal{L}^{Update}$ can be written as*

$$\mathcal{L}^{Update}(op, in) = \mathcal{L}'(op, \{(f_i, \mu_i)\}),$$

where f_i is the file identifier, μ_i is the number of modified keywords in file f_i and $\mathcal{L}'$ is stateless.

Note that, for our conjunctive queries, the leakage function is slightly modified and looks as follows:

$$\mathcal{L}^{Update}(op, w, bs) = \mathcal{L}'(op, bs),$$

where $\mathcal{L}'$ is stateless.

[1] In [1,33], the authors gave more general volume-hiding definitions, which include this basic requirement.

4.4 Backward Privacy

Informally, backward privacy ensures a server/adversary $\mathcal{A}$) cannot learn which files were added then deleted[2]. Previous backward privacy definitions only support single-keyword queries, making them unsuitable for conjunctive queries. We now introduce a new backward privacy definition, specifically designated Type-C, that supports our conjunctive queries.

- Type-C: Given two identical and consecutive conjunctive queries q, then it leaks file identifiers that currently match a query q, total number of updates for each keyword w and corresponding update times, where $w \in q$.

In the SSE literature, the authors have identified two types of leakage pattern (one for a search and the other for a result). A search pattern (sp) exposes a repetition of keywords in queries. A pattern of results (rp) reveals a final result for a search query. They are formally defined as follows:

$$\mathtt{sp}(q) = \{t : \{t, w\}_{w \in q}\}_{q \in Q}, \mathtt{rp}(q) = \{bs\}_{q \in Q},$$

where t is a timestamp, Q is the conjunctive queries, bs is the final result[3].

To formalize Type-C backward privacy, we introduce a new leakage function $\mathtt{Time}(q)$. For a conjunctive query q, it shows the update times t for each $w \in q$, specifically including $\mathtt{Time}(w)$ (update time of each keyword w). Formally,

$$\mathtt{Time}(q) = \{t : \{t, op, (w, bs)\}_{w \in q}\}_{q \in Q}.$$

Definition 3. *An $\mathcal{L}$-adaptively-secure DSSE scheme is Type-C backward private if the leakage functions $\mathcal{L}^{Search}$ and $\mathcal{L}^{Update}$ take the following forms:*

$$\mathcal{L}^{Update}(op, w, bs) = \mathcal{L}'(op, bs), \mathcal{L}^{Search}(q) = \mathcal{L}''(\mathtt{sp}(q), \mathtt{rp}(q), \mathtt{Time}(q)),$$

where $\mathcal{L}'$ and $\mathcal{L}''$ are stateless.

5 Scalable Bitmap Index Structure

The bitmap index (from ref. [36]) uses a bit string for each keyword: 1 denotes existence, 0 denotes negation. Though it enables forward/backward private DSSE (FB-DSSE), it only supports single-keyword queries. This section formalizes the bitmap index and extends it to handle conjunctive and disjunctive queries, yielding the scalable bitmap index.

[2] Note that the files are added and deleted during two same conjunctive queries q.
[3] Note that the $\mathtt{rp}(q)$ includes the $\mathtt{rl}(q)$.

5.1 Syntax of Scalable Bitmap Index Structure

The **scalable bitmap index** is an abstract index structure comprising four items of `make-index`, `add`, `delete`, and `query`.

- $I(l,d) \leftarrow$ `make-index`(λ): Upon the parameter λ, return an empty *key-value* bitmap index $I(l,d)$, where l is the number of files in a dataset and d is the maximum number of keywords in a conjunctive/disjunctive query. The bit length of *value* is $l \cdot \log d$.
- $I'(l,d) \leftarrow$ `add`$((key, \hat{value}); I(l,d))$: Insert a pair $(key, \hat{value})$ into the index $I(l,d)$, output the index structure $I'(l,d)$.
- $(I'(l,d)) \leftarrow$ `delete`$((key, \hat{value}); I(l,d))$: To delete a pair $(key, \hat{value})$ from the index $I(l,d)$, compute the complement of $\hat{value}$ denoted $\bar{value}$. Then perform `add`$((key, \bar{value}); I(l,d))$ and get the final $I'(l,d)$.
- *value* $\leftarrow$`query`$(\{key_1, \cdots, key_d\}, op \in \{\mathcal{C}, \mathcal{D}\})$: Query and return files including conjunctive (i.e. $op = \mathcal{C}$) or disjunctive (i.e. $op = \mathcal{D}$) keywords $\{key_1, \cdots, key_d\}$. For each $value_j$ corresponding key_j $(j = 1, \cdots, d)$, compute a $l \cdot \log d$-length bit string $value{=}(value_1 + \cdots, +value_d) \mod 2^{l \cdot \log d}$. If $op = \mathcal{C}$, for each $i \in \{0, \cdots, l-1\}$, check $\log d \cdot i$-th to $\log d \cdot (i+1) - 1$-th bits of *value*, if it is $\overbrace{11 \cdots 11}^{\log d}$, it means file i includes $key_1 \wedge \cdots \wedge key_d$; if it is not $\overbrace{00 \cdots 00}^{\log d}$, it means file i includes $key_1 \vee \cdots \vee key_d$.

5.2 An Instance of Scalable Bitmap Index

In `FB-DSSE`, file addition and deletion both involve modular operations on file identifiers. A better solution is a scalable bitmap index, which uses multiple bits to indicate file existence. To support conjunctive queries, `FB-DSSE` can process a conjunctive query as a sequence of single-keyword queries. However, this naïve approach has high communication overhead and leaks more information.

Suppose that the maximum number of keywords in a conjunctive query is d, then the communication overhead of the naïve solution is $O(\ell d)$ and the communication overhead of our new solution (scalable bitmap index) will be reduced to $O(\ell \log d)$, where ℓ is the maximum number of files in a database.

Specifically, assume that a dataset contains the maximum of ℓ files. Each file is assigned a bit string of length a. When bit strings assigned to all files are concatenated, we get a bit string bs of length $a\ell$ (multiplication of a and ℓ), which is initiated with all 0. Note that if $a = 1$, then the scalable bitmap index becomes the bitmap index from [36]. The maximum number of keywords b for conjunctive queries is $2^a - 1$. The ia-th bit of bs is set to 1, if the dataset contains file f_i. Figure 1 illustrates setup, addition, deletion and conjunctive query processing for a dataset with $\ell = 5$ and $a = 2$. In particular, Fig. 1(a) depicts a scalable bitmap index for five files, where only two files f_1 and f_3 exist. Figure 1(b) shows that file f_4 has been added to the dataset (the bit string 0100000000 is added to the original bit string 0001000100). Deletion can

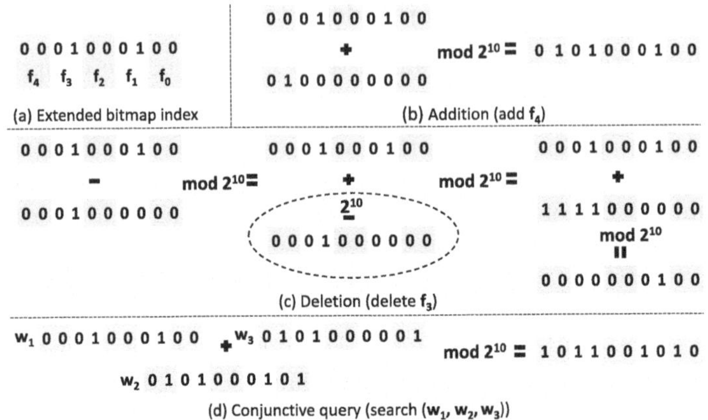

Fig. 1. Illustration of operations for scalable bitmap index

also be achieved by modular addition (see Fig. 1(c)), where f_3 is deleted from the dataset[4]. Deletion corresponds to modular subtraction of 0001000000 from 0001000100 (or alternatively modular addition of 0001000100 and 1111000000($=-0001000000 \bmod 2^{10}$)), which is similar to [36].

For each keyword, we assign a scalable bitmap index, which specifies files that contain the keyword. Consider a conjunctive query for keywords w_1, w_2, w_3 as shown in Fig. 1(d), a server first retrieves the scalable bitmap indices for keywords w_1, w_2, w_3 and adds them together. The result is sent to a client. If $2i$-th to $(2(i+1)-1)$-th bits of the result are equal to 11, then file f_i contains keywords w_1, w_2, w_3, where $i \in \{0, 1, \cdots, 4\}$. Note that, the scalable bitmap index also can support the disjunctive queries. In particular, if $2i$-th to $(2(i+1)-1)$-th bits of the result are different from 00, then the file f_i contains at least one keyword of the disjunctive query $(w_1 \vee w_2 \vee w_3)$.

6 Volume-Hiding Forward and Backward DSSE for Conjunctive Queries

In this section, we design two volume-hiding forward and backward DSSE schemes for conjunctive queries named `VFBDSSE-CQ`.

6.1 VFBDSSE-CQ

Algorithm 1 presents the scheme. To achieve all the properties (volume-hiding, forward and backward privacy, and conjunctive queries), `VFBDSSE-CQ` deploys the encryption $\Pi = (\texttt{Enc}, \texttt{Dec}, \texttt{Add})$, the scalable bitmap index and the framework of `FB-DSSE` [36]. From a bird's-eye view, the scheme works as follows: The setup

[4] The file f_3 should exist in the database.

algorithm determines the maximum number of files it can support (i.e., ℓ), and the number of bits used to denote each file (i.e., a). To add a keyword/file pair, the client initializes a zero bit string and sets the corresponding bit to 1 (the LSB of the bits used to denote the file). Then the client encrypts the bit string and sends it to the server. Deletion works similarly via modular subtraction transformed into addition (see Sect. 5.2). For a conjunctive query q, the client generates single keyword queries for each keyword (similar to FB-DSSE [36]). Then the server sums all results and returns the total to the client, who decrypts the bit-string and checks if the bits for each file equal the number of query keywords (e.g., for a 3-keyword query, matching files should show binary 11). The details are described below:

Algorithm 1. VFBDSSE-CQ

Setup(1^λ)

Client:

$K \xleftarrow{\$} \{0,1\}^\lambda$, $n \leftarrow$ integer
CT, **M** $\leftarrow$ empty map
return (EDB $=$ **M**, $\sigma = (n, K, \mathbf{CT})$)

Update$(w, bs, \sigma;$ EDB$)$

Client:

$K_w || K'_w \leftarrow F_K(w)$, $(ST_c, c) \leftarrow \mathbf{CT}[w]$
if $(ST_c, c) = \perp$ **then**
    $c \leftarrow -1$, $ST_c \leftarrow \{0,1\}^\lambda$
end if
$ST_{c+1} \leftarrow \{0,1\}^\lambda$, $\mathbf{CT}[w] \leftarrow (ST_{c+1}, c+1)$
$UT_{c+1} \leftarrow H_1(K_w, ST_{c+1})$, $C_{ST_c} \leftarrow H_2(K_w, ST_{c+1}) \oplus ST_c$
$sk_{c+1} \leftarrow H_3(K'_w, c+1)$, $e_{c+1} \leftarrow$ Enc(sk_{c+1}, bs, n)
Send $(UT_{c+1}, (e_{c+1}, C_{ST_c}))$ to the server.

Server:

Upon receiving $(UT_{c+1}, (e_{c+1}, C_{ST_c}))$
Set $\mathbf{M}[UT_{c+1}] \leftarrow (e_{c+1}, C_{ST_c})$

Search$(q, \sigma;$ EDB$)$

Client:

for $w \in q$ **do**
    $K_w || K'_w \leftarrow F_K(w)$, $(ST_c, c) \leftarrow \mathbf{CT}[w]$
    if $(ST_c, c) = \perp$ **then**
        return $\perp$
    end if
end for
Send $\{(K_w, ST_c, c)\}_{w \in q}$ to the server.

Server:

$Sum \leftarrow 0$
for each (K_w, ST_c, c) **do**
    $Sum_e \leftarrow 0$
    for $i = c$ to 0 **do**
        $UT_i \leftarrow H_1(K_w, ST_i)$, $(e_i, C_{ST_{i-1}}) \leftarrow \mathbf{M}[UT_i]$
        $Sum_e \leftarrow$ Add(Sum_e, e_i, n), Remove $\mathbf{M}[UT_i]$
        if $C_{ST_{i-1}} = \perp$ **then**
            Break
        end if
        $ST_{i-1} \leftarrow H_2(K_w, ST_i) \oplus C_{ST_{i-1}}$
    end for
    $\mathbf{M}[UT_c] \leftarrow (Sum_e, \perp)$, $Sum \leftarrow$ Add(Sum, Sum_e, n)
end for
Send Sum to the client.

Client:

$Sum_{sk} \leftarrow 0$
for $w \in q$ **do**
    for $i = c$ to 0 **do**
        $sk_i \leftarrow H_3(K'_w, i)$, $Sum_{sk} \leftarrow Sum_{sk} + sk_i \bmod n$
    end for
end for
$bs \leftarrow$ Dec(Sum_{sk}, Sum, n)
return bs

- (EDB, $\sigma = (n, K, \mathbf{CT})) \leftarrow$ **Setup**(1^λ): For an input of a security parameter λ, the client outputs a random secret key K for a Pseudorandom Function (PRF) F and an integer n, where $n = 2^{a\ell}$, a is the number of bits used to denote a file[5] and ℓ denotes the maximum number of files. Furthermore, he/she initializes two maps **CT** and **M**. The map **CT** is used to store the

[5] This means that the scheme can support the maximum of $b = 2^a - 1$ conjunctive keywords, see Sect. 5.2 for details.

newest search token and the corresponding number of updates c for every keyword w in the database. The map $\mathbf{M}$ holds the encrypted database EDB. Eventually, the client returns the state $\sigma = (n, K, \mathbf{CT})$ and the encrypted database EDB. Note that the client needs to keep $(K, \mathbf{CT})$ private.

- $(\sigma', \mathtt{EDB}') \leftarrow$ **Update**$(w, bs, \sigma; \mathtt{EDB})$: For an input (a keyword w, a bit string bs[6] and a state σ), the client first generates the secret key K_w and K'_w corresponding to w using the master key K. Here, K_w is used to compute tokens, while K'_w is used to generate new secret keys. Then, the client retrieves the current search token ST_c and the corresponding counter c. Next, he/she chooses a new random search token ST_{c+1} and increases the counter. To get a new state σ', they update $\mathbf{CT}$ appropriately. Moreover, he/she generates the update token UT_{c+1} through the hash function H_1 and the ciphertext of the previous search token C_{ST_c} using the specific hash function H_2. To save client storage, he/she uses H_3 to generate the one time secret key sk_{c+1} with the input of the counter $c+1$. With the secret key, he/she uses the Enc of Π to encrypt the bit string bs and outputs the ciphertext e. Eventually, he/she sends the update token UT_{c+1}, e and C_{ST_c} to the server. The server then updates the encrypted database accordingly and outputs EDB$'$.
- $bs \leftarrow$ **Search**$(q, \sigma; \mathtt{EDB})$: For an input (a conjunctive query q and a state σ, the client retrieves $\mathbf{CT}$ to get the current search token ST_c and the counter c and generates K_w and K'_w for each keyword w in the conjunctive query q. Then the client sends these search tokens to the server. Next, for each search token (or keyword w), the server searches EDB to get the ciphertexts e. Note that, to save server storage, the already searched entries can be removed and the server only needs to store the current summation Sum_e (corresponding to the keyword w, line 19 of **Search**). After that, the server adds these ciphertexts together using Add of Π, and the final result Sum is sent to the client. Eventually, the result can be decrypted by the client to get the final bit string bs, which points to the matching file identifiers.

Remark. VFBDSSE-CQ supports conjunctive queries and achieves volume-hiding, forward and backward privacy, which is more secure and expressive for practical use. However, the client storage of VFBDSSE-CQ is $O(|\mathbf{W}|)$, where $|\mathbf{W}|$ is the number of distinct keywords in a database. If a database has a large number of distinct keywords, the client requires large storage.

6.2 Small Client-Storage

Clearly, VFBDSSE-CQ's client storage grows linearly with the number of keywords. This section presents a new DSSE (SVFBDSSE-CQ) with small client storage, deploying and improving $\mathtt{SD}_a$ (from [11], which only supports single-keyword queries). At a high level, we implement a static SSE instance with a new Decrypt algorithm. To support the update, the client retrieves the corresponding files.

[6] Note that the bit string bs can denote many files. In other words, we can update many files during a single update.

Then the client re-encrypts the files together with the new file and sends them to the server. To reduce the number of retrievals (re-encryption), we initialize multiple SSE instances. The details are described below.

Before introducing our `SVFBDSSE-CQ`, we first describe `VSSE-CQ` (Algorithm 2), a static volume-hiding SSE supporting conjunctive queries used to construct `SVFBDSSE-CQ`. In [11], the authors added a **Decrypt** algorithm executed by the client with its secret key to instantiate updates. Additionally, each bit string bs is concatenated with its keyword w[7], allowing the client to decrypt all encrypted bit strings and re-encrypt them with the corresponding keyword w for new updates. Details are given below:

Algorithm 2. `VSSE-CQ`

Setup$(1^\lambda, \mathtt{DB}, n)$

Client:

$K \xleftarrow{\$} \{0,1\}^\lambda$, $\mathbf{M} \leftarrow$ empty map, $gc \leftarrow 0$
for $w \in \mathbf{W}$ **do**
  $c \leftarrow 0$, $K_w \leftarrow F_K(w)$
  for $bs \in \mathtt{DB}(w)$ **do**
    $K_{gc} \leftarrow F_K(gc)$, $l \leftarrow H_1(K_w, c)$, $e \leftarrow \mathtt{Enc}(K_{gc}, bs||w, n)$
    $\mathbf{GC} \leftarrow$ empty set, $\mathbf{GC} \leftarrow \mathbf{GC} \cup gc$
    Put $\mathbf{M}[l] = (e, \mathbf{GC})$ to the gc-th position of $\mathbf{M}$
    $c \leftarrow c + 1$, $gc \leftarrow gc + 1$
  end for
end for
return $(\mathbf{M}, K)$

Search$(q, K; \mathbf{M})$

Client:

for $w \in q$ **do**
  $K_w \leftarrow F_K(w)$
end for
Send $\{K_w\}_{w \in q}$ to the server.

Server:

$Sum \leftarrow 0$
for each K_w **do**
  $c \leftarrow 0$, $Sum_e \leftarrow 0$, $\mathbf{GC}_w \leftarrow$ empty set
  $(e, \mathbf{GC}) \leftarrow \mathbf{M}[H_1(K_w, c)]$
  while $(e, \mathbf{GC}) \neq \perp$ **do**
    $Sum_e \leftarrow \mathtt{Add}(Sum_e, e, n)$, $\mathbf{GC}_w \leftarrow \mathbf{GC}_w \cup \mathbf{GC}$
    Remove $\mathbf{M}[H_1(K_w, c)]$
    $c \leftarrow c + 1$, $(e, \mathbf{GC}) \leftarrow \mathbf{M}[H_1(K_w, c)]$
  end while
  Put $\mathbf{M}[H_1(K_w, 0)] = (Sum_e, \mathbf{GC}_w)$ to the smallest empty slot of $\mathbf{M}$, $Sum \leftarrow \mathtt{Add}(Sum, Sum_e, n)$
end for
Send $(Sum, \{\mathbf{GC}_w\}_{w \in q})$ to the client.

Client:

$Sum_{sk,w} \leftarrow 0$
for $w \in q$ **do**
  for $gc \in \mathbf{GC}_w$ **do**
    $K_{gc} \leftarrow F_K(gc)$, $Sum_{K,w} \leftarrow Sum_{K,w} + K_{gc} + w \bmod n$
  end for
end for
$bs||0s \leftarrow \mathtt{Dec}(Sum_{K,w}, Sum, n)$
return bs

Decrypt$(K, \mathbf{M})$

Client:

$\mathbf{R} \leftarrow$ empty set
for $c = 0$ to $|\mathbf{M}|$ **do**
  Get the c-th non-empty element $(e, \mathbf{GC})$ of $\mathbf{M}$
  if $\mathbf{GC}$ has one element gc **then**
    $K_{gc} \leftarrow F_K(gc)$, $bs||w \leftarrow \mathtt{Dec}(K_{gc}, e, n)$
    $\mathbf{R} \leftarrow \mathbf{R} \cup bs||w$
  else
    $Sum_{K,w} \leftarrow 0$
    for each $gc \in \mathbf{GC}_w$ **do**
      $K_{gc} \leftarrow F_K(gc)$
      $Sum_{K,w} \leftarrow Sum_{K,w} + K_{gc} + w \bmod n$
    end for
    $bs||0s \leftarrow \mathtt{Dec}(Sum_{K,w}, e, n)$
    $\mathbf{R} \leftarrow \mathbf{R} \cup bs||w$ ▷ Note that, if $\mathbf{GC}_w$ has more than one element, it means that the keyword has been searched before. Hence, the client knew the corresponding keyword.
  end if
end for
return $\mathbf{R}$

[7] For implementation, we can hash a keyword to a fixed length bit string.

- $(\mathbf{M}, K) \leftarrow$ **Setup**$(1^\lambda, \texttt{DB}, n)$: For an input (a security parameter λ, an integer n[8] and a database DB[9], the client chooses a random secret key K and uses it to encrypt the keyword/bit-string pairs. Moreover, he/she sets an empty map $\mathbf{M}$, which stores the encrypted bit strings. Eventually, the client outputs $\mathbf{M}$ and the client keeps K secret.
- $bs \leftarrow$ **Search**$(q, K; \mathbf{M})$: For an input (a conjunctive query q and the secret key K), the client produces the search token K_w for each keyword w in the conjunctive query q and sends the tokens to the server. Then the server searches $\mathbf{M}$ to get the results e and adds them together using Add of Π. The final result Sum and the global counters $\mathbf{GC}$ are sent to the client. To save server storage, the server removes the searched entries and stores the final result Sum_e and global counters $\mathbf{GC}_w$ in the smallest empty slot of $\mathbf{M}$. Eventually, the client decrypts Sum to get the final result bs.
- $\mathbf{R} \leftarrow$ **Decrypt**$(K, \mathbf{M})$: For an input (a secret key K and an encrypted bit strings $\mathbf{M}$), the client first generates one time secret key K_{gc} by applying the secret key K and global counters $\mathbf{GC}$. Now he/she can decrypt each encrypted bit string e by applying the corresponding one time secret key to Dec of Π. Eventually, the client outputs $\mathbf{R}$, which is a set of bit strings concatenated with the corresponding keywords.

Algorithm 3. SVFBDSSE-CQ

Setup(1^λ)

Client:

A set of keys $K_0, \cdots, K_{s-1} \leftarrow \perp$
$n \leftarrow$ integer
A set of Map $\mathbf{M}_0, \cdots \mathbf{M}_{s-1}$, the size of $\mathbf{M}_i = 2^i$, where $i \in \{0, \cdots, s-1\}$.
$\mathbf{M}_i \leftarrow$ empty map, $i \in \{0, 1, \cdots, s-1\}$
return $(\texttt{EDB} = \{\mathbf{M}_i\}, \sigma = (n, \{K_i\}))$

Update$(w, bs, \sigma; \texttt{EDB})$

Server:

Find the minimum j such that $\mathbf{M}_j = \varnothing$ or $\mathbf{M}_j$ is not full.
if $\mathbf{M}_j = \varnothing$ **then**
  Send $\mathbf{M}_0, \cdots, \mathbf{M}_{j-1}$ to the client, and set them to the empty at the server.
else
  Send $\mathbf{M}_j$ to the client.
end if

Client:

Set $\mathbf{R} \leftarrow$ empty set
if $\mathbf{M}_j$ is not full **then**
  $\mathbf{R} \leftarrow$ VSSE-CQ · **Decrypt**$(K_j, \mathbf{M}_j) \cup bs||w$
else
  for $i = 0$ to $j-1$ **do**
    $\mathbf{R} \leftarrow \mathbf{R} \cup$ VSSE-CQ · **Decrypt**$(K_i, \mathbf{M}_i)$
  end for
  $\mathbf{R} \leftarrow \mathbf{R} \cup bs||w$
end if
Parse $\mathbf{R}$ into DB.
$(\mathbf{M}'_j, K'_j) \leftarrow$ VSSE-CQ · **Setup**$(1^\lambda, \texttt{DB}, n)$
Update K_j with the new key K'_j, and send $\mathbf{M}'_j$ to the server.

Server:

Set $\mathbf{M}_j \leftarrow \mathbf{M}'_j$

Search$(q, \sigma; \texttt{EDB})$

Client and Server:

$bs \leftarrow 0$
for all i such that $\mathbf{M}_i \neq \varnothing$ **do**
  $bs_i||0s \leftarrow$ VSSE-CQ · **Search**$(q, K_i; \mathbf{M}_i)$
  $bs \leftarrow bs + bs_i \bmod n$
end for
return bs

---

[8] it is the output of the **Setup** of SVFBDSSE-CQ, which will be explained later.

[9] DB is a database with keyword/bit-string pairs.

We now introduce SVFBDSSE-CQ (Algorithm 3) for small client storage. Unlike VFBDSSE-CQ, it takes more time to update a keyword/bit-string pair—for each update, the client must retrieve and decrypt all pairs from the server, then re-encrypt them with the new pair and send back. Details are as follows:

- $(\mathtt{EDB} = \{\mathbf{M}_i\}, \sigma = (n, \{K_i\})) \leftarrow$ **Setup**(1^λ): For an input (a security parameter λ), a client outputs a set of random secret keys $\{K_i\}$ and a set of empty maps $\{\mathbf{M}_i\}$, where $i \in \{0, \cdots, s-1\}$ and s is the number of maps. The number of maps s means that this scheme can support the maximum of $2^s - 1$ updates. Moreover, he/she outputs an integer n, where $n = 2^{a\ell+|w|}$, a and ℓ are the same as the values in Algorithm 1 and $|w|$ is the length of the fixed length keyword w[10]. Eventually, the client outputs $\mathtt{EDB} = \{\mathbf{M}_i\}$ and the state $\sigma = (n, \{K_i\})$. The client keeps the set of keys $\{K_i\}$ secret.
- $(\sigma', \mathtt{EDB}') \leftarrow$ **Update**$(w, bs, \sigma; \mathtt{EDB})$: For an input (a keyword w, a bit string bs and a state σ), the client first retrieves certain maps from the server according to the technique of $\mathtt{SD}_a$. Then he/she decrypts the maps by using **Decrypt** of VSSE-CQ with the secret keys, parse them and the new keyword/bit string to DB. Next, he/she chooses new secret keys and re-encrypts DB using **Setup** of VSSE-CQ. Eventually, the client gets a new state σ' and keeps it secret. The server gets a new encrypted database EDB′.
- $bs \leftarrow$ **Search**$(q, \sigma; \mathtt{EDB})$: For an input (a conjunctive query q and a state σ), the client and the server execute **Search** of VSSE-CQ and get the result bit string bs_i for each non-empty map $\mathbf{M}_i \in \mathtt{EDB}$. Eventually, the client adds these bit strings together in sequence to get the final result, which accurately points to all matching files.

7 Security Analysis

The section evaluates the security of our DSSE schemes in detail. Note that we formulate a new backward privacy definition (called Type-C), which is well suitable for our conjunctive queries.

Theorem 1. *(Adaptive volume-hiding, forward and Type-C backward privacy of VFBDSSE-CQ). Let* $\Pi = (\mathtt{Enc}, \mathtt{Dec}, \mathtt{Add})$ *be a perfectly secure simple symmetric encryption with homomorphic addition,* F *be a secure PRF and* H_1*,* H_2 *and* H_3 *be random oracles. We define* $\mathcal{L}_{\mathit{VFBDSSE\text{-}CQ}} = (\mathcal{L}^{Search}_{\mathit{VFBDSSE\text{-}CQ}}, \mathcal{L}^{Update}_{\mathit{VFBDSSE\text{-}CQ}})$*, where* $\mathcal{L}^{Search}_{\mathit{VFBDSSE\text{-}CQ}}(q) = (\mathtt{sp}(q), \mathtt{rl}(q), \mathtt{Time}(q))$ *and* $\mathcal{L}^{Update}_{\mathit{VFBDSSE\text{-}CQ}}(op, w, bs) = (\mathtt{rl}(q))$*. Then VFBDSSE-CQ is* $\mathcal{L}_{\mathit{VFBDSSE\text{-}CQ}}$*-adaptively volume-hiding, forward and Type-C backward private.*

Note that the result size of each query(volume pattern) is fixed ($\mathtt{rl}(q)$), and the actual file count is not related to update count (c)—since c includes additions/deletions (each affecting ≥ 1 file), hiding the file count. Leakage functions

[10] We can use any hash functions to get the fixed length keyword.

reveal less information than forward and Type-C backward privacy leakages, so VFBDSSE-CQ achieves volume-hiding, forward and Type-C backward privacy. Full proof is deferred to Appendix A.1 due to page limits.

Theorem 2. *(Adaptive security and volume-hiding of VSSE-CQ). Let* $\Pi = (\mathtt{Enc}, \mathtt{Dec}, \mathtt{Add})$ *be a perfectly secure simple symmetric encryption with homomorphic addition, F be a secure PRF and H_1 be a random oracle. Given* $\mathcal{L}_{\mathtt{VSSE\text{-}CQ}} = (\mathcal{L}^{Setup}_{\mathtt{VSSE\text{-}CQ}}, \mathcal{L}^{Search}_{\mathtt{VSSE\text{-}CQ}})$, *where* $\mathcal{L}^{Setup}_{\mathtt{VSSE\text{-}CQ}}(DB, n) = (|DB|, \mathtt{rl}(q))$, *and* $\mathcal{L}^{Search}_{\mathtt{VSSE\text{-}CQ}}(q) = (\mathtt{sp}(q), \mathtt{rl}(q), \mathtt{Time}(q))$. *Then VSSE-CQ is* $\mathcal{L}_{\mathtt{VSSE\text{-}CQ}}$*-adaptively private and volume-hiding.*

Due to page limitation, we defer the full proof to the Appendix A.2. From Theorem 2, we can infer that SVFBDSSE-CQ achieves volume-hiding, forward and Type-C backward privacy.

Corollary 1. *(Adaptive volume-hiding, forward and Type-C backward privacy of SVFBDSSE-CQ). Given SVFBDSSE-CQ with a leakage function* $\mathcal{L}_{\mathtt{SVFBDSSE\text{-}CQ}} = (\mathcal{L}^{Search}_{\mathtt{SVFBDSSE\text{-}CQ}}, \mathcal{L}^{Update}_{\mathtt{SVFBDSSE\text{-}CQ}})$, *where* $\mathcal{L}^{Search}_{\mathtt{SVFBDSSE\text{-}CQ}}(q) = (\mathtt{sp}(q), \mathtt{rl}(q), \mathtt{Time}(q))$ *and* $\mathcal{L}^{Update}_{\mathtt{SVFBDSSE\text{-}CQ}}(op, w, bs) = (\mathtt{rl}(q))$. *Then SVFBDSSE-CQ is volume-hiding, forward and Type-C backward private.*

The leakage function $\mathcal{L}^{Update}$ of SVFBDSSE-CQ leaks the result length $\mathtt{rl}$, which is similar to the leakage function $\mathcal{L}^{Setup}$ of VSSE-CQ[11]. This is due to the fact that, for every update, the length of the bit string is leaked, and the client chooses a new secret key and re-encrypts all the entries. The leakage function $\mathcal{L}^{Search}$ of SVFBDSSE-CQ is the same as the search leakage function of VSSE-CQ, except that SVFBDSSE-CQ has multiple VSSE-CQ instances. Hence, SVFBDSSE-CQ is volume-hiding, forward and Type-C backward private.

8 Experiments

We evaluate our schemes' performance using two recent conjunctive DSSE benchmarks: VBTree [30] (forward private) and ODXT [25] (most efficient forward and backward private scheme). Experiments run on a single workstation (Intel Xeon E5-2609 v4 @ 1.70GHz, 64GB RAM, Ubuntu 20.04, Java) acting as both client and server, using JPBC [10] group $\mathbb{G}_T$[12] for ODXT's [25] modular operations.

Datasets. Following [12], we test on two datasets: Enron Email Dataset [8] (Enron) with 517,401 files ($\ell = 517{,}408$) and Chicago Crime Dataset [13] (Crime) with 7,120,931 records across 22 attributes. For Crime, we use the location description attribute containing 228 keywords ($\ell = 7{,}120{,}936$).

Experimental Evaluation. We evaluate the update and search time for four schemes on Enron and Crime datasets. Update experiments record the time needed for the keyword/file-identifier (or keyword/bit-string) pairs, with results

[11] $\mathcal{L}^{Setup}$ leaks update numbers. Note that it is also leaked in VFBDSSE-CQ.

[12] Compared with other groups ($\mathbb{G}_1, \mathbb{G}_2$), the modular exponentiation of $\mathbb{G}_T$ is fastest.

in Figs. 2 and 3. Search operations are executed in encrypted databases generated after updating many files, with the results in Figs. 4 and 5.

Experimental details: File identifiers are translated into scalable bitmap indices by converting bit strings into "BigInteger" equivalents[13]. The update time includes the generation of client tokens and the update time of the server. The result length of VFBDSSE-CQ and SVFBDSSE-CQ is $a\ell$ and $a\ell + |H(w) + 8|$, respectively. ℓ is the maximum number of files and a is the number of bits used to denote a file. $|H(w)|$ is the bit length of the output of a hash function H with input w. SVFBDSSE-CQ needs one more byte (8 bits) to produce a positive integer[14]. With parameter $a = 3$, bit string bs length is 1,552,224 and 21,362,808 bits for Enron and Crime respectively. For SVFBDSSE-CQ, keywords are concatenated with bit strings using SHA-1 for fixed length[15], with an extra byte added for positive binary hashed keywords, resulting in bs lengths of 1,552,392 and 21,362,976 bits, respectively.

Consider Fig. 2, as the number of updates grows, it clearly shows that the update time increases for all schemes when the Enron dataset is used. However, this is not always true. For the number of updates in the range $\langle 30, 40\rangle$, the update time of SVFBDSSE-CQ decreases slightly. This is due to the fact that, for java programming, certain times of modular addition of "BigInteger" with a certain length may cost less computation time. The update time of ODXT is slightly longer than the update time of VBTree. The update time of VFBDSSE-CQ is similar to the update time of SVFBDSSE-CQ. But our schemes (VFBDSSE-CQ and SVFBDSSE-CQ) have longer update time than VBTree and ODXT (see Crime dataset in Fig. 3). Notably, our schemes can let multiple files update via one keyword/bit-string pair, cutting encrypted database setup time. They also offer better privacy than VBTree and ODXT (Sect. 1) and efficient keyword deletions. Though their update is less efficient, search is far more so in practice —— this trade-off is discussed next.

We evaluate the search time for the four schemes with different numbers of keywords for the two datasets. As before, we set the parameter a to 3, which means that we can handle the maximum of $b = 2^3 - 1 = 7$ conjunctive keywords. In fact, we test the search for a maximum of 5 conjunctive keywords. This is due to the fact that five keywords are sufficient in practice[16]. Search time includes the time necessary to generate a token, to search and finally to decrypt. Figures 4 and 5 show that, when the number of keywords jumps from 1 to 2, the search time for ODXT increases dramatically. This is because, when we search for a single keyword, ODXT does not need to test the map named XSet, which greatly saves search time. It can also be seen that searching for a larger number of keywords

---

[13] The retrieval of the actual files that denoted by bit strings is not crucial and ignored in the paper.

[14] Although our schemes require comparable communication cost, our schemes achieve fast search, volume-hiding, forward privacy, backward privacy, and conjunctive queries simultaneously.

[15] The output length of SHA-1 is 20 bytes.

[16] In [30], the authors only tested three conjunctive keywords search.

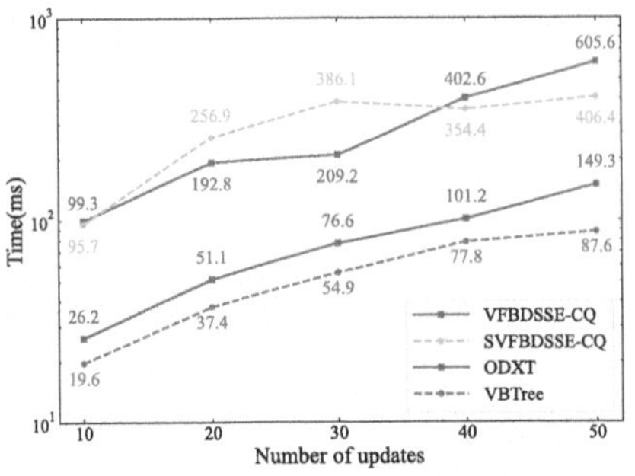

Fig. 2. Update time for the Enron dataset

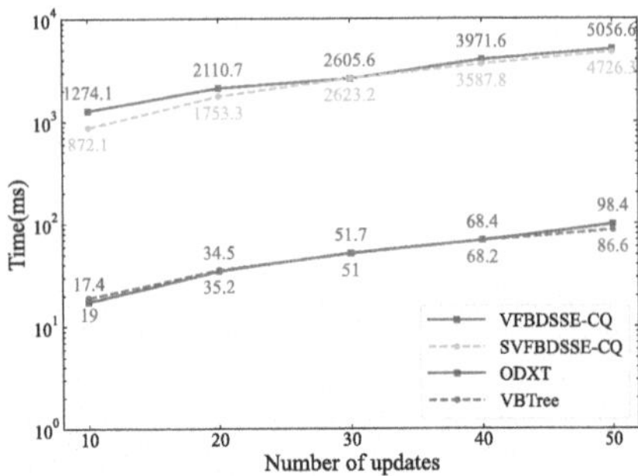

Fig. 3. Update time for the Crime dataset

results in a longer search time with some exceptions. For the Enron dataset, the search time of VBTree decreases when the number of keywords increases from 4 to 5. Interestingly, for the Crime dataset, search time for VBTree decreases if the number of keywords increases from 1 to 2 and from 3 to 5 keywords. Fewer files satisfy queries with more keywords, so searches stop at a certain tree depth and save time. For 2 to 3 keywords in Fig. 5, VFBDSSE-CQ's search time decreases; most of the time does not come from modular addition. From Fig. 4, our schemes have similar search times, while VBTree and ODXT take much longer: ours is 60× shorter than VBTree and 200× shorter than ODXT. Similarly, Fig. 5 shows VFBDSSE-CQ is 5× slower than SVFBDSSE-CQ; the two are 6× and 30× shorter than VBTree, and 600× and 3000× shorter than ODXT, respectively. The search time of our schemes outperforms the search time of VBTree and ODXT because the main operations of our schemes during the search are modular additions, which are very efficient.

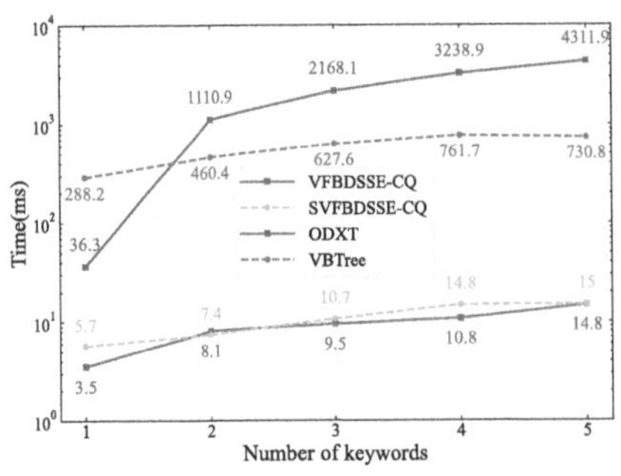

Fig. 4. Search time for the Enron dataset

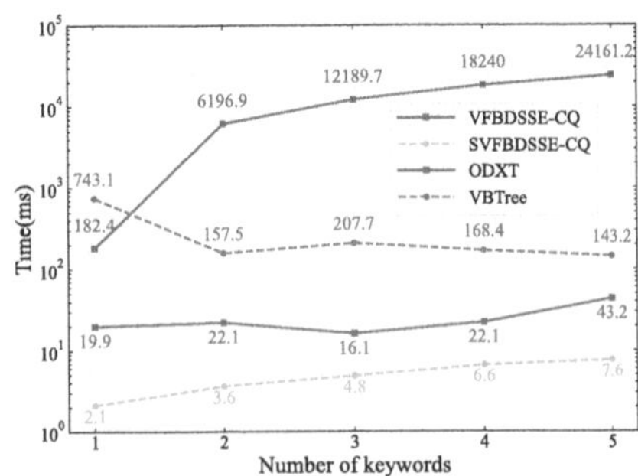

Fig. 5. Search time for the Crime dataset

Our experiments show our schemes outperform the VBTree and ODXT, except in updates. Though our updates take slightly longer, batch updates during setup can mitigate this by processing multiple file/keyword pairs together, thereby amortizing the cryptographic costs and reducing server communication. Notably, our search is more efficient and privacy is stronger. In summary, our schemes support conjunctive queries with volume-hiding, forward and Type-C backward privacy. `VFBDSSE-CQ` updates better than `SVFBDSSE-CQ`, but `SVFBDSSE-CQ` uses less client storage. Choose `VFBDSSE-CQ` for frequent updates or a few keywords; `SVFBDSSE-CQ` suits many keywords and rather infrequent updates in practice.

9 Conclusions

In this paper, we propose two DSSE schemes supporting conjunctive queries named `VFBDSSE-CQ` and `SVFBDSSE-CQ`, which achieve volume-hiding, forward and backward privacy and they can be tailored for different applications. The `VFBDSSE-CQ` scheme is suitable for applications with frequent updates or/and a small number of keywords. The `SVFBDSSE-CQ` scheme requires smaller client storage and is better for applications with a large number of keywords and infrequent updates. As the currently used backward privacy definition is not suitable for conjunctive queries, we introduce a new backward privacy definition for our conjunctive queries and have called it Type-C backward privacy.

Acknowledgments. This work is supported by the Key Research and Development Program of Shandong Province (Grant No.: 2021CXGC010106), Guangxi Key Research and Development Project(Guike AB25069120), Beijing Natural Science Foundation (L251002), National Natural Science Foundation of China (Grant No. 62372040, 62302037, 62272294, 62572045), Fundamental Research Funds for the Central Universities (2025MS023), in part by National Science Centre, Poland (Grant No. 2023/49/B/ST6/02580).

A Proof

A.1 Proof of Theorem 1

Proof. We argue that an adversary $\mathcal{A}$ cannot distinguish between two consecutive games. In particular, `REAL` is exactly the same game as the original scheme. `IDEAL` is simulated with the defined leakages.

Game G_0**:** The game follows precisely the original scheme. So we have

$$\Pr[\mathtt{REAL}_{\mathcal{A}}^{\mathtt{VFBDSSE\text{-}CQ}}(\lambda) = 1] = \Pr[G_0 = 1].$$

Game G_1**:** We replace PRF F with a truly random function. For a new keyword, we choose a random key with uniform probability for the keyword w and store the key and the corresponding keyword w in table `Key` for consistency. For a queried keyword, we retrieve the key from table `Key`. Then we can establish an adversary $\mathcal{B}_1$ to distinguish F from a truly random function if an adversary $\mathcal{A}$ can distinguish G_0 from G_1. Formally,

$$\Pr[G_0 = 1] - \Pr[G_1 = 1] \leq \mathbf{Adv}_{F,\mathcal{B}_1}^{\mathtt{prf}}(\lambda).$$

Game G_2: We replace the hash function H_1 with a random oracle. In particular, we pick a random value for every new update token UT. Moreover, we store it in table $\mathtt{UT}$ for the **Update**. To make it consistent with the **Search**, we generate random tokens through the random oracle H_1 such that $H_1(K_w, ST_c) = \mathtt{UT}[w, c]$. In addition, we store (K_w, ST_c) in table $\mathtt{H}_1$ for future queries. If an adversary has already queried the $c+1$-th entry, then $\mathtt{H}_1$ stores (K_w, ST_{c+1}), which means that we cannot choose a random token that is equal to an existing value (namely $H_1(K_w, ST_{c+1}) = \mathtt{UT}[w, c+1]$). Hence, the game terminates with a negligible probability. If an adversary wants to query the $(c+1)$-th entry, the adversary needs to guess the $(c+1)$-th search token ST_{c+1}, and the probability is $1/2^\lambda$ due to the fact that every search token ST is randomly chosen. Assuming the adversary makes $p(\lambda)$ (polynomial number) queries, then

$$\Pr[G_1 = 1] - \Pr[G_2 = 1] \leq p(\lambda)/2^\lambda.$$

Game G_3: Similarly, we can replace H_2 and H_3 with random oracles. Then assuming the adversary makes $p(\lambda)$ (polynomial number) queries, so

$$\Pr[G_2 = 1] - \Pr[G_3 = 1] \leq 2p(\lambda)/2^\lambda.$$

Game G_4: We replace bs with all zeros bit string. If $\mathcal{A}$ can distinguish G_4 from G_3, then we can establish an adversary $\mathcal{B}_2$ to break the perfect security of Π. Then we have

$$\Pr[G_3 = 1] - \Pr[G_4 = 1] \leq \mathbf{Adv}^{\mathtt{PS}}_{\Pi,\mathcal{B}_2}(\lambda).$$

Simulator. In this game, we simulate $\mathtt{IDEAL}$ with leakages defined in Algorithm 4. We first replace the conjunctive query q with $\mathtt{sp}(q)$ in G_4 and remove some parts of the original algorithm, which does not change the adversary view. Note that, for the conjunctive query q, we use the timestamp when it queried for the first time (namely $\hat{q} \leftarrow \mathtt{min}\ \mathtt{sp}(q)$).

Now, we are ready to show that G_4 and **Simulator** are indistinguishable. We first can easily find that the **Update** of these two games is indistinguishable since the values are randomly chosen for every update operation in both games. To simulate the **Search**, the simulator $\mathcal{S}$ needs to embed the previous search token to the current ciphertext C. Hence, $\mathcal{S}$ first chooses two search tokens. One is for the latest search token ST_c and the other one is for its previous search token ST_{c-1}, which is embedded into the current ciphertext C via H_2. This operation is executed in a sequence until the first search token ST_0. After that, the pairs (w, i) are mapped to the global update count t, which helps us to map the values randomly chosen in the **Update** to the corresponding values in the **Search**. In other words, we conclude that

$$\Pr[G_4 = 1] = \Pr[\mathtt{IDEAL}^{\mathtt{VFBDSSE\text{-}CQ}}_{\mathcal{A},\mathcal{S}}(\lambda) = 1].$$

Finally,

$$\Pr[\mathtt{REAL}^{\mathtt{VFBDSSE\text{-}CQ}}_{\mathcal{A}}(\lambda) = 1] - \Pr[\mathtt{IDEAL}^{\mathtt{VFBDSSE\text{-}CQ}}_{\mathcal{A},\mathcal{S}}(\lambda) = 1]$$
$$\leq \mathbf{Adv}^{\mathtt{prf}}_{F,\mathcal{B}_1}(\lambda) + \mathbf{Adv}^{\mathtt{PS}}_{\Pi,\mathcal{B}_2}(\lambda) + 3p(\lambda)/2^\lambda.$$

□

Algorithm 4. Simulator $\mathcal{S}$

```
Setup(1^λ)
  n ← integer, CT, M ← empty map
  return (EDB = M, CT, n)
Update(rl(q))
Client:
  sk[t] ← {0,1}^λ
  e[t] ← Enc(sk[t], 0s, n)      ▷ The length of 0s equals rl(q).
  C[t] ← {0,1}^λ
  UT[t] ← {0,1}^λ
  Send (UT[t], (e[t], C[t])) to the server.
  t ← t + 1
Search(sp(q), rl(q), Time(q))
Client:
  q̂ ← min sp(q)
  Parse rp(q̂) into bs.
  for w ∈ q̂ do
      K_w || K'_w ← Key(w)
      (ST_c, c) ← CT[w]
      Parse Time(w) into (t_0, ···, t_c)      ▷ Time(w) ∈ Time(q̂)
      if (ST_c, c) = ⊥ then
          return ⊥
      end if
      for i = c to 0 do
          ST_{i-1} ← {0,1}^λ
          Program H_1(K_w, ST_i) ← UT[t_i]
          Program H_2(K_w, ST_i) ← C[t_i] ⊕ ST_{i-1}
      end for
  end for
  Send {(K_w, ST_c, c)}_{w∈q̂} to the server.
```

A.2 Proof of Theorem 2

Proof. Similarly, we formulate a series of games from REAL to IDEAL and prove that every two consecutive games are indistinguishable.

Game G_0: This game follows precisely the original scheme, which is described in Algorithm 2, so

$$\Pr[\mathtt{REAL}_{\mathcal{A}}^{\mathtt{VSSE\text{-}CQ}}(\lambda) = 1] = \Pr[G_0 = 1].$$

Game G_1: We replace the PRF F by a truly random function. If an adversary $\mathcal{A}$ can distinguish between G_0 and G_1, then we can construct an adversary $\mathcal{B}_1$ that is able to distinguish F from a truly random function. Formally,

$$\Pr[G_0 = 1] - \Pr[G_1 = 1] \leq \mathbf{Adv}_{F,\mathcal{B}_1}^{\mathtt{prf}}(\lambda).$$

Game G_2: We model H_1 as a random oracle same as above. So we have

$$\Pr[G_1 = 1] - \Pr[G_2 = 1] \leq p(\lambda)/2^{\lambda}.$$

Game G_3: We encrypt all zeros bit string instead of the actual bit string. If the adversary $\mathcal{A}$ can distinguish between G_3 and G_2, then we can design an adversary $\mathcal{B}_2$ that is able to break the perfect security of Π. In other words,

$$\Pr[G_2 = 1] - \Pr[G_3 = 1] \leq \mathbf{Adv}_{\Pi,\mathcal{B}_2}^{\mathtt{PS}}(\lambda).$$

Simulator. We can build a simulator by replacing the conjunctive query q with $\mathtt{sp}(q)$ in G_3, which is similar to Algorithm 4. **Setup** is similar to **Update**. With the input $|\mathtt{DB}|$, we can simulate the encrypted database. Note that $\mathtt{Time(q)}$ denotes the insertion order of the setup phase. With the search leakages, we can simulate the **Search** protocol, which is similar to Algorithm 4. Thus

$$\Pr[G_3 = 1] = \Pr[\mathtt{IDEAL}_{\mathcal{A},\mathcal{S}}^{\mathtt{VSSE\text{-}CQ}}(\lambda) = 1].$$

Finally,

$$\Pr[\mathtt{REAL}_{\mathcal{A}}^{\mathtt{VSSE\text{-}CQ}}(\lambda) = 1] - \Pr[\mathtt{IDEAL}_{\mathcal{A},\mathcal{S}}^{\mathtt{VSSE\text{-}CQ}}(\lambda) = 1] \\ \leq \mathbf{Adv}_{F,\mathcal{B}_1}^{\mathtt{prf}}(\lambda) + \mathbf{Adv}_{\Pi,\mathcal{B}_2}^{\mathtt{PS}}(\lambda) + p(\lambda)/2^{\lambda}.$$

□

References

1. Amjad, G., Patel, S., Persiano, G., Yeo, K., Yung, M.: Dynamic volume-hiding encrypted multi-maps with applications to searchable encryption. IACR Cryptol. ePrint Arch. p. 765 (2023)
2. Bag, A., Patranabis, S., Mukhopadhyay, D.: Tokenised multi-client provisioning for dynamic searchable encryption with forward and backward privacy. In: AsiaCCS 2024, pp. 1691–1707 (2024)
3. Bost, R.: $\Sigma o\varphi o\varsigma$: forward secure searchable encryption. In: CCS 2016, pp. 1143–1154 (2016)
4. Bost, R., Minaud, B., Ohrimenko, O.: Forward and backward private searchable encryption from constrained cryptographic primitives. In: CCS 2017, pp. 1465–1482 (2017)
5. Cash, D., Grubbs, P., Perry, J., Ristenpart, T.: Leakage-abuse attacks against searchable encryption. In: CCS 2015, pp. 668–679 (2015)
6. Cash, D., Jarecki, S., Jutla, C., Krawczyk, H., Roşu, M.C., Steiner, M.: Highly-scalable searchable symmetric encryption with support for Boolean queries. In: Canetti, R., Garay, J.A. (eds.) CRYPTO 2013. LNCS, vol. 8042, pp. 353–373. Springer, Cham (2013). https://doi.org/10.1007/978-3-642-40041-4_20
7. Chamani, J.G., Papadopoulos, D., Papamanthou, C., Jalili, R.: New constructions for forward and backward private symmetric searchable encryption. In: CCS 2018, pp. 1038–1055 (2018)
8. Cohen, W.W.: Enron email dataset. https://www.cs.cmu.edu/~./enron/
9. Curtmola, R., Garay, J., Kamara, S., Ostrovsky, R.: Searchable symmetric encryption: improved definitions and efficient constructions. In: CCS 2006, pp. 79–88 (2006)
10. De Caro, A., Iovino, V.: JPBC: Java pairing based cryptography. In: ISCC 2011, pp. 850–855 (2011)
11. Demertzis, I., Chamani, J.G., Papadopoulos, D., Papamanthou, C.: Dynamic searchable encryption with small client storage. Cryptology ePrint Archive, Paper 2019/1227
12. Demertzis, I., Papamanthou, C., Talapatra, R.: Efficient searchable encryption through compression. Proc. VLDB Endow. 1729–1741 (2018)
13. Department, C.P.: Crimes - 2001 to present. https://data.cityofchicago.org/Public-Safety/Crimes-2001-to-Present/ijzp-q8t2
14. Fu, Z., Huang, F., Ren, K., Weng, J., Wang, C.: Privacy-preserving smart semantic search based on conceptual graphs over encrypted outsourced data. In: TIFS 2017, pp. 1874–1884 (2017)
15. Garg, S., Mohassel, P., Papamanthou, C.: Tworam: efficient oblivious ram in two rounds with applications to searchable encryption. In: Robshaw, M., Katz, J. (eds.) CRYPTO 2016. LNCS, vol. 9816, pp. 563–592. Springer, Heidelberg (2016). https://doi.org/10.1007/978-3-662-53015-3_2

16. Guo, C., Li, W., Tang, X., Choo, K.K.R., Liu, Y.: Forward private verifiable dynamic searchable symmetric encryption with efficient conjunctive query. In: TDSC 2023, pp. 746–763 (2023)
17. Jiang, Q., Chang, E.C., Qi, Y., Qi, S., Wu, P., Wang, J.: RPHX: result pattern hiding conjunctive query over private compressed index using intel SGX. In: TIFS 2022, pp. 1053–1068 (2022)
18. Kamara, S., Moataz, T.: Computationally volume-hiding structured encryption. In: Ishai, Y., Rijmen, V. (eds.) Eurocrypt 2019. LNCS, vol. 11477, pp. 183–213. Springer, Cham (2019). https://doi.org/10.1007/978-3-030-17656-3_7
19. Kamara, S., Papamanthou, C., Roeder, T.: Dynamic searchable symmetric encryption. In: CCS 2012, pp. 965–976 (2012)
20. Kornaropoulos, E.M., Moyer, N., Papamanthou, C., Psomas, A.: Leakage inversion: towards quantifying privacy in searchable encryption. In: CCS 2022, pp. 1829–1842 (2022)
21. Lai, S., et al.: Result pattern hiding searchable encryption for conjunctive queries. In: CCS 2018, pp. 745–762 (2018)
22. Liu, D., Wang, W., Xu, P., Yang, L.T., Luo, B., Liang, K.: D-DSE: distinct dynamic searchable encryption resisting volume leakage in encrypted databases. In: USENIX Security 2024, pp. 2563–2580
23. Mondal, P., Chamani, J.G., Demertzis, I., Papadopoulos, D.: {I/O-Efficient} dynamic searchable encryption meets forward & backward privacy. In: USENIX Security 2024, pp. 2527–2544 (2024)
24. Oya, S., Kerschbaum, F.: Hiding the access pattern is not enough: exploiting search pattern leakage in searchable encryption. In: USENIX Security 2021, pp. 127–142 (2021)
25. Patranabis, S., Mukhopadhyay, D.: Forward and backward private conjunctive searchable symmetric encryption. Cryptology ePrint Archive, Paper 2020/1342
26. Ren, K., et al.: Hybridx: new hybrid index for volume-hiding range queries in data outsourcing services. In: ICDCS 2020, pp. 23–33 (2020)
27. Song, D.X., Wagner, D., Perrig, A.: Practical techniques for searches on encrypted data. In: S&P 2000, pp. 44–55 (2000)
28. Sun, S.F., et al.: Practical backward-secure searchable encryption from symmetric puncturable encryption. In: CCS 2018, pp. 763–780 (2018)
29. Wang, J., Sun, S., Li, T., Qi, S., Chen, X.: Practical volume-hiding encrypted multimaps with optimal overhead and beyond. In: CCS 2022, pp. 2825–2839 (2022)
30. Wu, Z., Li, K.: VBTree: forward secure conjunctive queries over encrypted data for cloud computing. VLDB J. 25–46 (2019)
31. Zhang, X., Wang, W., Xu, P., Yang, L.T., Liang, K.: High recovery with fewer injections: practical binary volumetric injection attacks against dynamic searchable encryption. In: USENIX Security 2023, pp. 5953–5970 (2023)
32. Zhang, Y., Katz, J., Papamanthou, C.: All your queries are belong to us: the power of file-injection attacks on searchable encryption. In: USENI Security 2016, pp. 707–720 (2016)
33. Zhao, Y., Wang, H., Lam, K.Y.: Volume-hiding dynamic searchable symmetric encryption with forward and backward privacy. Cryptology ePrint Archive, Report 2021/786
34. Zuo, C., et al.: Searchable encryption for conjunctive queries with extended forward and backward privacy. In: PETS 2025, pp. 440–455 (2025)
35. Zuo, C., Sun, S.F., Liu, J.K., Shao, J., Pieprzyk, J.: Dynamic searchable symmetric encryption schemes supporting range queries with forward (and backward) security. In: ESORICS 2018, pp. 228–246 (2018)

36. Zuo, C., Sun, S.F., Liu, J.K., Shao, J., Pieprzyk, J.: Dynamic searchable symmetric encryption with forward and stronger backward privacy. In: ESORICS 2019, pp. 283–303 (2019)
37. Zuo, C., Sun, S.F., Liu, J.K., Shao, J., Pieprzyk, J., Wei, G.: Forward and backward private dynamic searchable symmetric encryption for conjunctive queries. Cryptology ePrint Archive, Paper 2020/1357
38. Zuo, C., Sun, S.F., Liu, J.K., Shao, J., Pieprzyk, J., Xu, L.: Forward and backward private DSSE for range queries. In: TDSC 2022, pp. 328–338 (2022)

Privacy-Preserving Fine-Grained Similarity Queries for Aging in Place System

Zhuliang Jia[1(✉)], Suprio Ray[1], Rongxing Lu[2], and Mohammad Mamun[3]

[1] Faculty of Computer Science, University of New Brunswick, Fredericton, NB E3B 5A3, Canada
zhuliang.jia@unb.ca

[2] School of Computing, Queen's University, Kingston, ON K7L 2N8, Canada

[3] National Research Council of Canada, Fredericton, NB E3B 9W4, Canada

Abstract. As the aging population continues to grow, healthcare systems face increasing pressure to support timely and personalized medical services to older adults. To address this need, Aging in Place (AiP) has emerged as a promising approach, enabling seniors to remain in their own homes while still receiving continuous medical support. AiP services increasingly rely on similarity search over sensitive electronic health records (EHRs) to enable personalized interventions. To support such queries with limited local resources, medical institutions outsource EHRs to cloud servers. However, outsourcing raises three key challenges: preserving data and query privacy, hiding access patterns, and allowing flexible similarity measures. To address these challenges, we propose an efficient, privacy-preserving scheme for fine-grained similarity queries tailored to AiP. Our design combines p-stable locality-sensitive hashing (p-stable LSH) with additive secret sharing (ASS) and function secret sharing (FSS) to return all records that satisfy users' fine-grained similarity requirements while ensuring privacy throughout the process. Our security analysis confirms privacy guarantees under the honest-but-curious model. Extensive experimental evaluations demonstrate computational efficiency and practical scalability for real-world AiP implementations.

Keywords: Privacy-preserving · aging in place · fine-grained · similarity queries

1 Introduction

With the increase in life expectancy and population growth, aging has become a social issue that cannot be ignored. One major challenge is the imbalance between the growing elderly population and the limited availability of healthcare and eldercare resources. Elders typically need more frequent and specialized medical attention, which places additional strain on existing healthcare systems.

W. Li et al. (Eds.): EISA 2025, CCIS 2897, pp. 25–39, 2026.
https://doi.org/10.1007/978-3-032-21177-4_2

At the same time, insufficient healthcare resources can lead to a decline in the quality of life for many elderly individuals, as not everyone has equal access to the care they need [2]. Additionally, many elders do not want to move into nursing homes. This reluctance arises for several reasons: first, there are not enough resources to build nursing homes for all elderly individuals; second, such facilities often involve higher economic costs; and finally, moving into a nursing home typically forces seniors to leave the communities where they have lived for decades, which can have negative psychological effects. As a result, many governments increasingly recommend the concept of Aging in Place (AiP), which allows older adults to remain in their own homes while aging [9].

Yet AiP also faces certain challenges. For example, many seniors suffer from chronic conditions that require continuous monitoring. The traditional approach involves home visits by healthcare professionals, but this method incurs additional costs and may not be feasible given the growing elderly population and the limited availability of medical staff. Moreover, healthcare workers cannot be present with patients at any time. This combination can enable real-time collection, transmission, and storage of various health data, allowing older adults to live independently and comfortably at home while receiving continuous medical support. In AiP systems, medical institutions typically maintain large-scale databases of electronic health records (EHRs) compiled from treatment records maintained over time. For example, when an AiP platform observes an abnormal trend in an older adult's vital signs, clinicians may want to search the cloud-stored EHRs for patients whose profiles are similar to this user in order to decide whether early intervention is necessary. Meanwhile, clients can perform similarity queries over these repositories to identify past cases that closely resemble their own health profiles, such as patients with similar vital signs, activity patterns, or medical histories, thereby enabling proactive health management, early disease prevention, and timely medical consultations based on evidence-driven insights [7].

However, as the volume, variety, and velocity of EHR data continue to grow with expanding AiP deployments, managing the storage capacity and computational requirements locally becomes increasingly impractical and cost-prohibitive. To address these challenges, medical institutions often outsource both data storage and query processing tasks to powerful cloud servers, which significantly improve system scalability, computational efficiency, and overall service availability. Despite these advantages, outsourcing sensitive health data and user queries to untrusted environments inevitably raises critical privacy concerns, creating an urgent need for robust mechanisms that protect the confidentiality of EHRs as well as the privacy of users' query intentions throughout the entire computation process [12].

In this paper, we study privacy-preserving similarity queries for AiP systems. We consider a practical setting with a healthcare data owner (DO) who outsources data and computation to two non-colluding honest-but-curious cloud providers, serving many query users simultaneously. To support flexible utility, we adopt the p-stable locality-sensitive hashing (LSH) technique and allow each user to specify a similarity threshold t: a record is returned only if at least t out of K LSH components match the query. This formulation captures common approximate matching needs while giving query users explicit control over the required similarity level.

Existing approaches [6,11] can secure similarity queries over sensitive EHRs but typically rely on heavy cryptographic primitives, which often lead to substantial computational overhead and consequently high latency. Such latency limits their practicality in real-world scenarios with large-scale data in AiP scenario. On the other hand, lightweight solutions [5,10] have been proposed to improve efficiency by reducing cryptographic complexity or adopting approximate query techniques. Although these schemes achieve lower latency, they cannot guarantee access-pattern privacy. These trade-offs highlight the necessity of a new design that simultaneously preserves access-pattern privacy, enables fine-grained similarity control, and remains efficient enough for interactive use in AiP services.

To address these challenges, we propose a privacy-preserving scheme for fine-grained similarity queries that combines p-stable LSH, additive secret sharing (ASS), and function secret sharing (FSS) to achieve thresholded similarity search without revealing sensitive data, queries, or matching results to any single server. Our main contributions are summarized as follows:

- First, we design a privacy-preserving similarity query framework for AiP that integrates p-stable LSH with an explicit similarity-threshold interface, allowing users tune retrieval quality to their needs.
- Second, our proposed scheme preserves access-pattern privacy. Leveraging ASS and FSS techniques, each query is decomposed into fixed-length shares and yields uniformly sized server responses, making the server-visible transcript independent of the number or location of matches.
- Finally, we provide rigorous security analyses confirming that our proposed scheme preserves data privacy against honest-but-curious adversaries. Experimental results further demonstrate computational and communication efficiency, affirming its practicality for real-world AiP healthcare applications.

The rest of this paper is organized as follows. In Sect. 2, we briefly introduce some preliminaries used in our scheme. Section 3 introduces system and security models, and some definition used in our scheme. Section 4 presents the scheme details, followed by the security analysis and performance evaluation in Sect. 5 and Sect. 6. Finally, we draw a conclusion in Sect. 7.

2 Preliminaries

In this section, we introduce some techniques that will be used in our proposed scheme.

2.1 P-Stable Locality-Sensitive Hashing (p-Stable LSH)

The p-stable LSH scheme [3] hashes high-dimensional vectors via random projections from p-stable distributions, ensuring that nearby points under the l_p norm collide with higher probability than distant ones.

Definition 1. *Let $\|\cdot\|_p$ denote the ℓ_p norm on $\mathbb{R}^d$, i.e., for any vector $\mathbf{v} \in \mathbb{R}^d$, $\|\mathbf{v}\|_p = \left(\sum_{i=1}^d |v_i|^p\right)^{1/p}$ with $0 < p \le 2$. For bucket width $r > 0$, sample a random vector $\mathbf{a} \in \mathbb{R}^d$ whose entries are i.i.d. p-stable, and a scalar $\beta \sim \mathrm{Unif}[0, r]$; define*

$$h_{\mathbf{a},\beta}(\mathbf{x}) = \left\lfloor \frac{\mathbf{a}^\top \mathbf{x} + \beta}{r} \right\rfloor, \quad \mathbf{x} \in \mathbb{R}^d. \tag{1}$$

The family $H = \{h_{\mathbf{a},\beta}\}$ is (r_1, r_2, p_1, p_2)-locality-sensitive under ℓ_p: if $\|\mathbf{x} - \mathbf{y}\|_p < r_1$ then $\Pr[h(\mathbf{x}) = h(\mathbf{y})] \ge p_1$; if $\|\mathbf{x}-\mathbf{y}\|_p > r_2$ then $\Pr[h(\mathbf{x}) = h(\mathbf{y})] \le p_2$. Given parameters $r_1 < r_2$ and probabilities $p_1 > p_2$, a family of hash functions $H = \{h_{\mathbf{a},b} : \mathbb{R}^d \to \mathbb{Z}\}$ is called (r_1, r_2, p_1, p_2)-p-stable locality-sensitive if for any $x, y \in \mathbb{R}^d$,

$$\begin{aligned} \|\mathbf{x} - \mathbf{y}\|_p < r_1 &\Rightarrow \Pr[h(\mathbf{x}) = h(\mathbf{y})] \ge p_1; \\ \|\mathbf{x} - \mathbf{y}\|_p > r_2 &\Rightarrow \Pr[h(\mathbf{x}) = h(\mathbf{y})] \le p_2. \end{aligned} \tag{2}$$

Hence, the collision probability decreases monotonically with $\|\mathbf{x} - \mathbf{y}\|_p$, enabling efficient approximate nearest-neighbor search. Concatenating K independent hashes to form

$$g(\mathbf{x}) = (h_1(\mathbf{x}), \ldots, h_K(\mathbf{x})) \tag{3}$$

reduces false positives by lowering the collision probability for far points; increasing K amplifies this effect (accuracy amplification). Note that, in our scheme, without loss of generality, we assume that all elements of $\mathbf{x}$ are integers.

2.2 Additive Secret Sharing (ASS)

We use standard two-party (2, 2) additive secret sharing over $\mathbb{Z}_p$ [8]. For $x \in \mathbb{Z}_p$, let $[\![x]\!] = ([\![x]\!]_{(0)}, [\![x]\!]_{(1)})$ with $[\![x]\!]_{(0)} + [\![x]\!]_{(1)} = x$. We use subscript $b \in \{0, 1\}$ to indicate the share held by party CSb. All arithmetic is over $\mathbb{Z}_p$.

$\mathsf{MulSS}([\![u]\!]_{(b)}, [\![v]\!]_{(b)}) \to [\![w]\!]_{(b)}$ denotes the Beaver-triple–based multiplication. Given $[\![u]\!]_{(b)}$, $[\![v]\!]_{(b)}$ at CSb, and a triple $([\![a]\!], [\![d]\!], [\![c]\!])$ with $c = a \cdot d$, each party b computes $e_b = [\![u]\!]_{(b)} - [\![a]\!]_{(b)}, f_b = [\![v]\!]_{(b)} - [\![d]\!]_{(b)}$, opens $e = e_0 + e_1$ and $f = f_0 + f_1$, and outputs the product share $[\![w]\!]_{(b)} = [\![c]\!]_{(b)} + e [\![d]\!]_{(b)} + f [\![a]\!]_{(b)} + b \cdot (ef) \bmod p$.

$\mathsf{MulVV}([\![\mathbf{u}]\!]_{(b)}, [\![\mathbf{v}]\!]_{(b)}) \to [\![\mathbf{w}]\!]_{(b)}$ denotes vector-wise (element-wise) multiplication. For $\mathbf{u}, \mathbf{v} \in \mathbb{Z}_p^\ell$, invoke MulSS per coordinate in parallel (one triple per coordinate) and batch the openings; i.e., $[\![w_j]\!] = \mathsf{MulSS}([\![u_j]\!], [\![v_j]\!])$ for all j.

2.3 Function Secret Sharing (FSS)

We follow the definition of function secret sharing (FSS) from [1]. For a function family $\mathcal{F}_{\mathbb{G}_{\text{in}},\mathbb{G}_{\text{out}}}$ with domain $\mathbb{G}_{\text{in}}$ and range $\mathbb{G}_{\text{out}}$, a two-party FSS scheme with key space $\mathcal{K}_0 \times \mathcal{K}_1$ has algorithms $(\mathsf{Gen}, \mathsf{Eval})$, both taking λ as an implicit input:

- $\mathsf{Gen}(1^\lambda, f)$ is a key-generation algorithm that, given 1^λ and a description of $f \in \mathcal{F}_{\mathbb{G}_{\text{in}},\mathbb{G}_{\text{out}}}$, outputs keys $(k_0, k_1) \in \mathcal{K}_0 \times \mathcal{K}_1$. We assume f explicitly includes the input/output groups $\mathbb{G}_{\text{in}}, \mathbb{G}_{\text{out}}$.

- $\mathsf{Eval}(b, k_b, x)$ is an evaluation algorithm that, given party index $b \in \{0,1\}$, key $k_b \in \mathcal{K}_b$, and $x \in \mathbb{G}_{\text{in}}$, the algorithm outputs $y_b \in \mathbb{G}_{\text{out}}$.

A particularly useful special case of FSS is Distributed Comparison Functions (DCF) [4].

DCF is FSS for comparison functions. For an ordered domain $\mathbb{G}_{\text{in}}$ (e.g., $\{0,1\}^k$ under integer ordering) and output group $\mathbb{G}_{\text{out}}$, let $f^{<}_{\tau,1}(x) = 1$ if $x < \tau$ and 0 otherwise.

Based on this, the range comparison function (DRF) $f_1^{[L,U)}(x)$ can be implemented via two DCFs: $f_1^{[L,U)}(x) = f^{<}_{U,1}(x) - f^{<}_{L,1}(x)$ outputs 1 if $L \leq x < U$ otherwise 0.

3 Problem Formulation

This section presents the system model, security model, and formal definitions for the proposed similarity query scheme.

3.1 System Model

Our system mainly involves three parties: a data owner DO, two cloud services $\mathbf{CS} = \{\text{CS0}, \text{CS1}\}$, and a set of query users, denoted as $\mathcal{U} = \{\mathcal{U}_1, \mathcal{U}_2, \cdots\}$ (Fig. 1).

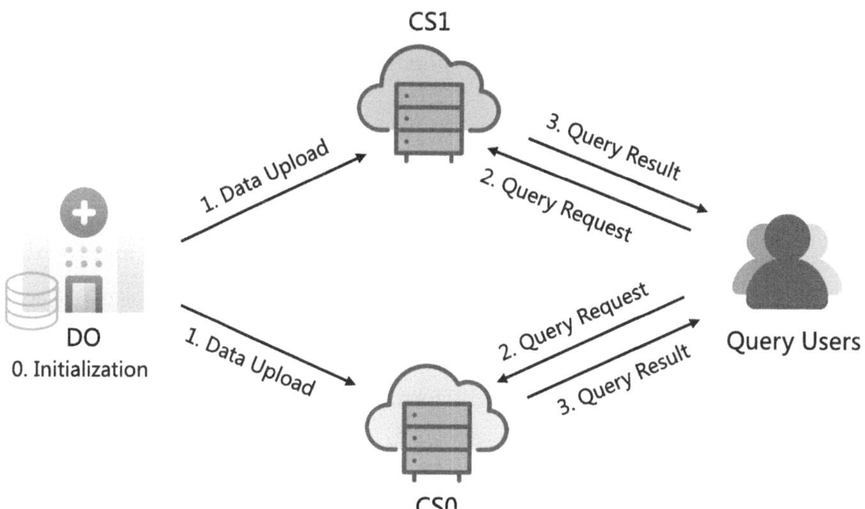

Fig. 1. System model under consideration

- Data Owner (DO): The DO is the healthcare center holding an electronic health records (EHRs) dataset $\mathcal{E} = \{\mathbf{e}_i\}_{i=1}^n$, where each record $\mathbf{e} = (e_1, \cdots, e_d)$, $\mathbf{e} \in \mathcal{E}$ contains multiple attributes. The DO aims to provide healthcare similarity services to query users. To achieve this goal with limited local computational and storage resources, the DO outsources the secret shares $[\![\mathcal{E}]\!]$ to powerful cloud servers.
- Cloud services $\mathbf{CS} = \{\text{CS0}, \text{CS1}\}$: Each CS$b, b \in \{0, 1\}$ is a cloud service provider, responsible for storing the secret shares of the dataset outsourced from DO and executing similarity query services for query users.
- Query Users $\mathcal{U}s = \{\mathcal{U}_1, \mathcal{U}_2, \cdots\}$: There are multiple query users in the system, denoted by $\mathcal{U}s = \{\mathcal{U}_1, \mathcal{U}_2, \ldots\}$. Each query user submit similarity query $\mathbf{q} = (q_1, q_2, \cdots, q_d)$ to $\mathbf{CS}$ and obtain the corresponding results returned by the cloud servers.

Note that our system focuses on the efficient and secure outsourcing and processing of similarity queries on the outsourced dataset; we do not discuss registration and authenticity in this paper.

3.2 Security Model

In our security model, the data owner is assumed to be honest. Each cloud server CSb for $b \in \{0, 1\}$ is assumed to be honest-but-curious, meaning that it faithfully executes all system processes but may attempt to infer information about the data or the queries from the information it receives during these processes. Moreover, we assume that the two cloud servers do not collude, as this assumption is widely accepted because cloud service providers must maintain their reputation. We also assume that query users are honest, since any misbehavior would be subject to legal penalties.

Note that our scheme is designed to prioritize privacy in similarity queries within the AiP system. Therefore, issues such as collusion among different parties and other active attacks (e.g., Denial of Service attacks) are beyond the scope of this paper and will be addressed in future work. Under the specified security model, our scheme aims to protect the privacy of both the queries and the data of the data owner.

3.3 Problem Formulation

Based on p-stable LSH, we can formally formulate the user fine-grained similarity query in our scheme.

Definition 2 (User Fine-Grained Similarity Query Based on p-Stable LSH). *Let $\mathcal{E} = \{\mathbf{e}_1, \ldots, \mathbf{e}_n\} \subset \mathbb{Z}_p^d$ be a dataset, where each record is a d-dimensional vector $\mathbf{e}_i = (e_{i1}, \ldots, e_{id})^\top$. Let $g(\mathbf{x}) = (h_1(\mathbf{x}), \ldots, h_K(\mathbf{x}))$ be a concatenated hash as described in Definition 1. Given a query vector $\mathbf{q} \in \mathbb{Z}_p^d$ and an integer threshold $t \in \{1, \ldots, K\}$, define the collision count*

$$C(\mathbf{e}_i, \mathbf{q}) = \sum_{j=1}^{K} \mathbf{1}\{h_j(\mathbf{e}_i) = h_j(\mathbf{q})\}. \tag{4}$$

The fine-grained similarity query *returns the result set*

$$\mathcal{R}(\mathbf{q}, t) = \{\mathbf{e}_i \in \mathcal{E} : C(\mathbf{e}_i, \mathbf{q}) \geq t\}, \tag{5}$$

i.e., all records for which at least t of the component hashes in $g(\cdot)$ collide with the query.

Definition 3 (Definition of Our Scheme). *Our privacy-preserving fine-grained similarity retrieval scheme over outsourced data consists of six algorithms:*

- $\mathsf{pp} \leftarrow \mathsf{SysInit}(1^\lambda)$ *is the system initialization algorithm. It inputs the security parameter λ, and outputs public parameters* pp.
- $\{[\![\mathcal{E}]\!]_{(b)}, [\![g]\!]_{(b)}, \mathsf{KeyList}_b\}_{b\in\{0,1\}} \leftarrow \mathsf{Upload}(\mathcal{E}, \mathsf{pp})$ *is the data upload algorithm executed by the data owner. It inputs the dataset $\mathcal{E}$ and the public parameter* pp, *and outputs to two non-colluding servers $CS0$, $CS1$ the secret-shared dataset $[\![\mathcal{E}]\!]$, the secret-shared LSH parameters $[\![g]\!]$, and the key list* $\mathsf{KeyList}_b$ *required during the online phase.*
- $\{\mathsf{token}_{(b)}\}_{b\in\{0,1\}} \leftarrow \mathsf{TokenGen}(\mathbf{q}, t, \mathsf{pp})$ *is the query token generation algorithm run by a user $\mathcal{U}$. It inputs a query vector $\mathbf{q}$ and a threshold $t \in \{1, \ldots, K\}$, and outputs the per-server query token* $\mathsf{token}_{(b)}$.
- $\{[\![\hat{\mathbf{e}}_i]\!]_{(b)}\}_{i=1}^n \leftarrow \mathsf{Query}([\![\mathcal{E}]\!]_{(b)}, \mathsf{token}_{(b)})$ *is the server-side query processing algorithm. Each server CSb inputs its received secret-shared data $[\![\mathcal{E}]\!]_{(b)}$ and the token* $\mathsf{token}_{(b)}$, *and outputs to the query user the corresponding secret-shared query result $\{[\![\hat{\mathbf{e}}_i]\!]_{(b)}\}_{i=1}^n$*
- $\hat{\mathcal{E}} \leftarrow \mathsf{Retrieve}(\{[\![\hat{\mathbf{e}}_i]\!]_{(0)}\}_{i=1}^n, \{[\![\hat{\mathbf{e}}_i]\!]_{(1)}\}_{i=1}^n)$ *is the client-side retrieval algorithm. It inputs the two sets of returned shares from $CS0$ and $CS1$, reconstructs the results, and outputs the final result set $\hat{\mathcal{E}}$.*

Definition 4 (Correctness Definition for Our Scheme). *Let $\mathcal{R}(\mathbf{q}, t) = \{\mathbf{e} \in \mathcal{E} : C(\mathbf{e}, \mathbf{q}) \geq t\}$. The scheme is correct if, for any $\mathcal{E}, \mathbf{q}, t$:*

- Completeness: *If $C(\mathbf{e}, \mathbf{q}) \geq t$, then $\mathbf{e} \in \hat{\mathcal{E}}$ after* $\mathsf{Retrieve}$.
- Soundness: *If $\mathbf{e} \in \hat{\mathcal{E}}$, then $C(\mathbf{e}, \mathbf{q}) \geq t$.*

4 Our Proposed Scheme

In this section, we first present our proposed scheme and then illustrate its correctness.

4.1 Scheme Construction

Our proposed privacy-preserving fine-grained similarity-based query scheme consists of five phases: (1) SysInit, (2) Upload, (3) TokenGen, (4) Query, and (5) Retrieve. We present each phase in detail below.

1. SysInit

Step 1. Based on the security parameter λ, DO initializes the system, and publishes the public parameters pp including the arithmetic field $\mathbb{Z}_p$ for additive secret sharing, and the total number K of all LSH functions.

2. Upload

Step 1. DO generates the p-stable LSH function $g(\mathbf{x}) = (h_1(\mathbf{x}), \ldots, h_K(\mathbf{x}))$. Then DO secret-shares the function $g(\mathbf{x})$ to the form:

$$[\![g]\!]_{(b)} = \{[\![h_1]\!]_{(b)}, \cdots, [\![h_K]\!]_{(b)}\},$$

where $[\![h_k]\!]_{(b)} = ([\![\mathbf{a}_k]\!]_{(b)}, [\![\beta_k]\!]_{(b)}, [\![r_k]\!]_{(b)})$ for $k \in [1, K]$.

Step 2. To avoid the division in Eq. 1 (i.e., $h_k(\mathbf{x}) = \lfloor (\mathbf{a}_k^\top \mathbf{x} + \beta_k)/r_k \rfloor$), DO transforms bucket-index computation into a range determination:

Let $s_k := \mathbf{a}_k^\top \mathbf{x} + \beta_k$, and define bucket intervals as

$$B_y^k := [L_y^k, U_y^k) = [yr_k, (y+1)r_k) \text{ where } y \in \mathbb{Z}_p. \tag{6}$$

Then

$$h_k(\mathbf{x}) = y \Leftrightarrow s_k(\mathbf{x}) \in B_y^k \Leftrightarrow L_y^k \leq \mathbf{a}_k^\top \mathbf{x} + \beta_k < U_y^k. \tag{7}$$

Subsequently, DO performs data preprocessing as the following steps:

- Based on the dataset $\mathcal{E} = \{\mathbf{e}_i\}_{i=1}^n$, the DO constructs K different LSH functions $H = \{h_1(\mathbf{x}), \ldots, h_K(\mathbf{x})\}$, where $h_k(\mathbf{x}) = \left\lfloor \frac{\mathbf{a}_k^\top \mathbf{x} + \beta_k}{r_k} \right\rfloor$ for $k \in [1, K]$.
- For each $k \in [1, K]$, the DO constructs

$$h_k(\mathbf{x}) = ([L_1^k, U_1^k), [L_2^k, U_2^k), \cdots, [L_{\max_k}^k, U_{\max_k}^k))$$

  based on Eqs. 6 and 7, where $\max_k$ is the maximum bucket number of $h_k(\mathbf{x})$.
- For each $k \in \{1, \cdots, K\}$ and $\gamma \in \{1, \ldots, \max_k\}$, the DO runs

$$(K_{k,\gamma}^{\mathrm{DRF},(0)}, K_{k,\gamma}^{\mathrm{DRF},(1)}) \leftarrow \mathsf{DRF.Gen}\left(1^\lambda, f_\beta^{[L_\gamma^k, U_\gamma^k)}\right).$$

Step 2. After that, DO prepares per-server key list $\mathsf{KeyList}_b$ that includes all required online keys and materials:

$$\{K_{k,\gamma}^{\mathrm{DRF},(b)}, K^{\mathrm{DRF},(1-b)}\}, \{[\![r]\!]_{(b)}, [\![K^{\mathrm{Beaver}}]\!]_{(b)}\}.$$

Step 3. For each entity $\mathbf{e} \in \mathcal{E}$, DO secret-shares $\mathbf{e}$ as

$$[\![\mathbf{e}]\!]_{(b)} = ([\![e_1]\!]_{(b)}, \cdots, [\![e_d]\!]_{(b)}),$$

then generates $[\![\mathcal{E}]\!]_{(b)} = \{[\![\mathbf{e}_i]\!]_{(b)}\}_{i=1}^n$.

Step 4. DO uploads $\{[\![\mathcal{E}]\!]_{(b)}, [\![g]\!]_{(b)}, \mathsf{KeyList}_b\}$ to CS_b for $b \in \{0,1\}$.

3. TokenGen

Step 1. The query user $\mathcal{U}$ first secret-shares its query vector $\mathbf{q}$ as

$$[\![\mathbf{q}]\!]_{(b)} = ([\![q_1]\!]_{(b)}, [\![q_2]\!]_{(b)}, \cdots, [\![q_d]\!]_{(b)}).$$

Step 2. For the required similarity threshold $t \in \{1, 2, \cdots, K\}$, the query user $\mathcal{U}$ invokes $\mathsf{DCF.Gen}(1^\lambda, f_1^t) \rightarrow (K_{\mathcal{U}}^{\mathrm{DCF},(0)}, K_{\mathcal{U}}^{\mathrm{DCF},(1)})$ to generate the keys of the DCF function.

Step 3. $\mathcal{U}$ generates the query token as $\mathsf{token}_{(b)} = \{[\![\mathbf{q}]\!]_{(b)}, K_{\mathcal{U}}^{\mathrm{DCF},(b)}, [\![t]\!]_{(b)}\}$. Then $\mathcal{U}$ sends the query request $\mathsf{token}_{(b)}$ to CSb, where $b \in \{0,1\}$.

4. Query

Step 1. After receiving $\{[\![\mathcal{E}]\!]_{(b)}, [\![g]\!]_{(b)}\}$ from DO, for each $[\![\mathbf{e}]\!]_{(b)} \in [\![\mathcal{E}]\!]_{(b)}$, CS$b$ performs the following steps:

For each $h_k \in H$, CSb proceeds as follows:

- Computes $[\![\mathbf{c}]\!]_{(b)} \leftarrow \mathsf{MulVV}([\![\mathbf{e}]\!]_{(b)}, [\![\mathbf{a}_k]\!]_{(b)})$, where $\mathbf{c} = (c_1, c_2, \cdots, c_d)$ is the d-dimensional vector obtained by element-wise multiplying $\mathbf{e}$ and $\mathbf{a}_k$.
- Computes $[\![Y_k]\!]_{(b)} \leftarrow (\sum_{j=1}^d [\![c_j]\!]_{(b)}) + [\![\beta_k]\!]_{(b)}$.
- Computes $[\![\mathbf{y}_k]\!]_{(b)} \leftarrow \mathsf{DRF.Eval}(K_{k,\gamma}^{\mathrm{RCF},(b)}, [\![Y_k]\!]_{(b)})$, for $\gamma \in [1, \max_k]$, where the result vector

$$[\![\mathbf{y}_k]\!]_{(b)} = ([\![y_{k,1}]\!]_{(b)}, \cdots, [\![y_{k,\max_k}]\!]_{(b)})$$

denotes the interval bucket (i.e., $[L_\gamma^k, U_\gamma^k)$) in which Y_k falls.

Step 2. After receiving query request $\mathsf{token}_{(b)}$ from the query user $\mathcal{U}$, for $h_k \in H$, CSb performs the following steps:

- Computes $[\![\tilde{\mathbf{c}}]\!]_{(b)} \leftarrow \mathsf{MulVV}([\![\mathbf{q}]\!]_{(b)}, [\![\mathbf{a}_k]\!]_{(b)})$, where $\tilde{\mathbf{c}} = (\tilde{c_1}, \tilde{c_2}, \cdots, \tilde{c_d})$ is the d-dimensional vector obtained by element-wise multiplying $\mathbf{q}$ and $\mathbf{a}_k$.
- Computes $[\![\tilde{Y_k}]\!]_{(b)} \leftarrow (\sum_{i=1}^d [\![\tilde{c_i}]\!]_{(b)}) + [\![\beta_k]\!]_{(b)}$.
- Computes $[\![\tilde{\mathbf{y}_k}]\!]_{(b)} \leftarrow \mathsf{DRF.Eval}(K_{k,\gamma}^{\mathrm{RCF},(b)}, [\![\tilde{Y_k}]\!]_{(b)})$ for $\gamma \in [1, \max_k]$, where the result vector

$$[\![\tilde{\mathbf{y}_k}]\!]_{(b)} = ([\![\tilde{y_{k,1}}]\!]_{(b)}, \cdots, [\![\tilde{y_{k,\max_k}}]\!]_{(b)})$$

denotes the interval bucket (i.e., $[L_\gamma^k, U_\gamma^k)$) in which $\tilde{Y_k}$ falls.

Step 3. For each $[\![\mathbf{e}]\!]_{(b)} \in [\![\mathcal{E}]\!]_{(b)}$, CS$b$ computes whether the similarity between the query vector $\mathbf{q}$ and the data entry $\mathbf{e}$ (using the previously obtained computation result $[\![\mathbf{y}_k]\!]_{(b)}$) satisfies the query user's requirement through the following steps:

- CSb computes $[\![\mathbf{V}_k]\!]_{(b)} \leftarrow \mathsf{MulVV}([\![\mathbf{y}_k]\!]_{(b)}, [\![\tilde{\mathbf{y}_k}]\!]_{(b)})$ for $k \in [1, K]$, where $\mathbf{V}_k = (v_{k,1}, v_{k,2}, \cdots, v_{k,\max_k})$ is the $\max_k$-dimensional vector obtained by element-wise multiplying $\mathbf{y}_k$ and $\tilde{\mathbf{y}_k}$. Then, it computes

$$[\![V_{sum}]\!]_{(b)} = \sum_{j=1}^{\max_k} [\![V_{k,j}]\!]_{(b)}.$$

- CSb invokes $[\![z]\!]_{(b)} \leftarrow \mathsf{DCF.Eval}(K_{\mathcal{U}}^{\mathrm{DCF},(b)}, [\![V_{sum}]\!]_{(b)})$, then uses the result to expand into a d-dimensional vector

$$[\![\mathbf{z}]\!]_{(b)} = ([\![z]\!]_{(b)}, \cdots, [\![z]\!]_{(b)}).$$

- CSb computes the secret-shared filter result of $[\![\mathbf{e}]\!]_{(b)}$ as follows:

$$[\![\hat{\mathbf{e}}]\!]_{(b)} \leftarrow \mathsf{MulVV}([\![\mathbf{z}]\!]_{(b)}, [\![\mathbf{e}]\!]_{(b)}).$$

Step 4. CSb returns the result $[\![\hat{\mathcal{E}}]\!]_{(b)} = \{[\![\hat{\mathbf{e}}]\!]_{(b)}\}_{\mathbf{e} \in \mathcal{E}}$ containing all records that satisfy the similarity requirement to the query user $\mathcal{U}$.

5. Retrieve

Step 1. After receiving $[\![\hat{\mathcal{E}}]\!]_{(b)}$ from CSb for $b \in \{0, 1\}$, the query user $\mathcal{U}$ reconstructs $\hat{\mathcal{E}}$. Removing all zero vectors from $\hat{\mathcal{E}}$ constitutes the final query result $\mathcal{R}$.

4.2 Correctness Analysis of Our Scheme

Theorem 1. *Let $\mathcal{E} = \{\mathbf{e}_i\}_{i=1}^n \subseteq \mathbb{Z}_p^d$ be the outsourced dataset and $g(\mathbf{x}) = (h_1(\mathbf{x}), \ldots, h_K(\mathbf{x}))$ the concatenated p-stable LSH. For a query $\mathbf{q} \in \mathbb{Z}_p^d$ and a threshold $t \in \{1, \ldots, K\}$, define $C(\mathbf{e}_i, \mathbf{q}) = \sum_{j=1}^K \mathbf{1}\{h_j(\mathbf{e}_i) = h_j(\mathbf{q})\}, \mathcal{R}(\mathbf{q}, t) = \{\mathbf{e}_i \in \mathcal{E} : C(\mathbf{e}_i, \mathbf{q}) \geq t\}$. When the scheme runs* TokenGen, Query, *and* Retrieve *as specified, the user reconstructs a set $\hat{\mathcal{E}}$ that satisfies $\hat{\mathcal{E}} = \mathcal{R}(\mathbf{q}, t)$.*

Proof. The proof proceeds as follows.

(i) Bucket Indication is Correct. For each component $k \in \{1, \ldots, K\}$, let $Y_k(\mathbf{x}) = \mathbf{a}_k^\top \mathbf{x} + \beta_k$ and the bucket intervals $[L_\gamma^k, U_\gamma^k)$ for $\gamma \in [1, \max_k]$ so that

$$h_k(\mathbf{x}) = \gamma \iff Y_k(\mathbf{x}) \in [L_\gamma^k, U_\gamma^k).$$

Evaluating $\mathsf{DRF.Eval}$ on $[\![Y_k(\mathbf{e})]\!]$ and $[\![Y_k(\mathbf{q})]\!]$ (with the pre-generated keys for all intervals) yields one-hot vectors

$$[\![\mathbf{y}_k]\!] = ([\![y_{k,1}]\!], \ldots, [\![y_{k,\max_k}]\!]), \quad [\![\tilde{\mathbf{y}}_k]\!] = ([\![\tilde{y}_{k,1}]\!], \ldots, [\![\tilde{y}_{k,\max_k}]\!]),$$

that open to the indicators of the unique buckets containing $Y_k(\mathbf{e})$ and $Y_k(\mathbf{q})$, respectively. Hence,

$$\sum_{\gamma=1}^{\max_k} y_{k,\gamma}\, \tilde{y}_{k,\gamma} = \mathbf{1}\{h_k(\mathbf{e}) = h_k(\mathbf{q})\}.$$

(ii) Collision Aggregation Equals the Collision Count. The servers compute $[\![\mathbf{V}_k]\!] \leftarrow \mathsf{MulVV}([\![\mathbf{y}_k]\!], [\![\tilde{\mathbf{y}}_k]\!])$ and then $[\![V_k^{\text{sum}}]\!] = \sum_{\gamma=1}^{\max_k} [\![V_{k,\gamma}]\!]$, which opens to $V_k^{\text{sum}} = \mathbf{1}\{h_k(\mathbf{e}) = h_k(\mathbf{q})\}$. Summing across all k in shares gives

$$[\![S(\mathbf{e}, \mathbf{q})]\!] = \sum_{k=1}^{K} [\![V_k^{\text{sum}}]\!] \Rightarrow S(\mathbf{e}, \mathbf{q}) = \sum_{k=1}^{K} \mathbf{1}\{h_k(\mathbf{e}) = h_k(\mathbf{q})\} = C(\mathbf{e}, \mathbf{q}).$$

(iii) Threshold Filtering Returns Exactly the Qualifying Records. Using the user-provided DCF keys for $f_{\geq t}(x) = \mathbf{1}\{x \geq t\}$, the servers evaluate

$$[\![z(\mathbf{e}, \mathbf{q})]\!] \leftarrow \mathsf{DCF.Eval}(K_{\mathcal{U}}^{\text{DCF}}, [\![S(\mathbf{e}, \mathbf{q})]\!]),$$

so that $z(\mathbf{e}, \mathbf{q}) = \mathbf{1}\{C(\mathbf{e}, \mathbf{q}) \geq t\}$. They expand $[\![z]\!]$ to a d-vector $[\![\mathbf{z}]\!]$ and output the masked record share $[\![\hat{\mathbf{e}}]\!] = \mathsf{MulVV}([\![\mathbf{z}]\!], [\![\mathbf{e}]\!])$. Thus, if $C(\mathbf{e}, \mathbf{q}) \geq t$ then $\hat{\mathbf{e}} = \mathbf{e}$; otherwise $\hat{\mathbf{e}} = \mathbf{0}$.

As a result, after Retrieve, the user discards all-zero vectors and obtains

$$\hat{\mathcal{E}} = \left\{\mathbf{e} \in \mathcal{E} \,:\, C(\mathbf{e}, \mathbf{q}) \geq t\right\} = \mathcal{R}(\mathbf{q}, t),$$

establishing completeness (all qualifying $\mathbf{e}$ appear) and the soundness (no non-qualifying $\mathbf{e}$ appear). Therefore, our proposed scheme meets the correctness requirement specified in Definition 4.

5 Security Analysis

In this section, we prove that our proposed scheme satisfies the security requirements of simulation-based security with leakage $\mathcal{L}$. We first give the definition of simulation-based security, and discuss the leakage function, then present the security of our scheme.

Definition 5 (Simulation-Based Security). *Let $\mathcal{A}_0$ and $\mathcal{A}_1$ be two probabilistic polynomial-time (PPT) adversaries respectively compromise CS0 and CS1. Our proposed scheme is said to be simulation-based secure with respect to leakage function $\mathcal{L}(\mathcal{S}_0)$ and $\mathcal{L}(\mathcal{S}_1)$, if there exist PPT simulators $\mathcal{S}_0$ and $\mathcal{S}_1$ such that for any honest-but-curious adversary $\mathcal{A}_0$ and $\mathcal{A}_1$, the views of the real interaction and the ideal interaction are computationally indistinguishable. Formally,*

$$Real^{\Pi}_{\mathcal{A}_{0(1)}}(1^{\lambda}) \stackrel{c}{\equiv} Ideal^{\mathcal{L}_{0(1)}}_{\mathcal{A}_{0(1)}, \mathcal{S}_{0(1)}}(1^{\lambda}), \tag{8}$$

where $\stackrel{c}{\equiv}$ denotes computationally indistinguishable. $Real^{\Pi}_{\mathcal{A}_{0(1)}}(1^{\lambda})$ is the view of $\mathcal{A}_{0(1)}$ interacting with the real scheme Π under security parameter λ. The $Ideal^{\mathcal{L}_{0(1)}}_{\mathcal{A}_{0(1)}, \mathcal{S}_{0(1)}}(1^{\lambda})$ is the view of $\mathcal{A}_{0(1)}$ interacting with simulator $\mathcal{S}_{0(1)}$, who only receives the leakage $\mathcal{L}_{0(1)}$.

Leakage Function. For any single cloud CSb, the view leaks only the following deterministic metadata:

- SysInit leakage $\mathcal{L}_{\mathsf{SysInit}}$: the security parameter λ, and the total number K of all LSH functions.
- Upload leakage $\mathcal{L}_{\mathsf{Upload}}$: the structure (number and length) of $\mathsf{KeyList}_b$, dataset size n, dimension d, number of hash components K, the number of buckets per component $\max_k$ (equivalently, the number of DRF keys), and the length of modulus p.
- Query leakage $\mathcal{L}_{\mathsf{Query}}$: the occurrence of a query, the bitlength of t, the vector dimension d, and the counts of FSS evaluations consistent with $(K, \max_k)$.

Theorem 2. *If FSS-based functions (e.g., DCF/DRF) are secure against chosen-plaintext attacks (CPA-secure), and Beaver triples are sampled correctly at random. Then our scheme is simulation-based secure against any PPT adversary corrupting a single cloud CSb under our security model with the leakage*

$$\mathcal{L} = \{\mathcal{L}_{\mathsf{SysInit}}, \mathcal{L}_{Upload}, \mathcal{L}_{Query}\}.$$

Proof. Real World. Let $\mathrm{Real}^{\Pi}_{\mathcal{A}_b}(1^\lambda)$ denote the view of CSb, including: online needed keys and materials $\mathsf{KeyList}_b$, $\{[\![\mathcal{E}]\!]_{(b)}, [\![g]\!]_{(b)}\}$ received in Data Upload phase; the query request $\mathsf{token}_{(b)}$ received in TokenGen phase; FSS evaluation internal results (shares).
Ideal World. We construct a PPT simulator $\mathcal{S}_b$ that, given only $\mathcal{L}$, produces a distribution computationally indistinguishable view $\mathrm{Ideal}^{\mathcal{L}_b}_{\mathcal{A}_b,\mathcal{S}_b}(1^\lambda)$ from $\mathrm{Real}^{\Pi}_{\mathcal{A}_b}(1^\lambda)$:
Upload Phase. Based on λ and the structure of $\mathsf{KeyList}_b$ in leakage $\mathcal{L}_{\mathsf{SysInit}}$, $\mathcal{S}_b$ invokes corresponding FFS-based functions' Gen over the same domain $\mathbb{Z}_p$ to generate randomly keys and materials $\mathsf{KeyList}^*_b$ with same structure as in the real execution. By the single-key privacy of FSS, a one-party key is independent of the underlying function, so the distribution is indistinguishable from the real one. Based on $\{n, d, K, \max_k\}$ from $\mathcal{L}_{\mathsf{Upload}}$, the simulator $\mathcal{S}_b$ creates $\{[\![\mathcal{E}^*]\!]_{(b)}, [\![g^*]\!]_{(b)}\}$ with the same length and structure as in the real execution. Marginally, a single additive share over $\mathbb{Z}_p$ is information-theoretically uniform and independent of the secret, hence identically distributed to the real execution.
Query Phase. Based on the $\mathcal{L}_{\mathsf{Query}}$, the simulator $\mathcal{S}_b$ samples $\mathsf{token}^*{}_{(b)}$ uniformly at random. It generates a DCF key $K^{*\mathrm{DCF},(b)}_{\mathcal{U}}$ for a random threshold t^*. For each FSS-based evaluation, the simulator outputs uniformly random shares in the same length with real evaluation; the marginal distribution of a single share matches that of the real evaluation outputs.

As the result, distinguishing the real world view and ideal world view is equivalent to distinguishing random values, thus

$$\mathrm{Real}^{\Pi}_{\mathcal{A}_{0(1)}}(1^\lambda) \stackrel{c}{\equiv} \mathrm{Ideal}^{\mathcal{L}_{0(1)}}_{\mathcal{A}_{0(1)},\mathcal{S}_{0(1)}}(1^\lambda).$$

Therefore, our proposed scheme is simulation-based secure against the honest-but-curious adversary CSb.

6 Performance Evaluation

In this section, we present the experimental evaluation of our scheme, focusing on computation overhead.

6.1 Experimental Setting

In our experiments, all experiments were executed on an Intel Core i7-14700F running Windows 11 with OpenJDK 23. Unless otherwise stated, the number of LSH tables is fixed at 10 and the security parameter is set to $\lambda = 128$. We vary three factors: dataset size $n \in \{1000, 2000, 3000, 4000, 5000\}$, number of attributes $d \in \{5, 10, 15, 20, 25\}$, and threshold $t \in \{2, 4, 6, 8\}$. When one factor varies, the others use their defaults ($n = 1000$, $d = 10$, $t = 4$).

First, we test the joint impact of n and d. The results are shown in Fig. 2. As both n and d increase, the runtime grows almost linearly and the surface is close to a plane, indicating that the total cost scales proportionally to $n{\cdot}d$ within the tested range.

Next, we test the effect of d under different thresholds while fixing $n = 1000$ (see Fig. 3). As d increases from 5 to 25, the runtime increases approximately linearly. Moreover, as t becomes larger, the slope becomes steeper; for example, at $d = 25$, the time at $t = 8$ is about 2.1× that at $t = 2$. These results indicate predictable scaling with respect to dimensionality.

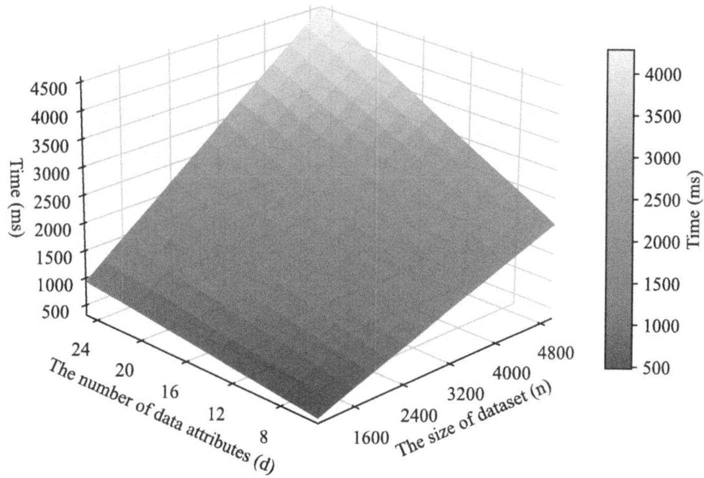

Fig. 2. Runtime surface vs. dataset size n and attributes d (fixed $t = 4$).

Then, we test the effect of n under different thresholds while fixing $d = 10$ (see Fig. 4). As n increases from 1000 to 5000, the runtime increases linearly; as t becomes larger, the growth rate increases accordingly. At $n = 5000$, the runtime

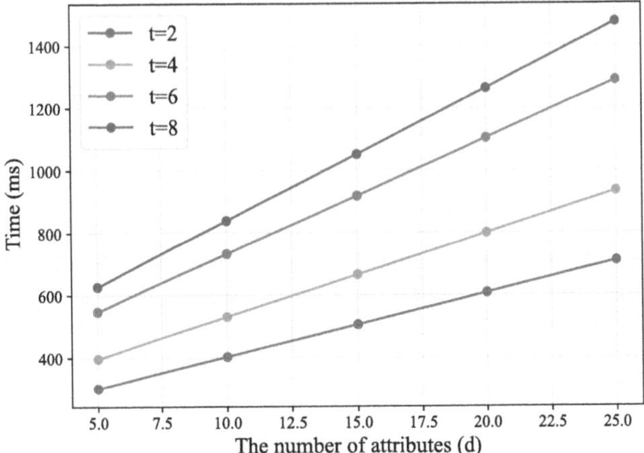

Fig. 3. Runtime vs. number of attributes d for different thresholds t (fixed $n = 1000$).

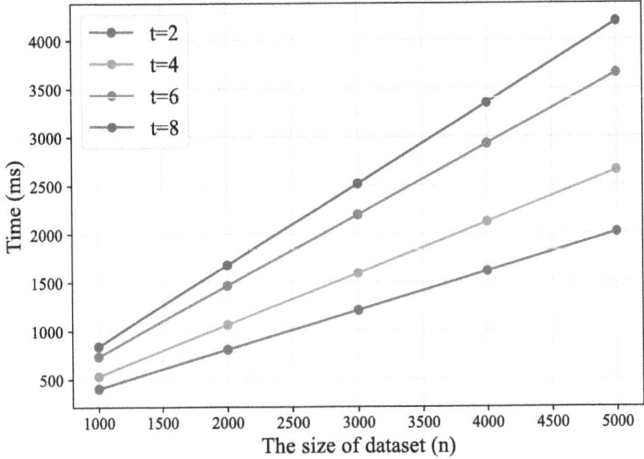

Fig. 4. Runtime vs. dataset size n for different thresholds t (fixed $d = 10$).

ranges from about 2.0 s ($t = 2$) to about 4.2 s ($t = 8$). This indicates that the system maintains stable throughput as data volume grows.

Overall, the experimental results show that our scheme exhibits near-linear scalability in both dataset size and attribute dimension, while the threshold t acts as a roughly linear amplifier of cost. The completion time remains within a few seconds even at the largest tested setting, demonstrating practical efficiency.

7 Conclusion

In this paper, we presented an efficient, privacy-preserving scheme for fine-grained similarity queries over EHRs in AiP services. By integrating p-stable

LSH with additive secret sharing and function secret sharing under the honest-but-curious model, our design supports thresholded matching that returns all records satisfying users' fine-grained similarity requirements while hiding access patterns. Extensive experiments demonstrate high computational and communication efficiency, privacy protection, and practical scalability, making the scheme well-suited for real-world AiP deployments. Future work will explore richer query types and stronger adversarial models.

Acknowledgments. This project was supported by collaborative research funding from the National Research Council of Canada's Aging in Place Challenge Program.

References

1. Boyle, E., Gilboa, N., Ishai, Y.: Function secret sharing. In: Oswald, E., Fischlin, M. (eds.) EUROCRYPT 2015. LNCS, vol. 9057, pp. 337–367. Springer, Heidelberg (2015). https://doi.org/10.1007/978-3-662-46803-6_12
2. Choi, M., Sempungu, J.K., Lee, E.H., Lee, Y.H.: Living longer but in poor health: healthcare system responses to ageing populations in industrialised countries based on the findings from the global burden of disease study 2019. BMC Public Health **24**(1), 576 (2024)
3. Datar, M., Immorlica, N., Indyk, P., Mirrokni, V.S.: Locality-sensitive hashing scheme based on p-stable distributions. In: Proceedings of the Twentieth Annual Symposium on Computational Geometry, pp. 253–262 (2004)
4. Gilboa, N., Ishai, Y.: Distributed point functions and their applications. In: Nguyen, P.Q., Oswald, E. (eds.) EUROCRYPT 2014. LNCS vol. 8441, pp. 640–658. Springer, Heidelberg (2014). https://doi.org/10.1007/978-3-642-55220-5_35
5. Gong, C., Wang, X., Zhu, D., Huang, C., Ma, Z., Ma, J.: Enabling efficient and privacy-preserving sequence similarity query on encrypted genomes. IEEE Trans. Depend. Secure Comput. (2025)
6. Huang, C., Lu, R., Zhu, H., Shao, J., Lin, X.: FSSR: fine-grained EHRS sharing via similarity-based recommendation in cloud-assisted ehealthcare system. In: Proceedings of the 11th ACM on Asia Conference on Computer and Communications Security, pp. 95–106 (2016)
7. Lewis, C., Buffel, T.: Aging in place and the places of aging: a longitudinal study. J. Aging Stud. **54**, 100870 (2020)
8. Shamir, A.: How to share a secret. Commun. ACM **22**(11), 612–613 (1979). https://doi.org/10.1145/359168.359176
9. Vanleerberghe, P., De Witte, N., Claes, C., Schalock, R.L., Verté, D.: The quality of life of older people aging in place: a literature review. Qual. Life Res. **26**(11), 2899–2907 (2017)
10. Zheng, Y., et al.: EPSet: efficient and privacy-preserving set similarity range query over encrypted data. IEEE Trans. Serv. Comput. **17**(2), 524–536 (2024)
11. Zheng, Y., Lu, R., Guan, Y., Zhang, S., Shao, J., Zhu, H.: Efficient and privacy-preserving similarity query with access control in ehealthcare. IEEE Trans. Inf. Forensics Secur. **17**, 880–893 (2022)
12. Zhou, X., et al.: Hierarchical federated learning with social context clustering-based participant selection for internet of medical things applications. IEEE Trans. Comput. Soc. Syst. **10**(4), 1742–1751 (2023)

VulFocus: Interpret AI Models in Software Vulnerability Detection

Yuejun Guo[1(✉)], Zeming Dong[2], and Qiang Tang[1]

[1] Luxembourg Institute of Science and Technology, Esch-sur-Alzette, Luxembourg
{yuejun.guo,qiang.tang}@list.lu
[2] University of Luxembourg, Esch-sur-Alzette, Luxembourg
zeming.dong@uni.lu

Abstract. In numerous academic work, Artificial Intelligence (AI) has demonstrated remarkable capabilities to detect software vulnerabilities from source code, particularly through transformer-based models like CodeBERT and Llama. However, in practice, these models often demonstrate limited generalization capability when applied to new codebases, raising critical questions about what they actually learn during training and whether they truly understand code semantics or merely recognize superficial patterns. By design, their black-box nature further complicates this issue by obscuring their decision-making process. This paper introduces VulFocus, an interactive visualization tool that facilitates interpreting the decision-making process of transformer-based models in vulnerability detection. VulFocus implements two interpretation approaches: attention-based analysis that highlights code regions of focus, and masked language modeling that identifies surprising or unexpected code segments. Our evaluations demonstrate that these visualizations help security analysts and researchers understand the reason behind model decisions, validate findings, assess model generalization capabilities, and understand ineffectiveness of variable-renaming based adversarial attacks. VulFocus bridges the gap between AI capabilities and human interpretability in software vulnerability detection, enabling more effective collaboration between automated systems and security analysts.

Keywords: Artificial intelligence · Interpretability · Software vulnerability detection

1 Introduction

Nowadays, cyberattacks exploiting software vulnerabilities have become increasingly sophisticated and frequent, posing significant risks to individuals, organization, and critical infrastructure. Traditional vulnerability detection typically relies on rule-based [16] and signature-based [31] approaches, which are constrained by predefined patterns and rules to identify emerging security threats. These approaches struggle to cover various vulnerabilities and often miss complex

W. Li et al. (Eds.): EISA 2025, CCIS 2897, pp. 40–58, 2026.
https://doi.org/10.1007/978-3-032-21177-4_3

security weaknesses. Recent advances in artificial intelligence (AI), particularly transformer-based models pre-trained on code repositories (e.g., CodeBERT [7], CodeT5 [39]) and newer large language models (LLMs) like Code Llama [30] and GPT-4 [27], have demonstrated remarkable capabilities to automate the detection of vulnerabilities.

Despite their immense potential in software vulnerability detection, these transformer models often exhibit limited generalization capability when evaluated on previously unseen codebases [13], raising critical concerns about their robustness and reliability in real-world deployment settings. A major contributing factor to this generalization challenge it the black-nature of these models, which obscures the decision-making process and makes it difficult for software researchers and security analysts to understand why a model classifies a specific code snippet as vulnerable-or conversely, why it fails to identify vulnerabilities. These state-of-the-art models typically consists of dozens of layers (e.g., 12 transformer layers for CodeBERT, and significantly more for LLMs like Code Llama and GPT-4) with millions to billions of parameters, incorporating complex non-linear activation functions, multi-head attention mechanisms, and intricate feature interactions across multiple representation levels. This architectural complexity, while enabling powerful representation learning capabilities, makes it becomes practically infeasible to trace the influence of specific code tokens or syntactic structures on the final vulnerability prediction.

This lack of interpretability creates a significant barrier to practical adoption. Without a deeper understanding of the rationale behind models' decision-making, practitioners cannot effectively validate model performance or build trust necessary for deploying these models in security-critical applications where false positives and false negatives can cause severe consequences. To address these pressing challenges, we present **VulFocus**[1], a novel visualization framework designed to enhance model interpretability in the domain of software vulnerability detection. VulFocus empowers researchers and security analysts with intuitive visual representations to better understand and evaluate models decisions of of software vulnerability detection models.

VulFocus has four main features: (1) VulFocus supports all transformer models for vulnerability detection, including large language models such as Code Llama [30]. Adding support for new models requires only linking (e.g., model card on Hugging Face [15]) the model into the existing implementation, making it highly extensible for future model integration; (2) VulFocus implements two interpretation approaches, attention-based analyais and masked language modeling (MLM) analysis, to enable users to understand model behaviour from different analytical perspectives; (3) VulFocus supports comparisons between model focus and human-annotated vulnerable lines, helping users evaluate whether or not the model is focusing on semantically meaningful regions of code, and further understand potential mismatches or failures; (4) VulFocus provides GUI

[1] The implementation of VulFocus is available at: https://github.com/Yuejun-GUO/VulFocus.

to enable users to interact with models, interpretation methods, and vulnerable source code.

The main contributions of this paper are as follows:

1. We introduce VulFocus, the first unified visualization framework specifically designed for interpreting transformer-based vulnerability detection models, addressing the critical gap in interpretability tools for this security-critical domain.
2. We demonstrate VulFocus's practical utility through systematic evaluation across three distinct scenarios: validating model predictions, assessing generalization capability, and analyzing variable renaming ineffectiveness for researchers, AI developers, and security analysts. These use cases provide concrete evidence of the framework's value in addressing real-world interpretability challenges.
3. We conduct systematic evaluations comparing model attention patterns with human-annotated vulnerable code lines, providing insights into model reliability and identifying cases where models may focus on semantically irrelevant code features.

2 Background

In this section, we briefly introduce the transformer models and two model interpretation methods adopted by VulFocus.

2.1 Transformer Models

Transformer models are a class of neural network architecture introduced by Vaswani *et al.* [37] in their seminal work "Attention Is All You Need". Unlike traditional convolutional neural networks (CNNs) and recurrent neural networks (RNNs) that rely on convolutional layers and recurrent connections to process data, transformer models use attention mechanisms to model contextual relationships between words within a sequence.

Core Architecture. Figure 1 shows the original architecture design of transformer, which consists of an encoder-decoder structure. Encoder-decoder models (e.g., CodeT5 [39]) are particularly effective for sequence-to-sequence tasks, such as machine translation [38] and program repair [8]. Nevertheless, various adaptations exist. For instance, encoder-only models (e.g., CodeBERT [7]) are designed for representation learning. Decoder-only models (e.g., GPT-4 [27], Code Llama [30]) are used for generative tasks like text generation. These variants modify the original encoder-decoder structure by retaining only the relevant components.

As shown in Fig. 1, the encoder (left side) is composed of multiple identical layers. Each layer includes a multi-head attention mechanism and a position-wise fully connected feed-forward network. The encoder takes the input embedding

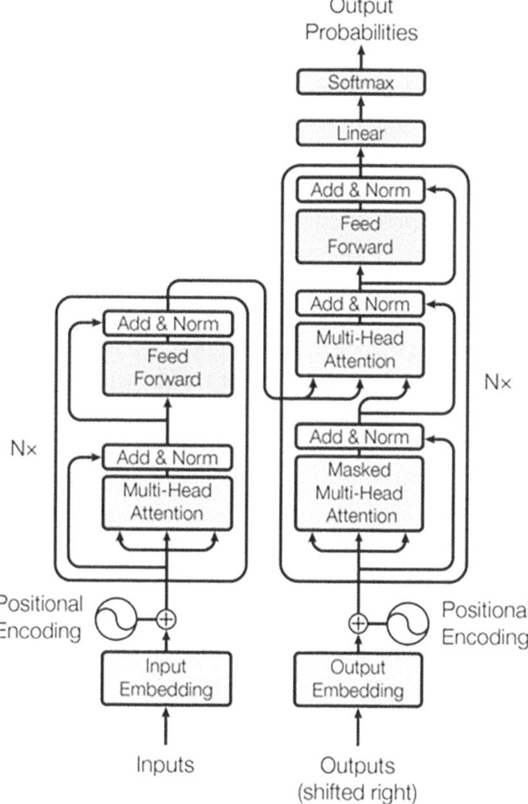

Fig. 1. The Transformer - model architecture. Image source: [37]

and processes it through these layers, allowing the model to capture contextual relationships between words in the input sequence. Residual connections and layer normalization are applied around each sub-layer to facilitate training and maintain stable gradients. The decoder (right side) also consists of multiple identical layers, but each layer has an additional **masked** multi-head attention mechanism which ensures that the predictions for a given position can depend only on the known outputs at positions before it.

Self-attention. The self-attention mechanism is a foundational component that enables transformer models to weigh the relevance of different tokens in a sequence with respect to each other. This is achieved through three learned linear transformations that create query (Q), key (K), and value (V) matrices from the input embedding. The attention function is computed as:

$$\text{Attention} = \text{softmax}\left(\frac{Q \cdot K^T}{\sqrt{d_k}}\right) V \tag{1}$$

where d_k represents the dimension of the key vectors.

Multi-head Attention. Multi-head attention extends this mechanism by performing multiple attention functions (heads) in parallel with independent projects of Q, K, and V. This allows the model to capture the information from different representation subspaces. The outputs of all attention heads are concatenated and linearly projected to produce the final output.

2.2 Model Interpretability Concepts

Attention-Based Interpretation. Leveraging the attention mechanism is the most widely used strategy to interpreting transformer-based models [2,3]. This approach works by extracting attention weights from the softmax operation in Equation(1), where the "attention scores" for each token correspond to the normalized dot-product values:

$$\text{attention\_score} = \text{softmax}\left(\frac{Q \cdot K^T}{\sqrt{d_k}}\right). \tag{2}$$

These attention scores indicate the relative importance that each token assigns to every other token in the sequence, with higher attention scores indicating parts that are more important for the model's decision. For instance, in machine translation [38], attention matrices can show alignment between source and target language words, while in image captioning [18], spatial attention maps highlight relevant image regions for each generated word.

Masked Language Modeling (MLM). MLM is a self-supervised pre-training objective used in transformer models such as CodeBERT [7]. It enables models to learn bidirectional contexual representations. In the case of CodeBERT, the model is trained on paired data of natural language (e.g., comment) and programming languages (e.g., Python and Java), allowing it to capture the semantic relationships between source code and its corresponding documentation or comments. During training, approximately 15% of input tokens in a code sequence are randomly replaced with a special `[MASK]` token, and the model is trained to predict the original masked tokens by using the context provided by the surrounding tokens. Formally, given a sequence, $\mathbf{x} = \omega_1\omega_2 \dots \omega_i \dots \omega_n$, where ω_i is a token, a masked version of the sequence is constructed as $\mathbf{x}^* = \omega_1[\text{MASK}] \dots [\text{MASK}] \dots \omega_n$. The objective is to recover the original tokens ω_2 and ω_i.

Additionally, MLM is commonly used in conducting adversarial attack research [41], where token importance is calculated to identify which parts of the code would most significantly influence the model's predictions. This approach works by assessing the importance of individual tokens through token substitution. Specifically, each token in the input sequence is independently replaced with a special token, such as `[MASK]` and `[unk]`, and the impact on the model's prediction confidence is measured. Following the approach of Yang et al. [42], token importance is quantified by computing the change in the model's output confidence before and after substitution. Let $\mathbf{x} = \omega_1\omega_2 \ldots \omega_i \ldots \omega_n$ be the original input, and $f(\mathbf{x})$ be the model's prediction confidence (e.g., the probability assigned to the correct label). For a token ω_i, a perturbed input $\mathbf{x}^*$ is formed by replacing ω_i with a special token (e.g., `[unk]`). The importance score of ω_i is then computed as:

$$\text{importance\_score} = |f(\mathbf{x}) - f(\mathbf{x}^*)| \tag{3}$$

A higher score indicates that the token has a larger influence on the model's prediction, as its removal or masking causes a significant change in the output confidence.

3 The Design of VulFocus

VulFocus provides an interactive visualization framework to interpret AI model reasoning in software vulnerability detection. Figure 2 provides a comprehensive overview of a web-based frontend built with the Streamlit framework [33] and a server-side backend (written in Python).

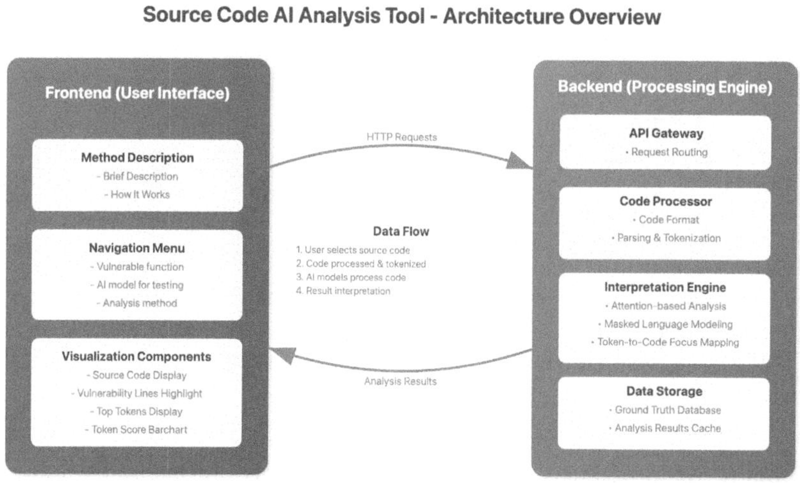

Fig. 2. Architecture design of VulFocus.

3.1 Frontend (User Interface)

The user interface comprises three primary components that work together to provide insights into model decision-making processes to researchers and security analysts, as illustrated in Fig. 2. Figure 3 gives a screenshot of the interface.

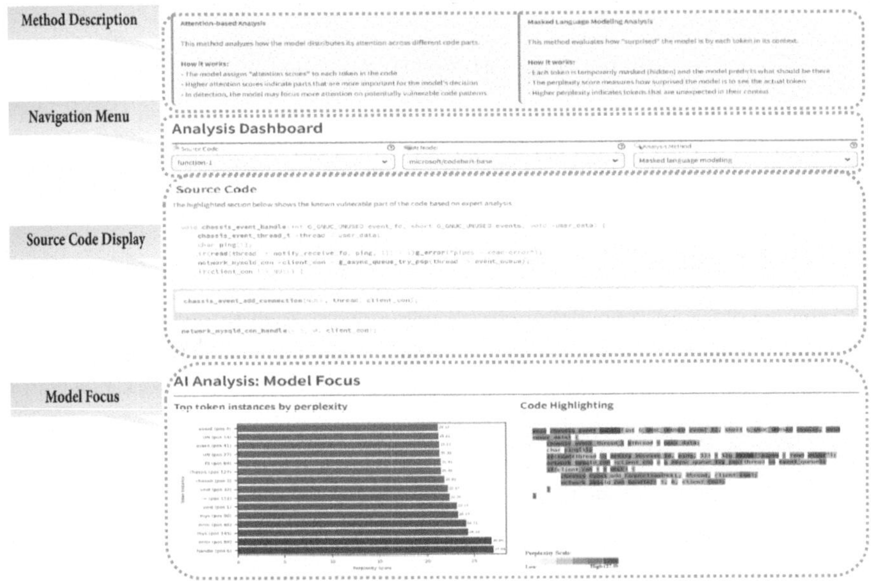

Fig. 3. VulFocus user interface overview design.

Method Description. This component presents users with detailed explanations of the underlying methodologies, including brief descriptions of the two interpretation approaches, attention-based analysis and masked language modeling (MLM) analysis. This helps users understand the underlying techniques and how to interpret their visualization outputs.

Navigation Menu. The menu delivers an interactive dashboard where users can configure their analysis by selecting:

1. **Source code** to analyze. The data used in VulFocus comes from the benchmark dataset Big-Vul [6] for software vulnerability detection. Each entry in the dataset represents a function with a specific Common Weakness Enumeration (CWE)[2] identifier where vulnerable lines have been explicitly annotated.

[2] https://cwe.mitre.org/.

Note that VulFocus is designed to be extensible, enabling seamless integration of new vulnerability detection datasets with minimal effort. Adding new datasets is straightforward–users simply need to format their data according to the same JSON schema as the Big-Vul dataset, regardless of whether the annotation of vulnerable lines is available.

2. **AI model** to interpret. VulFocus supports all transformer-based models for vulnerability detection. It currently integrates five pre-trained models from Hugging Face [15]: Microsoft's CodeBERT [24], Meta's Llama-3.2-1B [23], Mistral's Mistral-7B-v0.1 [25], and two specialized vulnerability detection models (Coderbert_finetuned_detect_vulnerability_on_MSR [35] and Vulnerability_Detection_Using_CodeBERT [28]). These two specialized models are fine-tuned versions of CodeBERT using different datasets. With its modular design, VulFocus seamlessly integrates any transformer model for vulnerabilty detection from Hugging Face's extensive ecosystem through a plugin-based architecture. Users can incorporate cutting-edge models with just a single configuration line, enabling rapid experimentation without core system modifications. This extensibility ensures VulFocus automatically benefits from the latest AI research advances.
3. **Analysis method** to apply, attention-based or MLM.

Visualization Components. As illustrated in Fig. 3, the visualization includes both "Source code" and "Model focus".

- **Source code display** shows the selected source code with vulnerable lines highlighted in pink when human annotations are available. The vulnerability lines highlight the pinpoint specific problematic code segments. Even without annotations, the component remains useful for code visualization and serves as a reference for evaluating whether the model is focusing on the correct code parts when performing vulnerability detection.
- **Model focus** reveals the model's reasoning by the selected interpretation method via two integrated visualization approaches:
  1. **Token importance ranking (left side)**: A bar chart displays tokens ordered by their computed scores (attention or perplexity), highlighting the most important or surprising elements. These tokens are mapped back to their corresponding code segments for meaningful interpretation.
  2. **Contextual code visualization (right side)**: The original source code is rendered with color-coded highlighting, where the intensity of each highlight directly reflects the token's importance score. This representation allows users to quickly identify which code segments capture the model's focus within their natural context. In vulnerability detection tasks, the most critical or vulnerable code lines should ideally exhibit the highest intensity scores.

3.2 Backend (Processing Engine)

The backend infrastructure is implemented in Python using the Pytorch framework, with all AI models loaded from Hugging Face. It consists of four integrated modules as illustrated in Fig. 2.

API Gateway. This module manages the request routing and handles HTTP communications between the frontend and backend services, ensuring smooth data flow and system response.

Code Processor. This module includes a critical preprocessing that transforms raw, unformatted source code from benchmark datasets into structured, readable representations suitable for users. This module addresses the inherent challenge that source code in datasets often lacks proper formatting and indentation, appearing as compressed single-line strings that are difficult for human interpretation, as shown in Fig. 4.


```
{"full_function": "void *arm_dma_alloc(struct device *dev, size_t size, dma_addr_t *handle, gfp_t gfp, struct dma_attrs *attrs) { pgprot_t prot = __get_dma_pgprot(attrs, pgprot_kernel); void *memory; if (dma_alloc_from_coherent(dev, size, handle, &memory)) return memory; return __dma_alloc(dev, size, handle, gfp, prot, false, __builtin_return_address(0));}", "vulnerable_part": "pgprot_t prot = __get_dma_pgprot(attrs, pgprot_kernel);"}
```


Fig. 4. Example of unformatted source code from benchmark datasets.

The processor implements language-specific formatting algorithms to restore proper code structure, applies intelligent indentation and spacing rules. Currently, VulFocus supports both C and Python, and can be extended to accommodate additional programming languages by implementing language-specific formatting rules. Additionally, this module performs tokenization to convert the formatted source code into standardized input representations for AI models.

Interpretation Engine. The core analytical component that performs attention-based and MLM analysis. For each token, the engine computes the attention score and importance score using Eq. (2) and Eq. (3), respectively. The engine renders token-level analysis directly onto the source code through precise positional alignment. Each token span is mapped to its corresponding character positions in the original code and visualized with color-coded highlighting. The visualization preserves the granular detail of individual token scores.

Data Storage. This module is responsible for maintaining persistent storage of both datasets and cached analysis results. It ensures reliable access to reference data and previously computed interpretations, supporting efficient retrieval and reuse across analytical workflows.

4 Use Cases

To demonstrate VulFocus's utility, we present three use cases that highlight how the tool helps researchers and security analysts understand and validate AI model decisions in software vulnerability detection. Figure 5 illustrates a code function with vulnerable lines highlighted.

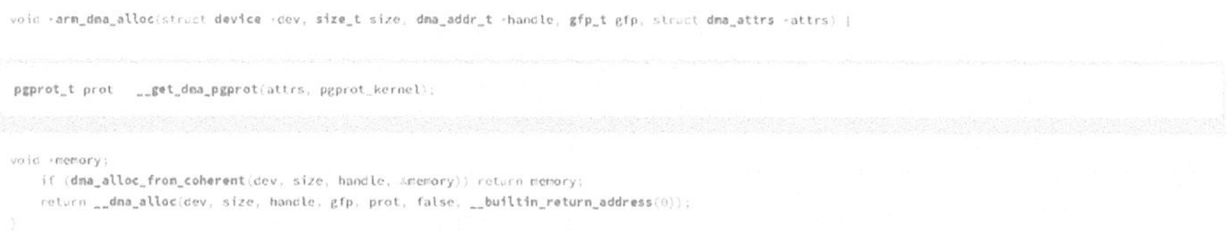

```
void *arm_dma_alloc(struct device *dev, size_t size, dma_addr_t *handle, gfp_t gfp, struct dma_attrs *attrs) {

pgprot_t prot = __get_dma_pgprot(attrs, pgprot_kernel);

void *memory;
    if (dma_alloc_from_coherent(dev, size, handle, &memory)) return memory;
    return __dma_alloc(dev, size, handle, gfp, prot, false, __builtin_return_address(0));
}
```

Fig. 5. Use case example (with human-annotated vulnerable lines).

4.1 Validating Model Predictions

The validation of model predictions serves different purposes depending on the availability of human-annotated vulnerable lines and target user groups.

When Annotation Is Available. Researchers and AI developers can visually compare model focus with human-annotated vulnerable lines to assess the reliability of model outputs before deploying in real-world applications. Based on the comparison, users can verify whether the model truly understand code semantics or merely learns superficial patterns from the training data.

As shown in Fig. 5, the vulnerable line is:
`pgprot_t prot = __get_dma_pgprot(attrs, pgprot_kernel);`.
However, interpreting by the attention scores, the CodeBERT model focuses on irrelevant code parts, mainly punctuations (e.g., `}`, `:`), as shown in Fig. 6(a). While Llama-3.2-1B [23] and Mistral-7B-v0.1 [25] focus on more meaningful code parts (e.g., `_dma`, `handle`, `_size`), they still fail to identify vulnerable lines. In contrast, Mistral-7B-v0.1 outperforms Llama-3.2-1B, as it demonstrates more selective attention and does not uniformly focus on all parts of the code. This may be due to its more advanced architecture or training on higher-quality data. Additionally, the MLM[3] shows that CodeBERT is less focused on the vulnerable line than the entire code. According to these visualizations, we can conclude that both models has not learnt useful patterns and are not ready for deployment in real-world applications.

[3] Note that MLM does not apply to Llama-3.2-1B and Mistral-7B-v0.1 because Llama and Mistral models use causal language modeling instead of MLM. Therefore, it cannot calculate token importance score as in Equation (3).

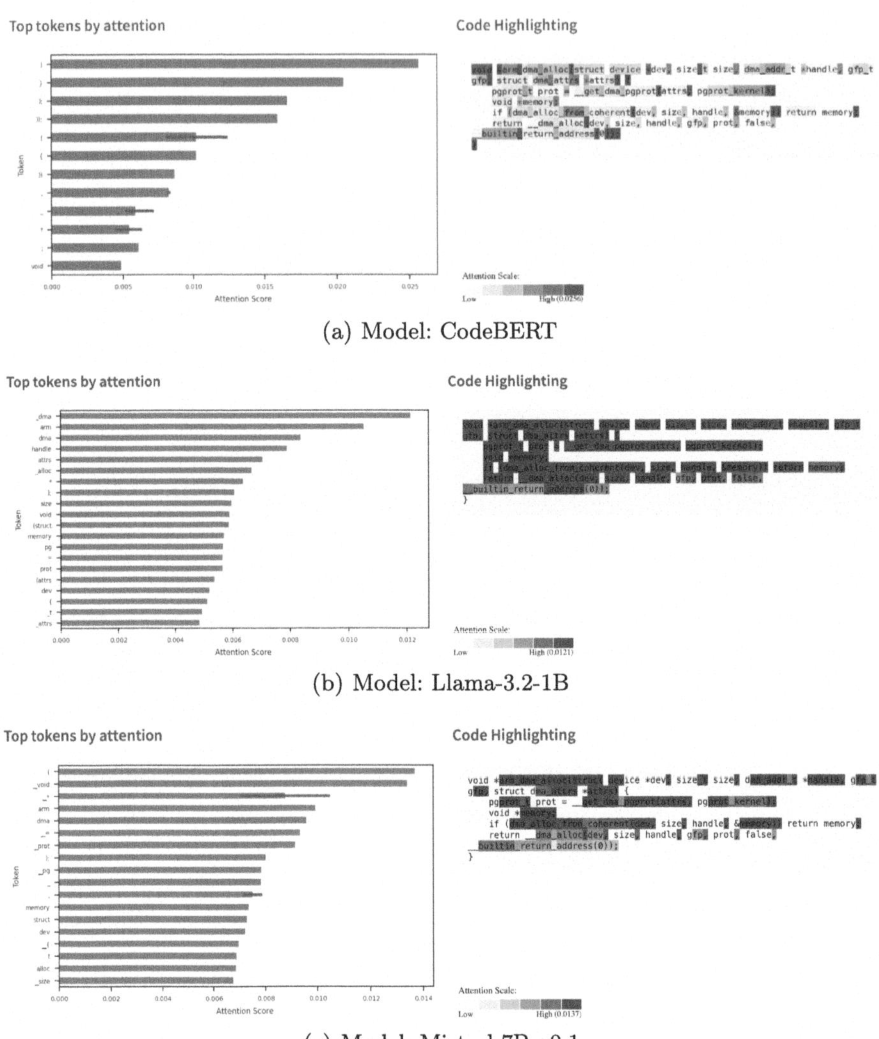

Fig. 6. Use case example: model focus by attention-based analysis.

When Annotation Is Unavailable. Security analysts can leverage VulFous to understand model predictions in operational scenarios. The visualization helps analysts assess the credibility of detected vulnerabilities and build trust in automated detection models by examining whether the model focus aligns with their domain expertise.

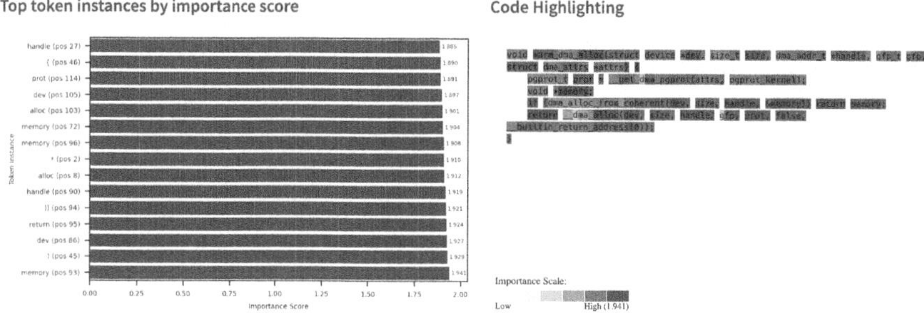

Fig. 7. Use case example: model focus by MLM-based analysis. Model: CodeBERT

4.2 Assessing Generalization Capabilities

While state-of-the-art performance is often reported in the literature, vulnerability detection models often demonstrate low generalization capability to new coedebases [13]. Researchers and AI developers can benefit from VulFocus to assess model generalization capabilities by comparing attention patterns across different models on identical input data. In this use case, the human annotation of vulnerable lines is not needed.

We demonstrate this capability by comparing CodeBERT and its two fine-tuned versions, Coderbert_finetuned_detect_vulnerability_on_MSR [35] and Vulnerability_Detection_Using_CodeBERT [28]. Both models have been fine-tuned specifically for software vulnerability detection and have reported 70% and 100% accuracy on their test sets, respectively. However, we observed that all these three models produce the same model focus (Fig. 8) on the example code function from the Big-Vul dataset [6], indicating that fine-tuning failed to improve the model's interpretative focus. Beyond the visual analysis, we examined the model parameters and found that only the `pooler.dense.weight` parameter differs between CodeBERT and both fine-tuned versions, with slight parameter changes, Coderbert_finetuned_detect_vulnerability_on_MSR (maximum: 0.126724) and Vulnerability_Detection_Using_CodeBERT (maximum: 0.133648). Since the `pooler` layer is primarily used for classification tasks and does not affect the attention mechanisms in the transformer layers, the identical attention score distributions are expected, as the core attention parameters remain unchanged during fine-tuning. This suggests that the fine-tuning process primarily adapted the classification head and both fine-tuned models may not have learned distinct, generalizable vulnerability features from their respective training datasets.

4.3 Understanding Variable Renaming Attack Ineffectiveness

Variable renaming [42] is a common adversarial attack against code analysis models, where attackers replace variable names with semantically similar alternatives to foo the model. This attack is particularly effective when targeting

```
void *arm_dma_alloc(struct device *dev, size_t size, dma_addr_t *handle, gfp_t
gfp, struct dma_attrs *attrs) {
    pgprot_t prot = __get_dma_pgprot(attrs, pgprot_kernel);
    void *memory;
    if (dma_alloc_from_coherent(dev, size, handle, &memory)) return memory;
    return __dma_alloc(dev, size, handle, gfp, prot, false,
__builtin_return_address(0));
}
```

Fig. 8. Code highlighting using attention-based analysis. All three models, CodeBERT [24], Coderbert_finetuned_detect_vulnerability_on_MSR [35] and Vulnerability_Detection_Using_CodeBERT [28], produce the same results.

variables that strongly influence model decisions. However, empirical studies [41] have demonstrated that these attacks often achieve low success rates when targeting vulnerability detection models. While existing studies generally attribute this issue to an insufficient search space of alternatives or ineffective search algorithm, VulFocus provides a different perspective by revealing which code elements actually influence model decisions.

Consider the example code function in Fig. 5, where the vulnerable line contains variables `prot`, `attrs`, and `pgprot_kernel`. When conducting variable-renaming based adversarial attacks, the attackers will assume they are critical for the model's vulnerability assessment. However, as shown in Fig. 7, the model's focus on these variables is actually minimal. This explains why variable renaming attacks targeting these elements show low success rates–the attacked variables have little influence on the model, making the adversarial modifications ineffective.

5 Related Work

We review related work across three foundational areas: AI-based vulnerability detection, interpretability techniques for code analysis models, and visualization tools that enhance understanding of AI-driven source code analysis.

5.1 AI for Software Vulnerability Detection

Compared to the traditional static analyzers [16,31] that often require manual feature engineering by security experts, AI facilitates the analysis without running the target program and is feasible to function at different granularities (e.g., file, function, and program slice) [11]. Various AI models have been developed and put in-use to support automated vulnerability detection. Simple examples including multi-layer perception (MLP), convolutional neural network (CNN), and recurrent neural network (RNN) have shown improved performance by better modeling sequential and structural code information. For instance, Grieco *et al.* [9] developed VDiscover that uses a MLP model to predict vulnerabilities.

Zhou *et al.* [44] proposed Devign, a graph neural network approach that represents code as heterogeneous graphs combining syntax and semantic information. Transformer-based models, such as CodeBERT [7] and CodeT5 [39], have demonstrated superior performance across various code-related tasks, including software vulnerability detection. These models benefit from pre-training on massive code repositories paired with natural language documentations, enabling them to learn rich representations of code syntax and semantics.

More recently, the advent of large language models (LLMs) is changing the vulnerability detection paradigm. Zhou *et al.* conducted a survey and revealed that LLMs like GPT-3.5, GPT-4 [27], Unixcoder [10], and Code Llama [30] have been frequently used in the literature for software vulnerability detection. Li *et al.* [19] demonstrated that both GPT-3.5 and GPT-4 have the ability to identify vulnerable code and provide detailed information on the detected vulnerabilities. However, studies have shown that these models suffer from generalization limitations [13] and robustness concerns against adversarial attacks [41].

5.2 Model Interpretability for Source Code Analysis

As AI model architectures grow more complex, understanding their decision-making processes becomes increasingly important and challenging. Techniques such as attention visualization [20], saliency maps [32], and feature attribution [36] methods are commonly used to offer insights into how AI models make decisions. Specific to transformer-based models, the most canonical explanation method relies on their attention mechanisms as they explicitly show which input tokens influence each output token and are an inherent part of the model's architecture [2,3]. While these approaches were initially developed for general purposes, they have since been adapted for code-specific interpretation. Mohammadkhani *et al.* [26] analyzed two pre-trained code modles—CodeBERT and GraphCodeBERT—using attention mechanisms as an intrinsic explainable AI approach. They revealed that models focus on different token types depending on the task: method signatures for code documentation, syntax tokens for code translation, and balanced attention for code refinement. Beyond attention-based analysis, model-agnostic techniques have also been employed to explain model baheviors. Wattanakriengkrai *et al.* [40] applied LIME [29], an explanation method, to explain a prediction of which code tokens lead the defect model to make decisions. Sotgiu *et al.* [34] utilized SHAP (SHapley Additive exPlanations) [21] to quantify the contribution of each code token to the model's prediction in vulnerability discovery.

On the other hand, adversarial robustness studies, particularly variable-renaming attacks, have inadvertently contributed interpretability insights through their methodologies. Most variable-renaming attacks, originally designed for robustness testing [41], employ masked language modeling (MLM) to quantify the influence of code tokens on model predictions. Yang *et al.* [42] measured token importance by replacing each token with `<unk>` and calculating the difference in model prediction confidence before and after the substitution. A larger difference indicates higher token importance, as removing that token significantly affects the model's predictive certainty. Wen *et al.* [41] followed the same methodology and used `unknown` as the mask token. Although these techniques were developed primarily for adversarial evaluation rather than interpretability, the underlying token importance calculations provide valuable insights into model dependencies that complement traditional attention-based and attribution methods.

5.3 Visualization Tools for AI-Based Source Code Analysis

Visualization tools have been developed to make the AI-based source code analysis understandable. Tools like CodeLens [12] and Comex [5] focus on visualizing code representations, such as token sequences and data flow graphs, enabling a deeper understanding of code structure for AI models. Several tools [1,14,17,22] focuses on parsing source code in different programming languages and extracting the abstract syntax tree (AST) representation. Zhang *et al.* [43] developed NeuralVis to support software engineers in visualizing and interpreting deep learning models. Specifically, NeuralVis provides interactive visualization of deep neural network architectures, rendering individual neurons, layers, and inter-layer connections. The tool focuses on convolutional neural networks, such as LeNet and VGG-12 architectures, while excluding transformer-based models from its current scope. Sam and Ravi [4] introduces a general-purpose framework for styling and visualizing source code using a CSS-inspired rule language. The visualization system allows developers and toolmakers to declaratively specify visual annotations over source code based on syntactic, semantic, and runtime properties. In summary, these tools typically visualize code representations or model outputs rather than explaining AI reasoning of model decisions.

Different from existing tools, VulFocus creates visualizations specifically designed to interpreting AI model decisions in the context of software vulnerability detection, addressing the critical need for transparency and trust in automated security analysis tools used by software developers and security practitioners.

6 Conclusion

This paper introduced VulFocus, an interactive visualization tool designed to interpret the decision-making process of transformer-based AI models in software vulnerability detection. By combining attention-based analysis with masked language modeling analysis, VulFocus bridges the gap between AI decisions and human interpretability in security applications. Our three use cases demonstrate that VulFocus can help researchers and security analysts validate model outputs, assess model generalization, and understand the ineffectiveness of variable-renaming based adversarial attacks. These features address critical challenges in deploying AI for real-world security applications where trust and generalization are critical.

Beyond its analytical capabilities, VulFocus's modular and extensible design positions it as a valuable platform for the evolving landscape of AI-driven cybersecurity research. The tool's plug-and-play architecture facilitates seamless integration with new models and datasets, ensuring researchers can leverage cutting-edge advances without development overhead.

Future work will focus on expanding VulFocus to support a wider range of additional interpretation approaches.

Acknowledges. This paper is funded by the European Commission through the Horizon Europe Programme as part of the LAZARUS project (Grant Agreement No. 101070303). The content of this article represents the sole responsibility of the authors and does not necessarily reflect the official views of the European Union.

References

1. Alon, U., Zilberstein, M., Levy, O., Yahav, E.: Code2vec: learning distributed representations of code. Proc. ACM Program. Lang. **3**(POPL) (2019). https://doi.org/10.1145/3290353
2. Chefer, H., Gur, S., Wolf, L.: Generic attention-model explainability for interpreting bi-modal and encoder-decoder transformers. In: 2021 IEEE/CVF International Conference on Computer Vision (ICCV), pp. 387–396. IEEE Computer Society, Los Alamitos, CA, USA (2021). https://doi.org/10.1109/ICCV48922.2021.00045
3. Chefer, H., Gur, S., Wolf, L.: Transformer interpretability beyond attention visualization. In: Proceedings of the IEEE/CVF Conference on Computer Vision and Pattern Recognition (CVPR), pp. 782–791 (2021). https://doi.org/10.1109/CVPR46437.2021.00084
4. Cohen, S., Chugh, R.: Code style sheets: CSS for code. Proc. ACM Program. Lang. **9**(OOPSLA1) (2025). https://doi.org/10.1145/3720421
5. Das, D., et al.: Comex: a tool for generating customized source code representations. In: Proceedings of the 38th IEEE/ACM International Conference on Automated Software Engineering, pp. 2054–2057. ASE '23, IEEE Press (2024). https://doi.org/10.1109/ASE56229.2023.00010
6. Fan, J., Li, Y., Wang, S., Nguyen, T.N.: A C/C++ code vulnerability dataset with code changes and CVE summaries. In: Proceedings of the 17th International Conference on Mining Software Repositories, pp. 508–512. MSR '20, Association for Computing Machinery, New York, NY, USA (2020). https://doi.org/10.1145/3379597.3387501
7. Feng, Z., et al.: CodeBERT: a pre-trained model for programming and natural languages. In: Findings of the Association for Computational Linguistics: EMNLP 2020, pp. 1536–1547. Association for Computational Linguistics, Online (2020). https://doi.org/10.18653/v1/2020.findings-emnlp.139
8. Fu, M., Tantithamthavorn, C., Le, T., Nguyen, V., Phung, D.: VulRepair: a T5-based automated software vulnerability repair. In: Proceedings of the 30th ACM Joint European Software Engineering Conference and Symposium on the Foundations of Software Engineering, pp. 935–947. ESEC/FSE 2022, Association for Computing Machinery, New York, NY, USA (2022). https://doi.org/10.1145/3540250.3549098

9. Grieco, G., Grinblat, G.L., Uzal, L., Rawat, S., Feist, J., Mounier, L.: Toward large-scale vulnerability discovery using machine learning. In: Proceedings of the Sixth ACM Conference on Data and Application Security and Privacy, pp. 85–96. CODASPY '16, Association for Computing Machinery, New York, NY, USA (2016). https://doi.org/10.1145/2857705.2857720
10. Guo, D., Lu, S., Duan, N., Wang, Y., Zhou, M., Yin, J.: UniXcoder: unified cross-modal pre-training for code representation. In: Proceedings of the 60th Annual Meeting of the Association for Computational Linguistics. Volume 1: Long Papers, pp. 7212–7225. Association for Computational Linguistics (2022)
11. Guo, Y., Bettaieb, S., Casino, F.: A comprehensive analysis on software vulnerability detection datasets: trends, challenges, and road ahead. Int. J. Inf. Secur. **23**(5), 3311–3327 (2024). https://doi.org/10.1007/s10207-024-00888-y
12. Guo, Y., Bettaieb, S., Hu, Q., Traon, Y.L., Tang, Q.: CodeLens: an interactive tool for visualizing code representations (2023). https://arxiv.org/abs/2307.14902
13. Guo, Y., Patsakis, C., Hu, Q., Tang, Q., Casino, F.: Outside the comfort zone: analysing LLM capabilities in software vulnerability detection. In: Computer Security – ESORICS 2024: 29th European Symposium on Research in Computer Security, Bydgoszcz, Poland, September 16–20, 2024, Proceedings, Part I, pp. 271–289. Springer-Verlag, Berlin, Heidelberg (2024). https://doi.org/10.1007/978-3-031-70879-4_14
14. Hirokazu, N.: AST visualization on browser - realtime JavaScript abstract syntax tree visualisation. http://nhiro.org/learn_language/AST-Visualization-on-browser.html. Accessed 24 Aug 2025
15. Hugging Face: hugging face models. https://huggingface.co/models/. Accessed 24 Aug 2025
16. Jang, C., Park, H., Choi, E., Lee, M., Cho, S.: A rule-based security auditing tool for software vulnerability detection. In: International Conference on Hybrid Information Technology, vol. 2, pp. 505–512. IEEE Computer Society, Los Alamitos, CA, USA (2006). https://doi.org/10.1109/ICHIT.2006.33
17. Katsumi, K.: Swift AST explorer - AST visualizer for swift source code. https://swift-ast-explorer.com/. Accessed 24 Aug 2025
18. Li, G., Zhu, L., Liu, P., Yang, Y.: Entangled transformer for image captioning. In: Proceedings of the IEEE/CVF International Conference on Computer Vision, pp. 8928–8937. IEEE (2019). https://doi.org/10.1109/ICCV.2019.00902
19. Li, H., Hao, Y., Zhai, Y., Qian, Z.: Assisting static analysis with large language models: a ChatGPT experiment. In: Proceedings of the 31st ACM Joint European Software Engineering Conference and Symposium on the Foundations of Software Engineering, pp. 2107–2111. ESEC/FSE 2023, Association for Computing Machinery, New York, NY, USA (2023). https://doi.org/10.1145/3611643.3613078
20. Liu, Y., Li, H., Guo, Y., Kong, C., Li, J., Wang, S.: Rethinking attention-model explainability through faithfulness violation test. In: Proceedings of the 39th International Conference on Machine Learning, pp. 13807–13824. PMLR (2022). https://proceedings.mlr.press/v162/liu22i/liu22i.pdf
21. Lundberg, S.M., Lee, S.I.: A unified approach to interpreting model predictions. In: Proceedings of the 31st International Conference on Neural Information Processing Systems, pp. 4768–4777. NIPS'17, Curran Associates Inc., Red Hook, NY, USA (2017). https://dl.acm.org/doi/10.5555/3295222.3295230
22. Mazko, O.: Online java parser & abstract syntax tree demo. https://mazko.github.io/jsjavaparser/ (2016). Accessed 24 Aug 2025
23. meta-llama: Model card of Llama-3.2-1B. https://huggingface.co/meta-llama/Llama-3.2-1B. Accessed 24 Aug 2025

24. microsoft: Model card of codebert-base. https://huggingface.co/microsoft/codebert-base. Accessed 24 Aug 2025
25. mistralai: model card of Mistral-7B-v0.1. https://huggingface.co/mistralai/Mistral-7B-v0.1. Accessed 24 Aug 2025
26. Mohammadkhani, A.H., Tantithamthavorn, C., Hemmatif, H.: Explaining transformer-based code models: what do they learn? When they do not work? In: 2023 IEEE 23rd International Working Conference on Source Code Analysis and Manipulation (SCAM), pp. 96–106. IEEE (2023). https://doi.org/10.1109/SCAM59687.2023.00020
27. OpenAI, Achiam, J., Adler, S., et al.: GPT-4 technical report. arXiv preprint arXiv:2303.08774 (2024). https://arxiv.org/abs/2303.08774
28. RayenLLM: model card of vulnerability_detection_using_codebert. https://huggingface.co/RayenLLM/Vulnerability_Detection_Using_CodeBERT. Accessed 24 Aug 2025
29. Ribeiro, M.T., Singh, S., Guestrin, C.: "Why should i trust you?": explaining the predictions of any classifier. In: Proceedings of the 22nd ACM SIGKDD International Conference on Knowledge Discovery and Data Mining, pp. 1135–1144. KDD '16, Association for Computing Machinery, New York, NY, USA (2016). https://doi.org/10.1145/2939672.2939778
30. Rozière, B., et al.: Code Llama: open foundation models for code. arXiv preprint arXiv:2308.12950 (2024). https://arxiv.org/abs/2308.12950
31. Senanayake, J., Kalutarage, H., Al-Kadri, M.O., Petrovski, A., Piras, L.: Android source code vulnerability detection: a systematic literature review. ACM Comput. Surv. **55**(9) (2023). https://doi.org/10.1145/3556974
32. Simonyan, K., Vedaldi, A., Zisserman, A.: Deep inside convolutional networks: visualising image classification models and saliency maps. In: 2nd International Conference on Learning Representations (ICLR), Workshop Track Proceedings (2014). http://arxiv.org/abs/1312.6034
33. Snowflake Inc.: Streamlit: a faster way to build and share data apps. https://streamlit.io/. Accessed 24 Aug 2025
34. Sotgiu, A., Pintor, M., Biggio, B.: Explainability-based debugging of machine learning for vulnerability discovery. In: Proceedings of the 17th International Conference on Availability, Reliability and Security. ARES '22, Association for Computing Machinery, New York, NY, USA (2022). https://doi.org/10.1145/3538969.3543809
35. starmage520: model card of coderbert_finetuned_detect_vulnerability_on_msr. https://huggingface.co/starmage520/Coderbert_finetuned_detect_vulnerability_on_MSR. Accessed 24 Aug 2025
36. Sundararajan, M., Taly, A., Yan, Q.: Axiomatic attribution for deep networks. In: Proceedings of the 34th International Conference on Machine Learning - Volume 70, pp. 3319–3328. ICML'17, JMLR.org (2017)
37. Vaswani, A., et al.: Attention is all you need. In: Proceedings of the 31st International Conference on Neural Information Processing Systems, pp. 6000–6010. NIPS'17, Curran Associates Inc., Red Hook, NY, USA (2017). https://dl.acm.org/doi/10.5555/3295222.3295349
38. Vo, H.N.K., et al.: Revitalizing Bahnaric language through neural machine translation: challenges, strategies, and promising outcomes. Proc. AAAI Conf. Artif. Intell. **38**(21), 23360–23368 (2024). https://doi.org/10.1609/aaai.v38i21.30385

39. Wang, Y., Wang, W., Joty, S., Hoi, S.C.: CodeT5: identifier-aware unified pre-trained encoder-decoder models for code understanding and generation. In: Proceedings of the 2021 Conference on Empirical Methods in Natural Language Processing, pp. 8696–8708. Association for Computational Linguistics, Online and Punta Cana, Dominican Republic (2021). https://doi.org/10.18653/v1/2021.emnlp-main.685
40. Wattanakriengkrai, S., Thongtanunam, P., Tantithamthavorn, C., Hata, H., Matsumoto, K.: Predicting defective lines using a model-agnostic technique. IEEE Trans. Software Eng. **48**(5), 1480–1496 (2022). https://doi.org/10.1109/TSE.2020.3023177
41. Wen, J., Hu, Q., Guo, Y., Cordy, M., Le Traon, Y.: Variable renaming-based adversarial test generation for code model: benchmark and enhancement. ACM Trans. Softw. Eng. Methodol. (2025). https://doi.org/10.1145/3723353, just Accepted
42. Yang, Z., Shi, J., He, J., Lo, D.: Natural attack for pre-trained models of code. In: Proceedings of the 44th International Conference on Software Engineering, pp. 1482–1493. ICSE '22, Association for Computing Machinery, New York, NY, USA (2022). https://doi.org/10.1145/3510003.3510146
43. Zhang, X., Yin, Z., Feng, Y., Shi, Q., Liu, J., Chen, Z.: NeuralVis: visualizing and interpreting deep learning models. In: Proceedings of the 34th IEEE/ACM International Conference on Automated Software Engineering, pp. 1106–1109. ASE '19, IEEE Press (2020). https://doi.org/10.1109/ASE.2019.00113
44. Zhou, Y., Liu, S., Siow, J., Du, X., Liu, Y.: Devign: effective vulnerability identification by learning comprehensive program semantics via graph neural networks. Curran Associates Inc., Red Hook, NY, USA (2019). https://dl.acm.org/doi/10.5555/3454287.3455202

Diffusion-Based Intrusion Detection: A Unified Comparison of Augmentation, Feature Extraction, and Purification with Bayesian Optimization

Zenghui Wang(✉)

Department of Electrical and Smart Systems Engineering, University of South Africa, Florida 1709, South Africa
wangzengh@gmail.com

Abstract. Diffusion models are being adopted in Intrusion Detection Systems (IDS) for data augmentation, representation learning, and defense against adversarial noise. This study offers a unified evaluation of three integration strategies—Diffusion Data Augmentation (DDA-IDS), Diffusion Feature Extraction (DFE-IDS), and Diffusion-based Adversarial Purification (DAP-IDS)—implemented with the same backbone and assessed under an identical protocol on NSL-KDD. Bayesian Optimization (BO) tunes diffusion and classifier hyperparameters against a minority-aware validation objective (macro-F1). On clean traffic, DDA-IDS without BO achieves the best class balance (highest macro-F1). DFE-IDS underperforms due to feature overlap with the `normal` class, depressing `r2l`/`u2r` detection. DAP-IDS is the only pipeline that consistently benefits from BO, which raises rare-class recall while preserving `dos` and `normal` performance. These results show that the value of BO is method-dependent and that macro-F1 together with confusion-matrix analysis is essential for fair assessment beyond overall accuracy. The findings provide practical guidance for choosing among augmentation, representation learning, and purification under different latency and robustness requirements, and motivate hybrid designs that combine these roles for real-world deployment.

Keywords: Intrusion Detection Systems · Diffusion Models · Hyperparameter Optimization · Bayesian Optimization

1 Introduction

As cyber threats grow in scale and sophistication, Intrusion Detection Systems (IDS) must address three persistent challenges: severe class imbalance, the need for discriminative feature learning, and robustness against adversarial perturbations [1]. Diffusion probabilistic models (DDPM) have recently demonstrated strong generative and denoising capabilities in computer vision and anomaly detection [2], making their integration into IDS both well-motivated and timely.

W. Li et al. (Eds.): EISA 2025, CCIS 2897, pp. 59–74, 2026.
https://doi.org/10.1007/978-3-032-21177-4_4

In IDS, diffusion can be inserted at different stages of the pipeline. Diffusion Data Augmentation (DDA-IDS) applies DDPM at training time to synthesize minority-class samples and mitigate imbalance [2]. Diffusion Feature Extraction (DFE-IDS) uses a diffusion model as a representation learner to produce compact embeddings for downstream classification [3]. Diffusion-based Adversarial Purification (DAP-IDS) performs inference-time denoising to suppress adversarial noise before classification [4]. Although each strategy targets a distinct bottleneck, controlled comparisons across these designs remain limited.

This study provides a unified evaluation of DDA-IDS, DFE-IDS, and DAP-IDS on NSL-KDD under identical preprocessing, the same diffusion backbone and MLP classifier, and a common training protocol. To avoid bias from manual settings and to expose each method's best attainable regime, Bayesian Optimization (BO) is employed to tune diffusion and classifier hyperparameters with a minority-aware validation objective [5]. The evaluation reports accuracy together with macro-F1, weighted-F1, and confusion-matrix analysis to reflect class-wise performance beyond overall accuracy.

The main contributions are:

1) a head-to-head comparison of DDA-IDS, DFE-IDS, and DAP-IDS on NSL-KDD under a unified experimental setup;
2) integration of BO to optimize key factors (e.g., diffusion steps, noise schedule, denoiser width, classifier depth/width, and the purification horizon for DAP-IDS);
3) quantitative assessment using accuracy, macro-/weighted-F1, and confusion matrices for fair, minority-aware evaluation;
4) practical guidance on method selection under latency and robustness constraints, and implications for hybrid designs that combine augmentation, feature learning, and purification.

The remainder of the paper is organized as follows. Section 2 reviews related work. Section 3 details the research methodology and optimization procedure. Section 4 presents results and discussion. Section 5 concludes with recommendations for future research.

2 Related Work

2.1 Intrusion Detection

The AI-based IDS in Fig. 1 represents each network flow as a normalized feature vector $\mathbf{x} \in \mathbb{R}^d$ (with dataset $\mathcal{D} = \{(\mathbf{x}_n, \mathbf{y}_n)\}_{n=1}^N$), followed by standard preprocessing and a train/test split. A classifier f_θ (e.g., BP, RNN/LSTM, or CNN) maps $\mathbf{x}$ to class probabilities in the simplex, typically instantiated as

$$\hat{\mathbf{y}} = \mathrm{softmax}(W\, h^{(L)} + b), \qquad h^{(\ell)} = f\Big(W^{(\ell)} h^{(\ell-1)} + b^{(\ell)}\Big), \quad h^{(0)} = \mathbf{x}, \quad (1)$$

where $\theta = \{W^{(\ell)}, b^{(\ell)}\}_{\ell=1}^{L}$ and W, b in the output layer are the final affine parameters. Training minimizes the multi-class cross-entropy

$$\mathcal{L}(\theta) = -\sum_{i=1}^{C} y_i \ln \hat{y}_i, \tag{2}$$

with $\mathbf{y}$ one-hot over C classes and $\hat{\mathbf{y}} = f_\theta(\mathbf{x})$.

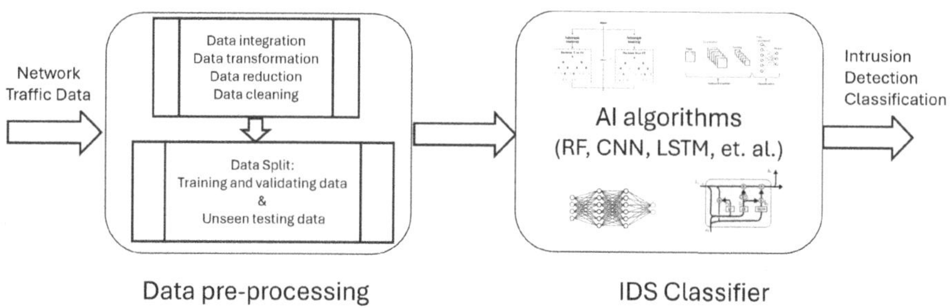

Fig. 1. Machine learning based intrusion detection system

IDS detect unauthorized activities in network traffic using signature-based or anomaly-based methods. ML-based anomaly detection has gained popularity due to flexibility and adaptability to new threats [6]. However, ML-IDS face challenges like class imbalance, feature redundancy, and adversarial vulnerability [7].

2.2 Diffusion Probabilistic Models

DDPM, initially designed for image generation [2], gradually injects and removes noise to model complex distributions in a robust manner. Recent applications extend to anomaly detection by leveraging its powerful generative properties, demonstrating success beyond vision tasks [8]. Diffusion Probabilistic Models formulate data generation as two opposite Markov chains: a forward diffusion that progressively adds Gaussian noise to a clean sample, and a reverse denoising that learns to remove noise step by step.

1) Forward process

Given an original sample $\mathbf{x}_0 \sim q(\mathbf{x}_0)$, define a noise schedule $\{\beta_t\}_{t=1}^{T}$, with $\alpha_t = 1 - \beta_t$ and $\bar{\alpha}_t = \prod_{i=1}^{t} \alpha_i$. At each timestep t,

$$q(\mathbf{x}_t \mid \mathbf{x}_{t-1}) = \mathcal{N}(\mathbf{x}_t; \sqrt{\alpha_t}\, \mathbf{x}_{t-1}, \beta_t \mathbf{I}), \tag{3}$$

which implies the marginal

$$q(\mathbf{x}_t \mid \mathbf{x}_0) = \mathcal{N}\big(\mathbf{x}_t; \sqrt{\bar{\alpha}_t}\, \mathbf{x}_0, (1 - \bar{\alpha}_t)\, \mathbf{I}\big). \tag{4}$$

Common noise schedules include linear and cosine variants; for non-vision data such as network traffic, smoother schedules are often preferred to mitigate excessive information loss at high noise levels.

2) Reverse process

We learn a neural network $\epsilon_\theta(\mathbf{x}_t, t)$ to predict the noise added at step t, defining

$$p_\theta(\mathbf{x}_{t-1} \mid \mathbf{x}_t) = \mathcal{N}\big(\mathbf{x}_{t-1}; \mu_\theta(\mathbf{x}_t, t), \sigma_t^2\mathbf{I}\big), \tag{5}$$

with prior $p(\mathbf{x}_T) = \mathcal{N}(\mathbf{0}, \mathbf{I})$. Sampling proceeds from $\mathbf{x}_T$ back to $\mathbf{x}_0$. Under the noise-prediction parameterization, the mean can be written as

$$\mu_\theta(\mathbf{x}_t, t) = \frac{1}{\sqrt{\alpha_t}}\left(\mathbf{x}_t - \frac{\beta_t}{\sqrt{1-\bar{\alpha}_t}}\,\epsilon_\theta(\mathbf{x}_t, t)\right), \tag{6}$$

with variance often set to the true posterior's diagonal term or its upper bound: $\sigma_t^2 \in \{\tilde{\beta}_t,\, \beta_t\}$. Alternative parameterizations include directly predicting $\hat{\mathbf{x}}_0$ or the v-prediction form, which can offer greater stability across noise levels.

3) Training objective

Maximizing likelihood yields the variational lower bound (VLB)

$$\begin{aligned}\mathcal{L}_{\text{VLB}} = {} & \underbrace{\mathrm{KL}[q(\mathbf{x}_T \mid \mathbf{x}_0) \,\|\, p(\mathbf{x}_T)]}_{L_T} + \sum_{t=2}^{T} \underbrace{\mathrm{KL}[q(\mathbf{x}_{t-1} \mid \mathbf{x}_t, \mathbf{x}_0) \,\|\, p_\theta(\mathbf{x}_{t-1} \mid \mathbf{x}_t)]}_{L_{t-1}} \\ & - \underbrace{\log p_\theta(\mathbf{x}_0 \mid \mathbf{x}_1)}_{L_0}.\end{aligned} \tag{7}$$

The true posterior $q(\mathbf{x}_{t-1} \mid \mathbf{x}_t, \mathbf{x}_0)$ is available in closed form:

$$q(\mathbf{x}_{t-1} | \mathbf{x}_t, \mathbf{x}_0) = \mathcal{N}\Big(\mathbf{x}_{t-1};\, \tilde{\mu}_t(\mathbf{x}_t, \mathbf{x}_0),\, \tilde{\beta}_t\mathbf{I}\Big), \tag{8}$$

$$\tilde{\mu}_t = \frac{\sqrt{\alpha_t}\,(1-\bar{\alpha}_{t-1})}{1-\bar{\alpha}_t}\,\mathbf{x}_t + \frac{\sqrt{\bar{\alpha}_{t-1}}\,\beta_t}{1-\bar{\alpha}_t}\,\mathbf{x}_0, \quad \tilde{\beta}_t = \frac{1-\bar{\alpha}_{t-1}}{1-\bar{\alpha}_t}\,\beta_t. \tag{9}$$

In practice, an equivalent and numerically stable "simplified objective" is used by sampling $t \sim \mathcal{U}\{1, \ldots, T\}$ and minimizing the noise MSE:

$$\mathcal{L}_{\text{simple}} = \mathbb{E}_{t, \mathbf{x}_0, \epsilon}\Big[\big\|\epsilon - \epsilon_\theta\big(\sqrt{\bar{\alpha}_t}\mathbf{x}_0 + \sqrt{1-\bar{\alpha}_t}\epsilon,\, t\big)\big\|_2^2\Big], \tag{10}$$

which is equivalent to $\mathcal{L}_{\text{VLB}}$ at the optimum.

4) Sampling and anomaly scoring (for IDS)

Reverse sampling can be performed via the original Markov chain (DDPM) or deterministic non-Markovian methods (DDIM). For latency-sensitive intrusion detection, few-step approximations or fast solvers are often employed to reduce inference time. In anomaly detection, diffusion models can score inputs using approximate log-likelihood or LBO, or by using the predicted $\hat{\mathbf{x}}_0$ or intermediate features as robust embeddings for a downstream classifier. When facing adversarial perturbations, a short forward-noise and denoise purification step can be applied at inference time to improve robustness without excessively degrading discriminative features.

2.3 Diffusion-Based IDS Approaches

There are important design considerations that determine how diffusion models are integrated into the IDS pipeline and what objectives they optimize. For augmentation-oriented systems, as in [2], a conditional DDPM can be trained on labeled flows and then used to synthesize minority-class traffic. In practice, the number of synthetic instances per class must be carefully calibrated so that the effective training prior matches the expected class distribution during deployment; otherwise, the classifier may become miscalibrated even if per-class F1 scores improve. It is also essential to prevent data leakage: synthetic samples should be generated exclusively from the training split, and any feature normalization statistics must be computed without referencing the test set.

In [2], the generative capability of diffusion is employed solely for training set augmentation, addressing class imbalance without changing the inference time process. By contrast, [3] uses diffusion as a deep feature extractor: network traffic is transformed into an alternative representation, passed through a trained U-Net DDPM, and the resulting embeddings are fed into a classifier. This approach prioritizes capturing rich structural patterns in the data rather than generating new samples.

A third approach, diffusion-based adversarial purification [4], applies diffusion at inference time. Here, each test sample is deliberately perturbed and then denoised to remove adversarial noise before classification. Unlike DDA-IDS, which addresses data imbalance, and DFE-IDS, which improves representation quality, purification functions as a defense mechanism aimed at enhancing robustness under adversarial attack.

Taken together, these three strategies demonstrate the versatility of diffusion models in IDS: they can be employed for targeted data augmentation, representation learning, or real-time input sanitization, depending on operational priorities.

2.4 Bayesian Optimization

Bayesian Optimization is a global optimization framework for black-box functions that are expensive to evaluate [11]. It is well-suited for tuning hyperparameters of machine learning models when gradients are unavailable and evaluations (e.g., model training) are costly. The core idea is to maintain a probabilistic surrogate model of the objective function $f(\mathbf{x})$, and to use this model to select the most promising candidates for evaluation.

Given an unknown objective $f : \mathcal{X} \to \mathbb{R}$, BO proceeds iteratively. At iteration n, a surrogate model $p(f \mid \mathcal{D}_n)$ is fit to the dataset $\mathcal{D}_n = \{(\mathbf{x}_i, y_i)\}_{i=1}^n$ where $y_i = f(\mathbf{x}_i) + \epsilon_i$. Gaussian Processes (GPs) are a common choice of surrogate, with prior

$$f(\mathbf{x}) \sim \mathcal{GP}(m(\mathbf{x}), k(\mathbf{x}, \mathbf{x}')) , \tag{11}$$

where $m(\cdot)$ is the mean function and $k(\cdot, \cdot)$ the covariance kernel.

The next query point is selected by maximizing an acquisition function $a(\mathbf{x} \mid \mathcal{D}_n)$ that balances *exploration* (searching uncertain regions) and *exploitation* (refining near the current optimum). A widely used acquisition function is the Expected Improvement (EI):

$$\mathrm{EI}(\mathbf{x}) = \mathbb{E}\left[\max\left(f(\mathbf{x}) - f(\mathbf{x}^+), 0\right)\right] , \tag{12}$$

where $f(\mathbf{x}^+)$ is the best observed value so far. For GP surrogates with predictive mean $\mu(\mathbf{x})$ and variance $\sigma^2(\mathbf{x})$, EI has a closed form:

$$\mathrm{EI}(\mathbf{x}) = (\mu(\mathbf{x}) - f(\mathbf{x}^+))\, \Phi(z) + \sigma(\mathbf{x})\, \phi(z), \quad z = \frac{\mu(\mathbf{x}) - f(\mathbf{x}^+)}{\sigma(\mathbf{x})}, \tag{13}$$

where Φ and ϕ are the standard normal CDF and PDF, respectively.

By iteratively selecting $\mathbf{x}_{n+1} = \arg\max_{\mathbf{x} \in \mathcal{X}} a(\mathbf{x} \mid \mathcal{D}_n)$ and updating the surrogate with the new observation, BO efficiently converges to high-performing configurations with significantly fewer evaluations than grid or random search.

3 Research Methodology

Different diffusion-based IDS variants, such as DDA-IDS [2], DFE-IDS [3], and DAP-IDS [4], integrate the generative process into intrusion detection pipelines in distinct ways. This study aims to systematically compare and evaluate these approaches within a unified framework, employing the same dataset, preprocessing procedures, and classifier architecture to ensure fairness in comparison. It is important to note that, because the diffusion-based preprocessing methods and classifier architectures used here differ from those in the original publications, the objective is not to replicate or surpass the reported results of the original works, but rather to assess their relative effectiveness under consistent experimental conditions. The performance of diffusion-based IDS methods depends strongly on hyperparameter choices in both the diffusion stage and the downstream classifier. To address this, Bayesian Optimization is employed to automatically identify effective configurations for each method. This approach allows the evaluation to reveal the true performance potential of the different pipelines, beyond the limitations of fixed, manually chosen parameter settings.

3.1 Dataset and Preprocessing

The NSL-KDD dataset [9] is selected for its widespread adoption as a benchmark in intrusion detection research and its improvements over the KDD'99 variant. Specifically, NSL-KDD removes duplicate and redundant entries, providing a cleaner and more challenging evaluation scenario where classifiers cannot rely on memorizing frequent patterns [9].

A defining characteristic of NSL-KDD is its inherent class imbalance across the aggregated categories: `dos`, `normal`, `probe`, `r2l`, and `u2r`. Moreover, the test set includes many rare or new attack variants unseen during training, making it ideal for analyzing an algorithm's sensitivity to both imbalance and distributional shifts.

Table 1 presents the approximate distribution of records across the five classes in the training and testing subsets (KDDTrain+ and KDDTest+):

Table 1. Approximate class-wise distribution in NSL-KDD train/test sets [17]

Class	Train (KDDTrain+)	Test (KDDTest+)
Normal	67,342	9,710
DoS	45,927	7457
Probe	11,656	2,421
R2L	995	2,754
U2R	52	200

These figures underscore the significant class imbalance, particularly for the `R2L` and `U2R` categories, which remain critically underrepresented in both splits.

For data preprocessing:

- The three categorical features—`protocol_type`, `service`, and `flag`—are one-hot encoded.
- Numeric and one-hot columns are standardized using a `StandardScaler` fitted on KDDTrain+ and then consistently applied to KDDTest+, ensuring no data leakage.
- Labels are mapped into the five categories via a single `LabelEncoder`.
- Model training uses the Adam optimizer with a batch size of 512.

3.2 Diffusion and Classifier Setup

To ensure fairness in performance comparison, the same DDPM (denoising diffusion probabilistic model) architecture, implemented with a lightweight 1D-U-Net backbone, is employed across all three methods. For DDA-IDS and DFE-IDS, the diffusion model is primarily used for data augmentation and feature enhancement, while for diffusion-based adversarial purification, it is used to denoise and restore potentially adversarially perturbed samples before classification. The diffusion core is the same U-Net-like MLP denoiser with sinusoidal time embedding The downstream classifier is a multi-layer perceptron (MLP) with three hidden layers (256 → 256 → 128 → num_classes), which is well-suited for network traffic data.

Table 2. Simulation results

Method	Setting	Accuracy	macro-F1	weighted-F1
DDA-IDS	No-opt	0.87	0.70	0.84
	BO-opt	0.86	0.66	0.82
DFE-IDS	No-opt	0.86	0.61	0.82
	BO-opt	0.85	0.59	0.82
DAP-IDS	No-opt	0.84	0.66	0.81
	BO-opt	0.86	0.67	0.83

Table 3. Performance of other methods

Method	Accuracy (%)	Method	Accuracy (%)
MCA-LSTM [10]	82.15	LSTM [15]	82.00
CNN-LSTM [12]	68.78	DNN [16]	75.75
GRU [13]	82.87	Simple RNN [18]	84.03
Semi-LSTM [14]	82.21	LSTM [18]	85.93
LSTM [13]	82.78	GRU [18]	85.65

3.3 Bayesian Optimization

Bayesian Optimization is employed to tune key hyperparameters for each method, ensuring the configurations are not biased by arbitrary manual selection. The optimization objective is validation macro-F1 on a stratified validation split, encouraging parameter sets that generalize well. The parameters and ranges are: 1) Diffusion process: Diffusion steps $T \in [40, 80]$; the denoiser hidden width $D_{hidden} \in [192,\ 384]$.
2) MLP classifier: Learning rate $\in \left[7 * 10^{-4}, 2 * 10^{-3}\right]$.
3) Purification step $t_{\text{purge}} \in [10, 60]$ (only for the adversarial purification method).
BO always evaluates on a stratified-by-class, group-by-raw-attack split (so that train/validation do not share sub-classes) and maximizes the same target: $\text{Score} = 0.5 \cdot \text{macro} - \text{F1} + 0.25 \cdot F1_{\text{r2l}} + 0.25 \cdot F1_{\text{u2r}}$. After BO selects a configuration, the model is retrained on train+val and reported on KDDTest+.

4 Experiments and Discussion

All pipelines were evaluated on NSL-KDD under a unified setup to avoid confounders. We report accuracy, macro-F1 and weighted-F1, and the associated confusion matrices.

4.1 Results

Table 2 summarizes six experimental settings across three diffusion-based pipelines and their normalized confusion matrices are given in Figs. 2 to 4. To show how is the performance comparing with some existing algorithms, some results from published papers are shown in Table 3. The compared methods include long short-term memory network (MCA-LSTM) [10], long-short-term memory based convolutional neural networks [12], Long-Short Term Memory (LSTM) [13] [18] [15], Gated Recurrent Unit (GRU) [13] [18], Simple RNN [18], Semantic parsing based LSTM model [14], and Deep Neural Network [16].

The comparative evaluation (Table 2) highlights that overall accuracy alone is insufficient for assessing IDS performance on NSL-KDD due to its severe class imbalance and presence of unseen attack variants in the test set. Across all settings, accuracy values are close (0.84–0.87), but macro-F1 reveals marked differences, particularly in the treatment of minority classes (`r2l` and `u2r`).

DDA-IDS without BO achieves the highest macro-F1 (0.70), balancing majority stability with improved minority detection. The confusion matrix (Fig. 2 (a)) shows almost perfect classification for `dos`, `normal`, and `probe`, with relatively few `r2l` and `u2r` misclassified as `normal`. However, after BO, macro-F1 drops to 0.66 despite stable accuracy. Figure 2 (b) reveals this decline stems from increased `r2l`→`normal` and `u2r`→`normal` misclassifications, suggesting that the BO-optimized parameters bias the classifier toward safer majority decisions at the expense of rare-class recall.

DFE-IDS performs less competitively in both base (macro-F1 = 0.61) and optimized (0.59) configurations. The confusion matrices (Fig. 3) show consistent collapse of `r2l` and `u2r` into `normal`, indicating that the frozen diffusion-based embeddings are not sufficiently discriminative for minority classes. Majority-class performance remains strong, but the representation overlap limits minority detection.

DAP-IDS shows a different trend: BO yields improvements in macro-F1 (0.66 → 0.67) and accuracy (0.84 → 0.86). The optimized confusion matrix (Fig. 4(b)) shows better `u2r` detection and stable `probe` recall without harming majority-class accuracy. Careful tuning of purification depth (t_{purge}) prevents over-smoothing, allowing the denoiser to remove perturbations without erasing features critical for minority detection.

To complement the visual confusion matrices, Table 4 condenses the key misclassification patterns. The diffusion data augmentation (DDA-IDS) pipeline without Bayesian Optimization (BO) achieves the most balanced performance, while BO optimization slightly shifts the decision boundary toward the majority

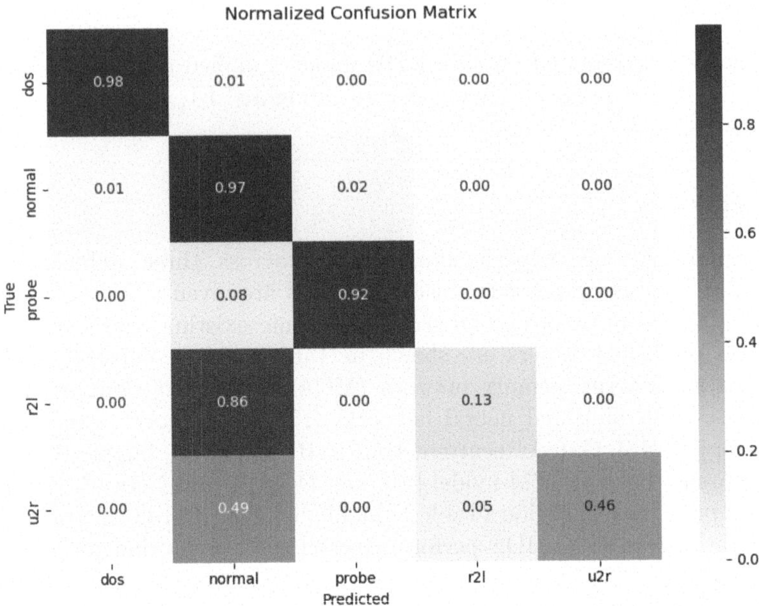

(a) Normalized Confusion Matrix of DDA-IDS without BO

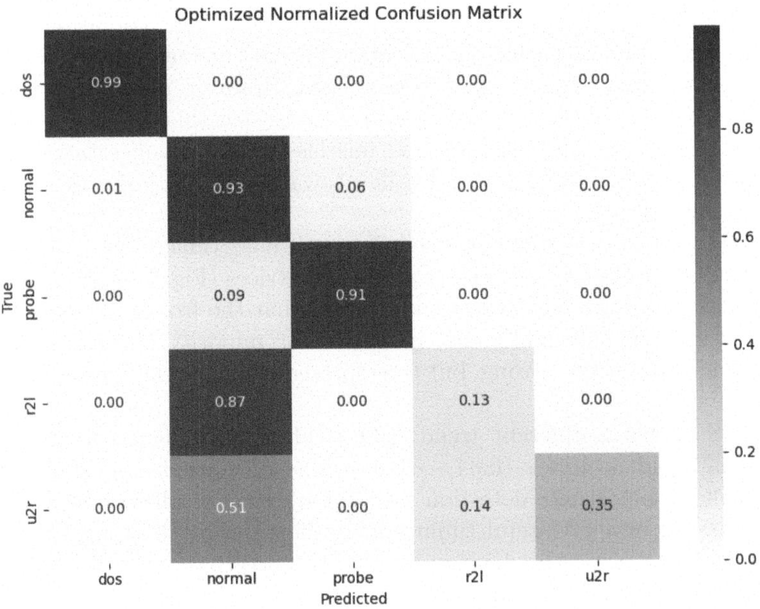

(b) Normalized Confusion Matrix of DDA-IDS with BO (optimized)

Fig. 2. Confusion matrices of DDA-IDS

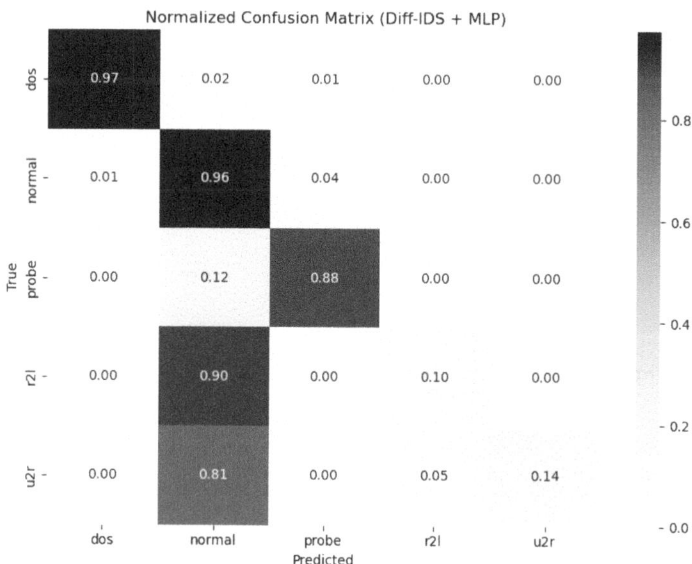

(a) Normalized Confusion Matrix of DFE-IDS without BO

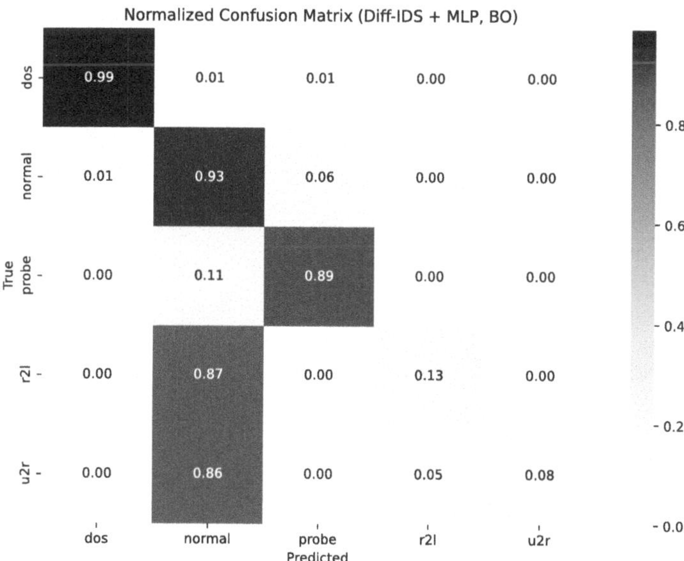

(b) Normalized Confusion Matrix of DFE-IDS with BO (optimized)

Fig. 3. Confusion matrices of DFE-IDS

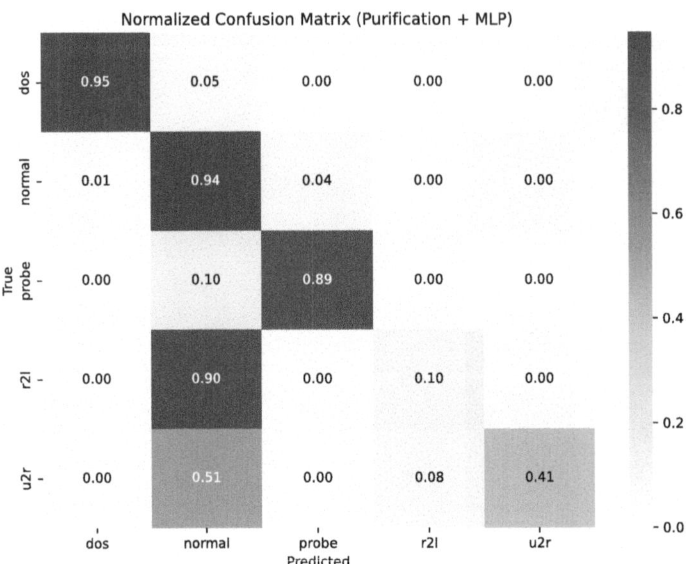

(a) Normalized Confusion Matrix of DAP-IDS without BO

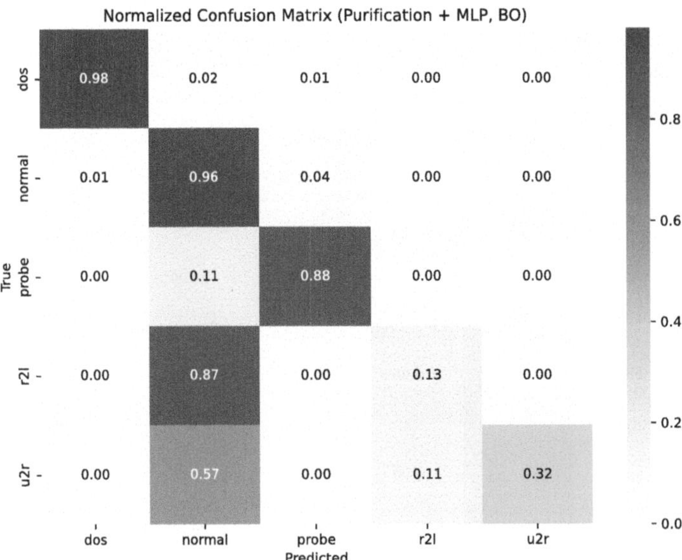

(b) Normalized Confusion Matrix of DAP-IDS with BO (optimized)

Fig. 4. Confusion matrices of DAP-IDS

class. Diffusion feature extraction (DFE-IDS) consistently suffers from embedding overlap, leading to systematic misclassification of minority attacks as normal traffic. Diffusion-based adversarial purification (DAP-IDS) benefits from BO tuning, which enhances *u2r* recall without sacrificing accuracy on major classes. This comparative summary underscores that diffusion models improve intrusion detection through distinct mechanisms—data balance, representation learning, and robustness—and that the observed misclassification tendencies should guide practitioners when selecting or tuning a diffusion-based IDS.

Table 4. Summary of confusion-matrix trends across diffusion-based IDS variants.

Method	BO	Dominant Error Trend	Minority-Class Behavior
DDA-IDS	No-opt	Few *r2l→normal*, *u2r→normal*	Highest macro-F1 (0.70); balanced overall
DDA-IDS	BO-opt	More *r2l/u2r→normal*	Slight recall drop for rare classes (0.66)
DFE-IDS	No-opt	Strong collapse of *r2l*, *u2r→normal*	Weak minority separation (0.61)
DFE-IDS	BO-opt	Similar collapse persists	No meaningful gain (0.59)
DAP-IDS	No-opt	Mild *u2r→normal*	Stable majority accuracy; moderate rare-class recall (0.66)
DAP-IDS	BO-opt	Reduced *u2r→normal*	Improved *u2r* detection (0.67)

Comparing with existing algorithms in Table 3, the diffusion-based pipelines, particularly DDA-IDS (no BO) and DAP-IDS (BO), outperform many conventional deep learning IDS architectures (e.g., MCA-LSTM, CNN-LSTM, GRU, Simple RNN, DNN) in terms of macro-F1 and minority-class recall, validating the integration of diffusion into IDS workflows.

4.2 Discussion and Practical Guidance

The results suggest the following practical insights:

1) Metric choice matters: macro-F1 and per-class confusion analysis are more reliable indicators than accuracy for imbalanced IDS tasks. Many accuracy gains can be illusory, driven by majority-class dominance.
2) Method selection depends on operational needs:
   For clean or mildly noisy environments with strict latency constraints, DDA-IDS without BO is optimal—highest macro-F1, minimal inference overhead, and balanced class performance.

For robustness under potential adversarial noise, DAP-IDS with BO is preferable—modest macro-F1 gains, improved `u2r` detection, and stable majority-class accuracy, with acceptable additional latency from denoising. DFE-IDS is suitable only when inference speed is paramount and minority detection is not critical. Its minority-class shortcomings could be mitigated by fine-tuning diffusion features or incorporating class-weighted/focal loss.

3) Hyperparameter optimization is context-dependent: BO's effectiveness depends on the objective function. The minority-aware score used here benefits purification but can degrade augmentation performance. Alternative BO targets—such as cost-sensitive loss or weighted macro-F1—may yield better-balanced outcomes for DDA-IDS and DFE-IDS.
4) Minority-class tracking is essential: Practitioners should monitor `r2l`→`normal` and `u2r`→`normal` transitions during model selection, as these dominate macro-F1 fluctuations.

In sum, diffusion models offer versatile benefits in IDS—augmenting scarce classes, improving representations, and enhancing robustness. The choice among DDA-IDS, DFE-IDS, and DAP-IDS should be guided by the threat model, performance priorities, and latency constraints of the deployment environment.

5 Conclusion

This work presented a unified, head-to-head comparison of three strategies for integrating diffusion models into IDS: Diffusion Data Augmentation for targeted minority-class synthesis, Diffusion Feature Extraction for representation learning, and Diffusion-based Adversarial Purification for inference-time defense against adversarial perturbations. All methods were implemented with a lightweight 1D-U-Net denoiser and a multi-layer perceptron (MLP) classifier, using identical preprocessing and training protocols on the NSL-KDD dataset to ensure a controlled comparison where only the role of diffusion varied.

The empirical findings show that DDA-IDS without BO achieved the highest macro-F1 score (0.70) on clean traffic, demonstrating balanced detection performance across majority and minority classes with minimal runtime overhead. DFE-IDS consistently underperformed in detecting rare categories (`r2l` and `u2r`) due to representation overlap with the `normal` class, a limitation that persisted regardless of BO tuning. In contrast, DAP-IDS was the only pipeline to consistently benefit from BO under a minority-aware objective, achieving a modest yet stable improvement in macro-F1 by enhancing `u2r` and `probe` detection while maintaining `dos` and `normal` stability.

These results underline two important conclusions for IDS design: (1) macro-F1 and confusion-matrix inspection are more faithful and informative metrics than accuracy in scenarios with severe class imbalance and unseen test attacks, and (2) the effectiveness of BO is method-dependent, with its benefit strongly tied to the alignment between the optimization target and the functional role of diffusion in the pipeline.

From a practical standpoint, the study suggests that DDA-IDS without BO is preferable in low-latency, clean-data settings where balanced class detection is the priority, whereas DAP-IDS with BO is recommended in environments where robustness to perturbations is critical. DFE-IDS, while offering faster inference, requires further enhancement—such as fine-tuning diffusion features or employing cost-sensitive training—to be competitive in rare-class detection.

This work also highlights several limitations. The evaluation was restricted to a single dataset (NSL-KDD) and a fixed classifier family (MLP), and did not explore cross-dataset generalization or multi-modal feature fusion. The impact of varying noise schedules, denoising architectures, and alternative optimization criteria was not exhaustively studied.

Future research will address these limitations by: (i) extending the evaluation to additional, more diverse IDS benchmarks with varying imbalance ratios and attack taxonomies; (ii) exploring hybrid pipelines that jointly integrate augmentation, representation learning, and purification stages; (iii) incorporating advanced imbalance-handling strategies such as focal loss, dynamic re-weighting, and meta-learning for class weighting; and (iv) investigating adaptive coupling between denoising strength and classifier confidence to dynamically trade off robustness and minority-class separability in real time.

Overall, the study reinforces the versatility of diffusion models as a foundational component for IDS and provides actionable guidance for selecting and tuning diffusion-based pipelines according to deployment constraints and operational priorities.

Acknowledgments. This work was partly supported by the South African National Research Foundation under Grant nos. CPRR240327211161, CHN231229201835, RA22112976288, KIC250321305600, and AJCR230704126719.

References

1. Denning, D. E.: An intrusion-detection model. IEEE Trans. Software Eng. **SE-13**(2), 222–232 (1987)
2. Tang, B., Lu, Y., Li, Q., Bai, Y., Yu, J., Yu, X.: A diffusion model based on network intrusion detection method for industrial cyber-physical systems. Sensors **23**(3), 1141 (2023). https://doi.org/10.3390/s23031141
3. Yang, Y., Tang, X., Liu, Z., Cheng, J., Fang, H., Zhang, C.: Diff-IDS: a network intrusion detection model based on diffusion model for imbalanced data samples. Comput. Mater. Continua **82**(3), 4389–4408 (2025)
4. Merzouk, M.A., Beurier, E., Yaich, R., Boulahia-Cuppens, N., Cuppens, F.: Diffusion-based adversarial purification for intrusion detection. arXiv:2406.17606 [cs.CR] (2024)
5. Snoek, J., Larochelle, H., Adams, R. P.: Practical Bayesian optimization of machine learning algorithms. In: Advances in Neural Information Processing Systems, vol. 25, pp. 2951–2959 (2012)
6. Sun, Y., Wang, Z.: Intrusion detection in IoT and wireless networks using image-based neural network classification. Appl. Soft Comput. **177**, 113236 (2025)

7. Chinnasamy, R., Subramanian, M., Easwaramoorthy, S.V., Cho, J.: Deep learning-driven methods for network-based intrusion detection systems: a systematic review. ICT Express **11**(1), 181–215 (2025)
8. Liu, J., et al.: A survey on diffusion models for anomaly detection. arXiv:2501.11430 [cs.LG] (2025)
9. Tavallaee, M., Bagheri, E., Lu, W., Ghorbani, A.: A detailed analysis of the KDD CUP 99 data set. In: Proceedings of the IEEE Symposium on Computational Intelligence for Security and Defense Applications, pp. 1–6 (2009)
10. Dong, R., Li, X., Zhang, Q., Yuan, H.: Network intrusion detection model based on multivariate correlation analysis - long short-term memory network. IET Inf. Secur. **14**(2), 166–174 (2020)
11. Shahriari, B., Swersky, K., Wang, Z., Adams, R.P., de Freitas, N.: Taking the human out of the loop: a review of Bayesian optimization. Proc. IEEE **104**(1), 148–175 (2016)
12. Hsu, C.-M., Hsieh, H.-Y., Prakosa, S., Azhari, M., Leu, J.-S.: Using long-short-term memory based convolutional neural networks for network intrusion detection. In: Wireless Internet. 11th EAI International Conference, WiCON 2018, Taipei, Taiwan, October 15–16, 2018, Proceedings. Lecture Notes in Computer Science, vol. 264, pp. 86–94 (2019)
13. Li, Z., Rios, A. L., Xu, G., Trajkovic, L.: Machine learning techniques for classifying network anomalies and intrusions. In: Proceedings of 2019 IEEE International Symposium on Circuits and Systems (ISCAS), pp. 1–5 (2019)
14. Li, Z., Qin, Z. A.: A semantic parsing based LSTM model for intrusion detection. In: International Conference on Neural Information Processing (ICONIP 2018). Lecture Notes in Computer Science, vol. 11304, pp. 600–609 (2018)
15. Wang, S., Xia, C., Wang, T.: A novel intrusion detector based on deep learning hybrid methods. In: IEEE 5th International Conference on Big Data Security on Cloud (BigDataSecurity), IEEE International Conference on High Performance and Smart Computing (HPSC) and IEEE International Conference on Intelligent Data and Security (IDS), Washington, DC, USA, pp. 300–305 (2019)
16. Tang, T.A., Mhamdi, L., McLernon, D., Zaidi, S.A.R., Ghogho, M.: Deep learning approach for network intrusion detection in software defined networking. In: 2016 International Conference on Wireless Networks and Mobile Communications (WINCOM), Fez, Morocco, pp. 258–263 (2016). https://doi.org/10.1109/WINCOM.2016.7777224
17. Ravipati, R.D., Abualkibash, M.: Intrusion detection system classification using different machine learning algorithms on KDD-99 and NSL-KDD datasets – a review paper. Int. J. Comput. Sci. Inf. Technol. (IJCSIT) **11**(3), 65–80 (2019)
18. Kasongo, S.M.: An intrusion detection framework using different types of recurrent neural networks. Comput. Commun. **199**, 113–125 (2023)

Flower Gone? Exploring Insider Attacks and the Effects on Federated Learning

Adam Copeland and Weizhi Meng(✉)

School of Computing and Communications, Lancaster University, Lancaster LA1 4YR, UK
weizhi.meng@ieee.org

Abstract. Federated learning (FL) is a privacy-aware machine-learning paradigm due to its decentralised data silos. However, its distributed nature introduces new risks for malicious insiders to compromise model integrity. In this work, we aim to investigate the empirical impacts of insider attacks on global model performance. We take advantage of a simulated Flower federated learning environment with an MNIST classification task to evaluate several attacks, including general and targeted label flipping, general and targeted model poisoning, fixed and random free-riding and backdoor and parameter scaling attacks. We establish a comprehensive view of model performance using the classification metrics–accuracy, precision, recall, F1 score and model loss. We perform a benchmark assessment and then varied the ratio of insiders for each attack type to detail how this impacted performance. The results indicate a decrease in model performance as the insider ratio increased for most attack types, with random free-riding and parameter scaling being the most impactful at low insider ratios. Targeted model poisoning and backdoor attacks remained consistent with the benchmark, making them challenging to detect. We conclude that a high insider ratio is required for most attacks to have a noticeable impact on model performance, which is unfeasible in larger-scale federated learning systems.

Keywords: Federated learning · Insider attack · Backdoor attack · Security analysis · Model poisoning

1 Introduction

The fields of artificial intelligence and machine learning have experienced rapid development in recent years due to their widespread commercial adoption. One such development is the introduction of federated learning by Google in 2016 [28]. Federated learning is the concept of multiple distributed devices training a single machine learning model under the supervision of a central server, without sharing their private training data [26]. This is a powerful tool because it allows for the training of large machine learning models across multiple distributed clients securely; however, it also introduces numerous risks from malicious actors.

W. Li et al. (Eds.): EISA 2025, CCIS 2897, pp. 75–96, 2026.
https://doi.org/10.1007/978-3-032-21177-4_5

Federated learning (FL) is an important step in the right direction for data privacy in the domain of machine learning [23], which can be vital in sensitive sectors such as healthcare and finance, but it is also of greater importance for the general public due to recent developments in social trends (e.g., Internet-of-Things [10] and user authentication [20]). However, it also introduces many new risks that have not been fully realised or explored. Investigating these risks is crucial for developing robust FL models and frameworks in the future.

FL aggregates the training results from individual clients or nodes through a central server; however, the server lacks access to the client's private training data, verifying the authenticity of these results can be challenging. Therefore, the process can be vulnerable to intentional attacks from malicious insider clients, such as inference attacks, backdoor attacks, poisoning attacks and more.

Contributions. Motivated by the popularity of FL, in this work, we focus on investigating the effects on federated learning model performance under various insider attack scenarios from compromised participants, aiming to evaluate the potential risks introduced. We aim to conduct a comprehensive study of attack types under various malicious client proportions and compare the results against a benchmark carried out under normal operating conditions. This allows us to determine the empirical impacts on performance from insider attacks and the critical proportion of insiders before model collapse occurs. The contributions are summarized as follows:

- We introduce the experimental design including FL platform, used datasets, insider attack scenarios, and how to implement these attacks on FL.
- We discuss the model evaluation by analyzing each attack type and varying the insider ratios, and indicate that free-riding and parameter scaling attacks are the most impactful threats to FL.

The structure of this paper is organized as follows. Section 2 introduces related studies on federated learning and different types of insider attacks. Section 3 describes the evaluation settings and metrics. Section 4 presents how to implement each insider attack scenario and Sect. 5 evaluates the impact of each attack type. In the end, Sect. 6 concludes our work.

2 Related Work

Data security is a vital part of any machine learning process, as the training data often contains sensitive information, such as financial, personal or confidential details. Federated learning processes have security risks similar to standard machine learning processes; however, their distributed nature introduces several new weaknesses from malicious participants. One such weakness is privacy leakage, where outsiders can infer information by intercepting model update communications despite federated learning being a privacy-aware paradigm that allows users to participate freely without sharing data between clients [24].

Threats to federated learning processes can be performed at both the training and inference stages [2]. For example, Bouacida and Mohapatra [6] investigated vulnerabilities and threats in federated learning, providing detailed explanations of various common attack types, and a summary of many defence mechanisms and the attacks they defend against. They focus the discussion on methods for establishing a trusted environment between clients of distributed systems through confidentiality and integrity, and introduce federated learning-specific techniques, including robust aggregation. Some recent surveys on FL and relevant attacks can refer to [3,11,30,32,33,35].

Potential Attacks on FL. Zhang et al. [37] stated that attack types on federated learning processes can be divided into model threats, jeopardising the robustness of the machine learning model, or data leakage, which endangers the privacy of users' data. There are numerous different types of attacks, each with different objectives. Poisoning attacks aim to undermine the quality of the global model, an example of a model threat, whilst inference attacks extract sensitive information from the model, an example of data leakage.

Both insiders and outsiders can perform attacks on the federated learning process, but attacks by insiders are often more successful and more impactful [24]. This is because they have a greater understanding and access to the process, and can therefore inflict a greater range of attacks at critical points. From the prior work [37], we know that threat models can be categorised into either semi-honest adversaries or malicious adversaries. A semi-honest adversary is one which passively attempts to infer sensitive information without directly contradicting the training and communication protocols of the network. A malicious adversary is one which actively deviates from network protocols in an attempt to tamper with the global model or steal sensitive information. Based on the type of adversaries, we can derive various attack types.

Poisoning attacks can be categorised into data poisoning and model poisoning, depending on what the attacker uses to attack the model [33]. Data poisoning occurs during the data collection phase, where a malicious adversary injects manipulated training data to impact model learning by altering the label, the features, or both. A simple example of a data poisoning attack is label-flipping, as it does not require any advanced knowledge. The adversary needs to do is to change the label assigned to a feature; this can be done randomly or deterministically, depending on the desired goal [37]. If done randomly, it will mismatch the feature and sample spaces of clients, causing the model to learn incorrect patterns. If done deterministically, this could be used to modify the perceived data distribution and increase the non-IID-ness of the training data, using model overfitting to reduce overall performance.

Another class of attack type is **inference attacks**. This is a privacy attack rather than degrading the performance of the global model, and is where an adversary attempts to infer details of the training data through model inference. This can be used to extract sensitive information from other clients that have trained the model. The two types of inference attacks are membership inference attacks and property inference attacks. Membership inference determines whether a data point is used during training through a Stochastic Gradient Descent algorithm. Property inference attacks infer desired properties that are uncorrelated with the global model's objective. Property inference attacks require an insider understanding of the model, but are often still effective when utilising secure model aggregation schemes, making it challenging to prevent.

Free-riding attacks are the simplest form of threat to federated learning. This is where the adversary does not participate in the honest local model training. It occurs when an adversary wishes to benefit from utilising a machine learning model, but either lacks training data in the domain or wants to save computing resources. To avoid detection, adversaries create false weights to return to the global model, appearing to participate fairly; however, as these weights have not been calculated, they are inaccurate. This can lead to a performance reduction of the global model, harming the performance of honest members while benefiting themselves. This attack type requires few resources and can be challenging to detect for federated learning processes [37].

Another simple attack is **backdoor attacks** [22]. Here, the attacker injects a subtle feature into the training data to force a desired prediction by the model when this feature is present. This embedded trigger enables the adversary to manipulate model inference. This attack can be challenging to detect, as model performance degradation depends on the proportion of data that is poisoned, whilst the backdoor can still be effective for even low poisoning rates [24]. For defence, Zhu et al. [38] introduced ADFL, an adversarial distillation-based backdoor defense scheme for federated learning. It can generate fake samples containing backdoor features by deploying a generative adversarial network (GAN) on the server side and relabeling the fake samples to obtain the distillation dataset.

Discussion. Federated learning processes are an example of distributed computer systems and, therefore have the same possible threats to security, such as Byzantine, Sybil, and Man-in-the-Middle attacks. Distributed systems rely on trust between client nodes, enforced by security measures that authenticate communications between actors, such as encryption, consensus protocols, and message authentication [1]. This provides authentication, confidentiality, integrity and data protection to the network [6]. Similar security measures, such as collaborative intrusion detection [14,17,18,25,34], blockchain technique [15,16,19,21,29] and user authentication [8,12,13,20,31], can be implemented in federated learning communications to improve trust between participants and reduce the risk of security threats.

Our main contribution in this work is experimentally evaluating the impacts of malicious insider attack scenarios on a simple federated learning simulation and verifying whether the experimental data aligns with the theoretical predictions of current literature.

3 Our Experimental Design

To experiment with different insider attack scenarios on federated learning processes, we need a federated learning environment that could be customised to integrate malicious clients. For this process, we decided to use Python-based framework–Flower [5]. Flower is a comprehensive, open-sourced research framework that allows large-scale federated learning experiments to be performed efficiently, without requiring excessive computing power to study distributed systems with up to millions of edge devices. It is a machine learning framework–agnostic framework, meaning it can be used to experiment with numerous popular frameworks, such as PyTorch, TensorFlow, and scikit-learn. This allows much flexibility to design experiments for any possible machine learning task, from image classification to natural language processing and numerical models. Other federated learning frameworks exist, such as TFF (TensorFlow Federated) [9] and FedLab [36]; however, these frameworks are not as flexible or scalable as Flower. For these reasons and potential benefits, we decided on Flower as the best framework to use in this work.

The Flower framework provides a built-in command to construct simple template projects based on the machine learning framework being used. We built the foundations of the code for this experiment using this feature for simplicity. We selected the PyTorch template as it is a popular framework for machine learning tasks, and edited the dataset, partitioning method and evaluation metrics used by the server and client apps to match the objectives of this study.

For this experiment, we used 100 client nodes in the simulation, representing a large cross-silo federated learning system. This provides a balance between network and computational complexity. A larger number of clients would be more resource-intensive to run, whilst this number allows us to simulate different attacker proportions to build a more comprehensive image.

The model we used as a classifier is a simple convolutional neural network, which follows the structure displayed in Fig. 1. This structure is a modified version and has been adapted for use with the MNIST dataset structure. This neural network consists of two convolution layers and two max-pooling layers, followed by three linear layers. This is a computationally inexpensive and straightforward structure for learning features in a low-resolution image classification task, whilst maintaining high levels of accuracy.

3.1 Our Dataset

For this work, we decided to utilise a popular benchmarking dataset to perform a simple, computationally inexpensive task. This can help reduce system overhead, making the experimentation process quicker and easier to carry out. For this reason, we used a Modified NIST (MNIST) dataset[1]. This dataset is often used for image classification tasks and contains 70,000 28 by 28-pixel, greyscale images of handwritten digits. It is split into 60,000 training and 10,000 testing

[1] https://huggingface.co/datasets/ylecun/mnist.

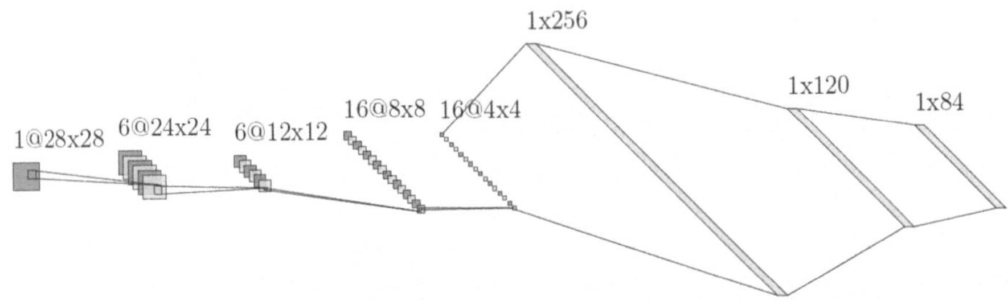

Fig. 1. A LeNet-5 architecture visualisation of the convolutional neural network

images, evenly distributed between ten classes, resulting in 6,000 training and 1,000 testing images per class. The simple nature of the data makes it ideal for fast model training, but the dataset is large enough to model any relationships defined in the sample space. A well-structured dataset leads to higher model accuracy and faster convergence, making it easier to monitor the effects of insider attack scenarios on model performance. MNIST is a comprehensive and accessible dataset for testing and validating classification systems and has seen widespread use due to its ease of access, compatibility and small size [7].

In a federated learning task, the datasets used for training are distinct, as no client has access to other's data. Therefore, the dataset must be partitioned to simulate distinct data silos per client. We used a Dirichlet distribution partitioner to split the dataset into n partitions based on the number of clients used in the simulation. A Dirichlet distribution partitions the classes in a dataset unevenly, based on a configurable α variable. This is used to simulate realistic non-IID data partitions. A higher α value equates to more uniform distributions, and we used a fixed seed value for the randomness to ensure robustness and repeatability for the experiment. We used an α value of 1 because this value produces an almost-even balanced class distribution, with some randomness that would be present in real scenarios.

3.2 Insider Attack Scenarios

The distinctive aspect of this work is the introduction of insider clients into the simulation. For the experiments, we introduced a configuration file to define the attack type and the insider ratio, the proportion of clients acting maliciously. Both being in a single location made it easy to update regularly. If the client is an insider, it will use a modified training function based on the selected attack type instead. For this study, we simulated various combinations of insider ratios and attack types to form a detailed view of how model performance changes. Initially, the simulation was run 10 times with an insider ratio of 0.00, and the results averaged to form a benchmark for comparing the impacts of the attacks on model performance. Next, each attack type was simulated under the following insider ratios and the results were recorded: 0.10, 0.25, 0.40, 0.50 and 0.70. This selection provides a detailed view without requiring many experiments.

The attack types we simulated are general label flipping, targeted label flipping, general model poisoning, targeted model poisoning, fixed free-riding, random free-riding, and backdoor and parameter scaling attacks. We briefly define each type of attack as below.

- **General label flipping:** It modifies all labels across the training data to degrade model accuracy. Malicious model weights will not reflect the same patterns in the data as non-malicious clients, disrupting the aggregation.
- **Targeted label flipping:** It flips specific labels to a target class to mislead the model into making particular incorrect predictions.
- **General model poisoning:** It injects arbitrary noise into the training data to disrupt global model convergence. Noise will be added using random numbers from a standard normal distribution multiplied by a scaling factor. Multiple scaling factors will be investigated to see the impact on model performance: 0.2x, 0.5x, and 0.7x.
- **Targeted model poisoning:** It injects arbitrary noise into a target class to degrade performance on selected inputs using the same method as general model poisoning.
- **Fixed free-riding:** It sends fixed or stale updates without performing local training, aiming to benefit without contributing. The incorrect weights will impact the aggregation from clients, degrading the performance.
- **Random free-riding:** It submits random gradients to simulate participation while avoiding computational cost. It is noted that random weights are harder to detect, whilst having a similar influence on model performance as fixed free-riding.
- **Backdoor attack:** It embeds a specific pattern into the global model that activates under specific triggers to manipulate results. Multiple poison rates will be investigated to evaluate the impact on model performance: 5%, 20%, 50% and 100%.
- **Parameter scaling attack:** It multiplies calculated local parameters to influence the global model aggregation. Multiple scaling factors will be investigated to see the impact on model performance: 2x, 5x, 7x and 10x.

3.3 Evaluation Metrics

Models trained using FL still use common machine learning metrics to evaluate their performance. For our experiment, the primary evaluation metrics will be centralised loss and accuracy, alongside averaged precision, recall, and F1 scores. Precision, recall and F1 score are per-class metrics, but macro-averaging will be used to reduce impacts from class imbalances in the data separation. These have been selected because they are the benchmark metrics used for classification tasks in the field and can account for the distributed nature of federated learning. This combination of metrics provides a comprehensive view of the impacts of insider attacks on model performance. The Flower simulation calculates two different versions of these metrics: centralised and distributed. Centralised values use the global model on the testing data, whereas distributed is calculated by averaging the performance of the local models individually. For this study, we use the following centralised metrics to analyse the impacts on the global model. Here is a brief explanation of each of the metrics mentioned.

- **Loss:** A loss function calculates the difference between a model's predictions and the actual label values. Model training aims to minimise the loss function. In this study, we utilised PyTorch's Cross-Entropy loss function, which takes into account the model's confidence in predictions to calculate the loss, not just whether it is correct or not [4,27].
- **Accuracy:** The proportion of correctly predicted instances over the total number of predictions.
- **Precision:** It indicates the proportion of true positive predictions out of all instances predicted as positive, reflecting how many positive predictions were correct.
- **Recall:** The proportion of true positive predictions out of all real positive instances, reflecting how many positive cases were missed.
- **F1 Score:** The harmonic mean of precision and recall, providing a balanced measure that considers both false positives and false negatives.

The code created for this study is open-source and can be accessed freely on our GitHub repository[2].

3.4 Federated Learning Structure

The federated learning model follows a simple convolutional neural network structure, consisting of two convolutional layers, two max pooling layers and three fully-connected linear layers, resulting in 10 outputs that represent the model's prediction confidence in the ten classes of the MNIST dataset. The Code Snippet is shown as below.

Listing 1.1. Convolutional Neural Network Code Snippet

```
self.conv1 = nn.Conv2d(1, 6, 5)
self.pool = nn.MaxPool2d(2, 2)
self.conv2 = nn.Conv2d(6, 16, 5)
self.fc1 = nn.Linear(16 * 4 * 4, 120)
self.fc2 = nn.Linear(120, 84)
self.fc3 = nn.Linear(84, 10)
```

The standard training loop used by the model under normal operation uses a cross-entropy loss function alongside an Adam optimiser to update neural network parameters. The system splits each client's data into batches, iterating through each batch with a fixed learning rate, learning features between the inputs and the labels. The Code Snippet is shown as below.

[2] https://github.com/alcopeland/421_fed_ML.

Listing 1.2. Federated Learning Training Loop Code Snippet

```
criterion = torch.nn.CrossEntropyLoss().to(device)
optimizer = torch.optim.Adam(net.parameters(), lr=lr)

for _ in range(epochs):
    for batch in trainloader:
        images = batch["image"]
        labels = batch["label"]
        optimizer.zero_grad()
        loss = criterion(net(images.to(device)),
        labels.to(device))
        loss.backward()
        optimizer.step()
        running_loss += loss.item()
```

4 Attack Scenario Implementation

To implement the insider attack scenarios into the federated learning process, we modified the basic training loop structure in distinct ways. Each client can retrieve the correct training function via a function call and substitute that into the training loop, allowing for configurable training of malicious clients. The clients access a shared insider ratio and seed value from the project's TOML configuration file, which ensures consistency between all client processes.

Each client will generate a list of malicious insider client IDs: if the ID is present in the list of insiders, it will perform a different training loop depending on the configured attack type. In the following parts, we will describe how each of the training loops was modified for each attack type.

4.1 Label Flipping Attack

General. To simulate a general label flipping attack, the malicious clients will cycle the labels used for training by adding one and then calculating the modulus based on the number of classes. This changes all the labels by 1 and wraps around back to the start, meaning that none of the training data matches up to its true label value. The Code Snippet is shown as below.

Listing 1.3. General Label Flipping Attack Code Snippet

```
# Change the labels of all classes by one, wrapping around
labels = (labels + 1) % 10
```

Targeted. To simulate a targeted label flipping attack, the malicious clients will only attack a single class by changing all instances of that label to a different one. In our simulation, we changed the labels from one to seven, whilst leaving the rest unchanged. This simulates a malicious client that wants to degrade the performance of identifying a specific class. The Code Snippet is shown as below.

Listing 1.4. Targeted Label Flipping Attack Code Snippet

```
# Flip labels of a specific class to another class, 1 -> 7
labels = torch.where(labels == 1, 7, labels)
```

4.2 Model Poisoning Attack

General. To simulate a general model poisoning attack, malicious clients will generate a list of random numbers the same shape as the images (following a standard normal distribution), multiply these by a scaling factor, and then add them to the input images. The resulting values are then clamped to ensure all values are valid. This will reduce the quality of the input images by adding different amounts of noise. The scaling factor can be varied to study the impact on the model performance at multiple intensity levels. The Code Snippet is shown as below.

Listing 1.5. General Model Poisoning Attack Code Snippet

```
# Add noise to images based on a scaling factor
images += torch.randn_like(images) * 0.2
# Ensure images are in the valid range
images = torch.clamp(images, 0, 1)
```

Targeted. To simulate a targeted model poisoning attack, the malicious clients will loop through each image in the batch to find instances of the target class, then add noise using the same technique as the general model poisoning function explained previously. The Code Snippet is shown as below.

Listing 1.6. Targeted Model Poisoning Attack Code Snippet

```
# Cycle through each image in the batch
for i in range(images.shape[0]):
    # If the current label is the target class
    if labels[i] == 1:
        # Add noise to images based on a scaling factor
        images[i] += torch.randn_like(images[i]) * 0.2
        # Ensure images are in the valid range
        images[i] = torch.clamp(images[i], 0, 1)
```

4.3 Free-Riding Attack

Fixed. To simulate a fixed free-riding attack, the malicious clients will not perform any actions at all. They will not perform any of the stages of the training loop, so the model weights returned do not change. This means that the client does not have to spend any computational power. The Code Snippet is shown as below.

Listing 1.7. Fixed Free-riding Attack Code Snippet

```
# Does not perform any training stages
return 0.01
```

Random. To simulate a random free-riding attack, the malicious clients will not perform any stages of the training loop, instead setting the neural network weights using random number generation following a standard normal distribution. The program cycles through each of the parameter weights in the neural network and sets the data to a list of randomly generated numbers. The Code Snippet is shown as below.

Listing 1.8. Random Free-riding Attack Code Snippet

```
# Does not perform any training stages
with torch.no_grad():
    # Cycles through each weight of the neural network
    for name, param in net.named_parameters():
        # Sets the weight to a random value
        param.data = torch.randn_like(param.data)
```

4.4 Backdoor Attack

To simulate a backdoor attack, the malicious clients will modify a portion of the training inputs with a solid square shape in the top left corner of the images, setting each one to a target label. The client will only insert the trigger into some of the training images, using a random chance based on a configurable poisoning rate. If this occurs, the client will iterate through each image in the batch, modifying the pixels and setting the labels for the batch to the target class. The poisoning rate can be varied to investigate its impacts on model performance. The Code Snippet is shown as below.

Listing 1.9. Backdoor Attack Code Snippet

```
# Chance to insert backdoor into batch
if random.random() < 0.7:
    # Iterates through each image in the batch
    for i in range(images.shape[0]):
        # Inserts the trigger shape in the image
        images[i, 0:5, 0:5] = 1.0
    # Sets the labels for the batch to the target class
    labels = torch.full_like(labels, 7)
```

4.5 Parameter Scaling Attack

To simulate a parameter scaling attack, the malicious clients will perform the normal training loop first, then they will iterate through each of the model weights calculated and multiply them by a configurable scaling factor to disproportionately influence the global model when aggregated. The scaling factor can be varied to examine the impacts on the model's performance. The Code Snippet is shown as below.

Listing 1.10. Parameter Scaling Attack Code Snippet

```
# Iterate through each parameter of the model
```

```
for name, param in net.named_parameters():
    # Scale the parameter value by a scaling factor
    param.data *= 5
```

5 Evaluation and Results

To evaluate the model's performance on the testing split of the dataset, we used common classification metrics: loss, accuracy, precision, recall and F1 score. To calculate the model's loss, we used PyTorch's criterion function using Cross Entropy to calculate a running loss value, which is then averaged. The accuracy of the model is calculated by counting the number of correct model predictions and then dividing by the total length of the data.

We used scikit-learn to derive the model's precision, recall, and F1 scores. These metrics are usually calculated for each class, but a *macro* averaging function can be used to calculate an unweighted mean, reducing the number of metrics to compare. The Code Snippet is shown as below.

Listing 1.11. Model Evaluation Code Snippet

```
from sklearn.metrics import precision_score, recall_score, f1_score

loss += criterion(outputs, labels).item()
correct += (torch.max(outputs.data, 1)[1] == labels).sum().item()

accuracy = correct / len(testloader.dataset)
loss = loss / len(testloader)

precision = precision_score(all_labels, all_preds,
    average='macro', zero_division=0)
recall = recall_score(all_labels, all_preds,
    average='macro', zero_division=0)
f1 = f1_score(all_labels, all_preds,
    average='macro', zero_division=0)
```

Our simulations were run using Flower and PyTorch on the MNIST dataset in a simple classification task. These tasks were evaluated using the metrics of loss, accuracy, precision, recall, and F1 score aiming to provide a comprehensive view of model performance after five training rounds. These metrics are centralised so they are calculated using the global model, rather than averaging the performance of the distributed models. Each attack type was run at each of the targeted insider ratios.

5.1 Benchmark

Initially, we ran the simulation ten times with an insider ratio of zero. These results represent the model's performance without any adversarial behaviour, establishing a baseline for comparison. The results and mean values calculated for these simulations are shown in Table 1. These averages are included with all results tables for easy comparison.

The results show that under normal operating conditions, the federated learning system consistently performs well. The low loss value of 0.276 signifies successful model convergence, and the high average accuracy of 93.2% shows that the model performs well without adversarial conditions. The four performance metrics are evenly balanced, showing stable learning from the training process. This proves consistent foundational model performance, ensuring the following impacts on results are by insider attacks.

Table 1. Model performance results under non-adversarial conditions.

Attempt	Loss	Accuracy	F1	Precision	Recall
1	0.262	0.930	0.929	0.931	0.930
2	0.347	0.916	0.915	0.916	0.915
3	0.235	0.943	0.942	0.942	0.942
4	0.325	0.918	0.915	0.919	0.917
5	0.291	0.938	0.937	0.938	0.937
6	0.265	0.938	0.937	0.937	0.937
7	0.239	0.944	0.944	0.944	0.944
8	0.254	0.935	0.934	0.935	0.935
9	0.286	0.927	0.925	0.927	0.927
10	0.255	0.935	0.934	0.936	0.934
Average	0.276	0.932	0.931	0.933	0.932

5.2 Label Flipping Attack

General. For the general label flipping attack, the aim is to degrade overall model performance by changing the labels of all classes in the training set. The results from Table 2 indicate that the attack had a little impact at the lower insider ratios of 0.10 and 0.25, with the 0.25's performance increasing above the baseline results. This could have a minimal impact due to the random variation of simulations and the aggregation technique used.

However, from 40% insiders, there is a consistent, marked decrease in performance as the number of insiders increases, reaching as low as 18.1% model accuracy at 70% insiders; therefore, approximately 40% is the critical point. A large proportion of insiders can inflict serious damage to the global model's convergence, making it unusable for other clients.

For higher insider ratios, the precision was noticeably lower than the other metrics, meaning that the model predicts a high number of false positive values. The model learning incorrectly and overfitting to the manipulated inputs can cause this, leading to frequent incorrect predictions due to classification degradation. On the other hand, these results also show that these processes can be robust to this attack when using FedAvg aggregation, even with as many as 25% malicious clients.

Table 2. Model performance results under a general label flipping attack at various insider ratios.

Insider Ratio	Loss	Accuracy	F1	Precision	Recall
0.00	0.276	0.932	0.931	0.933	0.932
0.10	0.416	0.915	0.914	0.917	0.914
0.25	0.352	0.936	0.935	0.936	0.935
0.40	0.835	0.723	0.716	0.759	0.724
0.50	1.504	0.323	0.276	0.252	0.328
0.70	2.007	0.181	0.146	0.122	0.185

Targeted. In the case of targeted label flipping attack, the direct impacts are difficult to realise from the selected evaluation metrics. The targeted attack decreases performance for a particular class, but the metrics are averaged so we cannot directly deduce the impacts on a specific class. However, we can infer conclusions by comparison to the general label flipping attack. Whilst the model's performance does decrease as the insider ratio increases, the change in these results is much less severe than the general label flipping attack, with the accuracy of the model only decreasing by 11.9% at 70% insiders, rather than a 75.1% decrease seen by the general attack. Furthermore, the model's loss at 70% insiders is noticeably lower than the same result for the general attack, meaning the model is learning more efficiently and is more confident in predicting answers close to the true labels. Therefore, the targeted attack is harder to notice, even at higher insider ratios.

We can predict that the class-based performance of the target class in this attack will follow a similar trend to the general label attack, with its performance decreasing compared to that of the other classes, which would remain similar to the benchmark results. This allows an adversary to manipulate the results of the model less noticeably than in a general label flipping attack (Table 3).

Table 3. Model performance results under a targeted label flipping attack at various insider ratios.

Insider Ratio	Loss	Accuracy	F1	Precision	Recall
0.00	0.276	0.932	0.931	0.933	0.932
0.10	0.223	0.947	0.946	0.946	0.946
0.25	0.447	0.879	0.872	0.881	0.877
0.40	0.325	0.928	0.928	0.930	0.929
0.50	0.421	0.826	0.805	0.888	0.839
0.70	0.692	0.813	0.792	0.774	0.825

5.3 Model Poisoning Attack

General. Model poisoning occurs when an adversary attempts to reduce the performance of the global model by degrading the quality of their training data. The results for these simulations show that at low insider ratios, the model performance shows a small decrease for each of the scaling factors. The highest scaling factor, (0.7x), only presents a maximum decrease of 20.8% in model accuracy, whereas 0.2x and 0.5x only saw a 3.8% and 4% decrease, respectively. These results show that the input data must be highly corrupted by a large number of malicious clients for this attack to be impactful, making the risk low as these conditions can be challenging to implement in practice.

The results in Table 4 show a slow decline in performance from 10% to 40% insiders; however, the change is more pronounced over 50%. Such behaviour implies this is the critical value for model collapse. Therefore, if an adversary wants to cause a collapse of a shared model, perhaps to inhibit a competitor, they must have control over a large proportion of client processes. In cross-device learning, this can be challenging due to the high number of clients, but cross-silo federated learning uses fewer clients, so this is more achievable.

Table 4. Model performance results under a general model poisoning attack (0.7x Scaling Factor) at various insider ratios.

Insider Ratio	Loss	Accuracy	F1	Precision	Recall
0.00	0.276	0.932	0.931	0.933	0.932
0.10	0.196	0.946	0.945	0.946	0.945
0.25	0.314	0.913	0.911	0.913	0.912
0.40	0.337	0.900	0.896	0.902	0.899
0.50	0.535	0.820	0.807	0.825	0.825
0.70	0.808	0.724	0.702	0.731	0.716

Targeted. The targeted model poisoning attack is in a similar situation to the targeted label flipping, in that we do not have class-wise performance metrics, so we cannot conclude whether the attack had the desired influence on performance. The results for this attack type show that it is difficult to detect through the global model's performance. For each of the scaling factors and insider ratios, the model's performance remains consistent with the benchmark. Table 5 shows the highest scaling factor, which would have the most impact on model performance, but each test performs similarly to the benchmark. The variation seen in the results could easily be attributed to natural variation in the machine learning process, as no two runs are identical.

However, this does not mean that the attack was unsuccessful in decreasing the performance of classifying the targets. Since the general poisoning attack resulted in a decrease in model performance at higher scaling factors and insider ratios, we predict that this pattern will carry over to the class-wise performance after targeted model poisoning. This attack type is high-risk because it can decrease the performance of a target class, whilst remaining undetected due to consistent global model performance.

Table 5. Model performance results under a targeted model poisoning attack (0.7x Scaling Factor) at various insider ratios.

Insider Ratio	Loss	Accuracy	F1	Precision	Recall
0.00	0.276	0.932	0.931	0.933	0.932
0.10	0.289	0.928	0.928	0.928	0.928
0.25	0.476	0.867	0.863	0.865	0.865
0.40	0.214	0.946	0.945	0.947	0.946
0.50	0.284	0.930	0.929	0.929	0.929
0.70	0.274	0.931	0.930	0.931	0.930

5.4 Free-Riding Attack

Fixed. Free-riding clients benefit from using a machine learning model without contributing to the training process, reducing costs. In distributed systems, selfish participants can be common. Whilst the malicious client may not deliberately target model performance, their inaction can cause this. If enough client processes act selfishly and avoid participating, the quality of the global model might decrease. This is proven by Table 6, which shows all metrics decrease as the insider ratio increases; however, the changes are minimal until 70% insiders, with a larger decrease of 11.8% from 89% accuracy to 77.2%. This shows if a majority of clients are selfish, it can cause the global model to collapse and be too inaccurate for honest clients to utilise effectively. However, the impacts are insignificant at lower insider ratios, meaning that systems can still produce effective models if they contain some free-riding clients due to aggregation.

Table 6. Model performance results under a fixed free-riding attack at various insider ratios.

Insider Ratio	Loss	Accuracy	F1	Precision	Recall
0.00	0.276	0.932	0.931	0.933	0.932
0.10	0.297	0.933	0.932	0.933	0.933
0.25	0.346	0.922	0.921	0.922	0.920
0.40	0.465	0.901	0.898	0.899	0.899
0.50	0.464	0.890	0.880	0.895	0.887
0.70	1.247	0.772	0.748	0.804	0.765

Random. The results of the random free-riding attack, shown in Table 7, tell a very different story from that of the fixed attack. This attack still does not perform any training stages, only returning random neural network model weights, saving the malicious client's computing power. However, its impact on the global model's performance is significantly more profound. Even at only 10% malicious clients, there is a 6.5% and 6.9% decrease in accuracy and F1 score, respectively, to the benchmark. This is much greater than the fixed free-riding attack, whose performance at both 10% and 25% insiders matched that of the benchmark. As low as 25% adversaries already caused the model to collapse, an accuracy of 68.4% is not feasible to apply effectively in the industry. At higher insider ratios, the model has completely collapsed, falling to as low as F1 score of 2.8% at 70% adversaries.

These results also contain loss values greater than 2 at as low as 40% insiders, reaching 2.427 at its peak. This is the highest recorded loss value during these experiments (excluding the loss values of the parameter scaling, which are unusually high). A high loss value implies that a model has poor convergence and makes uncertain class predictions, indicating worse training. This attack is the most disruptive to federated learning and is also one of the easiest to perform due to low computational complexity, as it skips the training loop. Furthermore, this attack can be challenging to detect when analysing model updates because the random values may not be inherently fake, as the server does not know the client's training data. Attacks like parameter scaling and fixed free-riding have more blatant malicious weights. These factors combined make random free-riding a dangerous attack in federated learning that can cause rapid model degradation with a small number of low-effort adversaries.

Table 7. Model performance results under a random free-riding attack at various insider ratios.

Insider Ratio	Loss	Accuracy	F1	Precision	Recall
0.00	0.276	0.932	0.931	0.933	0.932
0.10	0.730	0.867	0.862	0.879	0.867
0.25	1.359	0.684	0.657	0.722	0.680
0.40	2.087	0.285	0.242	0.492	0.277
0.50	2.375	0.070	0.038	0.099	0.073
0.70	2.427	0.100	0.028	0.031	0.099

5.5 Backdoor Attack

Backdoor attacks attempt to inject a hidden mechanism into a machine learning model, allowing manipulation of the model by using a known trigger feature in the inputs to increase the likelihood of a desired output. They do not often intend to decrease model performance because this could lead to a greater chance of discovery of the backdoor.

These attacks are usually performed with lower poisoning rates (5–10%) on large datasets to avoid detection whilst still inserting the trigger into the model. Table 8 shows results for poisoning rate at 20%, which on larger training sets, it can effectively implement a successful trigger, but even at 70% insiders, it shows performance comparable to the benchmark. Therefore, backdoor attacks can be very challenging to detect based on model performance alone, especially because the server and other clients cannot access the malicious actor's training data.

Higher poisoning rates, in our experiment, are unlikely to be applied in practice but have been included to study their effects. Both higher poison rates have a more notable impact on model performance, with the 50% model's accuracy decreasing to around 85% at 50% insiders. The 70% model achieves this at 40%, reaching a low of 54.6% F1 score. This shows that as the poisoning rate increases, model performance decreases; however, the impact will depend on the intensity of the trigger feature used. In our simulation, we use a very intrusive trigger, a solid box in the corner of the image, which reduces the quality of the training data greatly. If the trigger feature introduced was more subtle, the impacts on performance may be less pronounced.

In conclusion, backdoor attacks are high-risk insider attacks because they can be easily injected into a global model, which are difficult to detect and provide malicious clients with an unfair advantage over other clients.

Table 8. Model performance results under a backdoor attack (20% Poisoning Rate) at various insider ratios.

Insider Ratio	Loss	Accuracy	F1	Precision	Recall
0.00	0.276	0.932	0.931	0.933	0.932
0.10	0.294	0.945	0.947	0.947	0.947
0.25	0.401	0.932	0.931	0.932	0.931
0.40	0.467	0.854	0.837	0.877	0.852
0.50	0.413	0.924	0.923	0.924	0.924
0.70	0.356	0.925	0.924	0.924	0.924

5.6 Parameter Scaling Attack

Parameter scaling occurs after model training, where the calculated model weights are scaled to disproportionately influence the aggregation process, as large outlier values can disrupt an average. The large model weights caused the cross-entropy loss values calculated to be abnormal. Based on Table 9, the lowest scaling factors still have reasonable performance at low insider ratios, however, the results are also unstable, often increasing and decreasing randomly as the insider ratio changes, showing the disruptive nature of the attack.

At the higher scaling factors, model performance decreases greatly. Table 10 shows the results for the highest scaling factor tested, 10x. Even at an insider ratio of 10%, the model's accuracy decreases to 85.6%, down to 60% at 40% insiders. At the highest ratio of malicious clients, the model performs poorly with an F1 score of 1.8%, indicating the damage the attack can inflict. However, this attack, particularly at higher scaling factors, is very blatant if the central server analyses the incoming model updates for anomalies, as the values are very disparate from normal. Another downside to performing this attack type is that the malicious client must use computing power to perform model training before parameter scaling can be applied. Forming a composite attack type with random free-riding, scaling random values, could alleviate this. This combination would be computationally cheap to perform and combines the devastating impact of both attack types to rapidly degrade the global model.

Table 9. Model performance results under a parameter scaling attack (7x Scaling Factor) at various insider ratios.

Insider Ratio	Loss	Accuracy	F1	Precision	Recall
0.00	0.276	0.932	0.931	0.933	0.932
0.10	20.812	0.870	0.869	0.869	0.869
0.25	138564.714	0.822	0.819	0.819	0.819
0.40	14568984781.651	0.786	0.785	0.797	0.783
0.50	119011173122.549	0.604	0.597	0.603	0.597
0.70	66910721814472.930	0.482	0.474	0.483	0.476

Table 10. Model performance results under a parameter scaling attack (10x Scaling Factor) at various insider ratios.

Insider Ratio	Loss	Accuracy	F1	Precision	Recall
0.00	0.276	0.932	0.931	0.933	0.932
0.10	272.319	0.856	0.853	0.854	0.854
0.25	486515706.607	0.753	0.748	0.751	0.749
0.40	2526172195568.460	0.592	0.583	0.588	0.586
0.50	30321997026104.434	0.483	0.468	0.474	0.477
0.70	426012720073776.250	0.096	0.018	0.102	0.100

6 Concluding Remarks

In this work, we investigated the empirical impacts of insider attack scenarios on the performance of learning models trained through federated learning. We built a simulated federated environment with the Flower framework to perform a simple MNIST classification task. We utilised the performance metrics loss, accuracy, precision, recall and F1 score to create a comprehensive view of how different insider attacks affect model performance at various proportions of malicious clients. Finally, we evaluated the potential strengths and weaknesses of the attacks tested.

One key insight from these experiments is that federated learning processes are not inherently resistant to malicious actors because of the aggregation function. Many of the different attack types caused the global model to collapse, sometimes at as low as a 10% or 25% insider ratio for the more aggressive attacks. The riskiest attack types identified in this work are *random free-riding* and *parameter scaling attacks*. These attacks caused the global model to collapse rapidly, usually around 40 and 50% insiders.

A backdoor is another risky attack because it can be injected into the model without impacting the performance of the global model, even with a 20% data poisoning rate. It can be challenging to detect, as the other clients will not notice a perceivable change in performance, and they cannot access the training data of the malicious clients. Similarly, attacks that target a specific class have a minimal impact on model performance at low insider ratios. Combining various attacks into one composite attack, such as random free-riding and parameter scaling, could produce more noticeable impacts on model performance by utilising the strengths of each attack.

References

1. Security threats scenarios in trust and reputation models for distributed systems. Comput. Secur. **28**(7), 545–556 (2009)
2. Federated learning vulnerabilities: threats and defenses: a systematic review and future directions. Internet Things **24**, 100947 (2023)
3. Bai, L., Hu, H., Ye, Q., Li, H., Wang, L., Xu, J.: Membership inference attacks and defenses in federated learning: a survey. ACM Comput. Surv. **57**(4), 89:1–89:35 (2025)
4. Bergmann, D., Stryker, C.: What is a loss function? (2024). https://www.ibm.com/think/topics/loss-function. Accessed 15 May 2025
5. Beutel, D.J., et al.: Flower: A friendly federated learning research framework (2022)
6. Bouacida, N., Mohapatra, P.: Vulnerabilities in federated learning. IEEE Access **9**, 63229–63249 (2021)
7. Cohen, G., Afshar, S., Tapson, J., van Schaik, A.: EMNIST: extending MNIST to handwritten letters. In: 2017 International Joint Conference on Neural Networks (IJCNN), pp. 2921–2926 (2017)
8. Fu, H.C., Li, W., Wang, Y.: PassFile: graphical password authentication based on file browsing records. In: Kim, D.D., Chen, C. (eds.) Machine Learning for Cyber Security - 5th International Conference, ML4CS 2023, Yanuca Island, Fiji, December 4-6, 2023, Proceedings. Lecture Notes in Computer Science, vol. 14541, pp. 28–43. Springer (2023)
9. Google: TensorFlow federated: Machine learning on decentralized data (2019). https://www.tensorflow.org/federated. Accessed 12 May 2025
10. Jiang, Y., et al.: Blockchained federated learning for internet of things: a comprehensive survey. ACM Comput. Surv. **56**(10), 258 (2024)

11. Kapoor, A., Kumar, D.: Federated learning for urban sensing systems: a comprehensive survey on attacks, defences, incentive mechanisms, and applications. IEEE Commun. Surv. Tutorials **27**(2), 1293–1325 (2025)
12. Li, C., Meng, W., Li, W.: Enhancing EEG-based authentication with transformer in Internet of Things. IEEE Trans. Inf. Forensics Secur. **20**, 7197–7210 (2025)
13. Li, W., Meng, W., Furnell, S.: Exploring touch-based behavioral authentication on smartphone email applications in IoT-enabled smart cities. Pattern Recognit. Lett. **144**, 35–41 (2021)
14. Li, W., Meng, W., Kwok, L.F.: Surveying trust-based collaborative intrusion detection: state-of-the-art, challenges and future directions. IEEE Commun. Surv. Tutorials **24**(1), 280–305 (2022)
15. Li, W., Meng, W., Wang, Y., Li, J.: Enhancing blackslist-based packet filtration using blockchain in wireless sensor networks. In: Liu, Z., Wu, F., Das, S.K. (eds.) Wireless Algorithms, Systems, and Applications - 16th International Conference, WASA 2021, Nanjing, China, June 25-27, 2021, Proceedings, Part II. Lecture Notes in Computer Science, vol. 12938, pp. 624–635. Springer (2021)
16. Li, W., Meng, W., Yang, L.T.: Enhancing trust-based medical smartphone networks via blockchain-based traffic sampling. In: 20th IEEE International Conference on Trust, Security and Privacy in Computing and Communications, TrustCom 2021, Shenyang, China, October 20-22, 2021, pp. 122–129. IEEE (2021)
17. Li, W., Rosenberg, P., Glisby, M., Han, M.: Designing energy-aware collaborative intrusion detection in IoT networks. J. Inf. Secur. Appl. **81**, 103713 (2024)
18. Li, W., Stidsen, C., Adam, T.: A blockchain-assisted security management framework for collaborative intrusion detection in smart cities. Comput. Electr. Eng. **111**(Part A), 108884 (2023)
19. Li, W., Tan, J., Wang, Y.: A framework of blockchain-based collaborative intrusion detection in software defined networking. In: Kutylowski, M., Zhang, J., Chen, C. (eds.) Network and System Security - 14th International Conference, NSS 2020, Melbourne, VIC, Australia, November 25-27, 2020, Proceedings. Lecture Notes in Computer Science, vol. 12570, pp. 261–276. Springer (2020)
20. Li, W., Wang, Y., Li, J., Xiang, Y.: Toward supervised shape-based behavioral authentication on smartphones. J. Inf. Secur. Appl. **55**, 102591 (2020)
21. Li, Y., Zhang, J., Zhu, J., Li, W.: HBMD-FL: heterogeneous federated learning algorithm based on blockchain and model distillation. In: Chen, J., He, D., Lu, R. (eds.) Emerging Information Security and Applications - Third International Conference, EISA 2022, Wuhan, China, October 29-30, 2022, Proceedings. Communications in Computer and Information Science, vol. 1641, pp. 145–159. Springer (2022)
22. Li, Z., Lan, J., Yan, Z., Gelenbe, E.: Backdoor attacks and defense mechanisms in federated learning: a survey. Inf. Fusion **123**, 103248 (2025)
23. Lian, Z., Zeng, Q., Wang, W., Xu, D., Meng, W., Su, C.: Traffic sign recognition using optimized federated learning in Internet of Vehicles. IEEE Internet Things J. **11**(4), 6722–6729 (2024)
24. Lyu, L., Yu, H., Yang, Q.: Threats to federated learning: A survey (2020). https://arxiv.org/abs/2003.02133
25. Ma, Z., Liu, L., Meng, W., Luo, X., Wang, L., Li, W.: ADCL: toward an adaptive network intrusion detection system using collaborative learning in IoT networks. IEEE Internet Things J. **10**(14), 12521–12536 (2023)
26. Mammen, P.M.: Federated learning: Opportunities and challenges. CoRR abs/2101.05428 (2021)

27. Mao, A., Mohri, M., Zhong, Y.: Cross-entropy loss functions: Theoretical analysis and applications (2023). https://arxiv.org/abs/2304.07288
28. McMahan, B., Ramage, D.: Federated learning: collaborative machine learning without centralized training data. Google Res. Blog **3** (2017)
29. Meng, W., Li, W., Zhu, L.: Enhancing medical smartphone networks via blockchain-based trust management against insider attacks. IEEE Trans. Eng. Manag. **67**(4), 1377–1386 (2020)
30. Mohamed, H., Koroniotis, N., Moustafa, N., Schiliro, F., Zomaya, A.Y.: Harnessing federated learning for digital forensics in IoT: a survey and introduction to the IoT-LF framework. IEEE Open J. Commun. Soc. **6**, 3161–3191 (2025)
31. Qin, X., Li, W., Rosenberg, P.: RoundImage: toward secure graphical password authentication via rounded image selection in IoT. IEEE Internet Things J. **12**(12), 20473–20483 (2025)
32. Rao, B., Zhang, J., Wu, D., Zhu, C., Sun, X., Chen, B.: Privacy inference attack and defense in centralized and federated learning: a comprehensive survey. IEEE Trans. Artif. Intell. **6**(2), 333–353 (2025)
33. Wan, Y., Qu, Y., Ni, W., Xiang, Y., Gao, L., Hossain, E.: Data and model poisoning backdoor attacks on wireless federated learning, and the defense mechanisms: a comprehensive survey. IEEE Commun. Surv. Tutorials **26**(3), 1861–1897 (2024)
34. Wardana, A.A., Sukarno, P.: Taxonomy and survey of collaborative intrusion detection system using federated learning. ACM Comput. Surv. **57**(4), 88:1–88:36 (2025)
35. Xue, B., Zhang, J., Chen, B., Li, W.: Tackling Non-IID for federated learning with components alignment. In: Kim, D.D., Chen, C. (eds.) Machine Learning for Cyber Security - 5th International Conference, ML4CS 2023, Yanuca Island, Fiji, December 4-6, 2023, Proceedings. Lecture Notes in Computer Science, vol. 14541, pp. 131–144. Springer (2023)
36. Zeng, D., Liang, S., Hu, X., Wang, H., Xu, Z.: FedLab: a flexible federated learning framework. J. Mach. Learn. Res. **24**(100), 1–7 (2023)
37. Zhang, J., Zhu, H., Wang, F., Zhao, J., Xu, Q., Li, H.: Security and privacy threats to federated learning: issues, methods, and challenges. Secur. Commun. Netw. **1**, 2886795 (2022)
38. Zhu, C., Zhang, J., Sun, X., Chen, B., Meng, W.: ADFL: defending backdoor attacks in federated learning via adversarial distillation. Comput. Secur. **132**, 103366 (2023)

Privacy Paradox in Health Monitoring: Towards Future Privacy Predictive Model Development

Luyi Sun[1(✉)] and Bian Yang[2]

[1] Zhejiang University, Hangzhou 310058, China
luyis@zju.edu.cn
[2] Norwegian University of Science and Technology, Gjøvik 2815, Norway
bian.yang@ntnu.no

Abstract. Assisted living technologies have been introduced to support patients in staying in private homes longer in the digital era. Despite the convenience they offer, various factors influence patients' adoption of them, with privacy being a crucial consideration. Therefore, it is imperative to gather information on patients' privacy attitudes to effectively implement health monitoring systems. From another perspective, collecting patients' privacy attitudes and constructing privacy predictive models empower monitoring systems to make informed decisions in situations where patients lose their capacity. However, the discrepancy between privacy attitudes and privacy decisions in real-life situations, known as privacy paradox, can impact the predictive performance of these models. In this paper, we present the results of two experiments, one conducted via questionnaires, and the other one conducted via a combination of questionnaires and a VR platform. We investigate whether participants' situation-specific privacy attitudes in VR and questionnaires deviate from their stated privacy attitudes. The results of the studies have reflected two findings. First, privacy paradox phenomenon exists, and it was observed among most of the participants. Second, participants' privacy attitudes exhibited variability during all phases of the study. The findings suggest avenues for future research.

Keywords: Privacy paradox · Assisted living · Health monitoring · Virtual reality · Privacy behavior · Privacy attitudes

1 Introduction

The development of various assisted living technologies has significantly alleviated the burden on healthcare providers and enhanced the quality of life for care receivers. Privacy attitudes, serving as a critical factor influencing the adoption of assisted living technologies and health monitoring systems in private homes, have garnered increased attention from researchers in recent years [1,2].

Privacy attitudes play a pivotal role when care receivers encounter medical incidents in their daily lives. These attitudes encompass users' willingness to be

W. Li et al. (Eds.): EISA 2025, CCIS 2897, pp. 97–118, 2026.
https://doi.org/10.1007/978-3-032-21177-4_6

monitored, their handling of personal information (such as storing and sharing data with family members or clinical staff), and more [3]. Privacy attitudes may vary in different scenarios, depending on the sensitivity of activities and the urgency of medical incidents. For instance, a care receiver might prefer not to be monitored during financial activities but may consent to monitoring while doing household chores. Additionally, a care receiver may prefer family assistance for daily activities while opting for clinical staff help during medical emergencies. These privacy preferences reflect the privacy attitudes of care receivers.

Collecting care receivers' privacy attitudes and developing privacy predictive models can benefit both care receivers and healthcare providers in the digital era. For care receivers, personalized predictive models can aid in predicting privacy-related decisions during urgent cases or as decision-making capacity diminishes. These models help manage decisions regardless of large quantities of assisted living technologies and assistive applications. For healthcare providers, consideration of care receivers' preferences enhances the delivery of health services.

Nevertheless, developing privacy predictive models presents several challenges. Firstly, researchers encounter difficulty in comprehensively covering all scenarios that users may encounter. Users with diverse health conditions may face varying medical incidents while engaging in different activities at home. A predictive model might know how to handle a fall during meal preparation, but it could fail to address the privacy concerns of a person who has a seizure while bathing, a scenario it wasn't trained on. Additionally, in monitoring environments involving more than one person, such as care receivers and bystanders like family members or friends, care receivers may possess distinct privacy attitudes, influenced by the potential assistance from other bystanders. Consequently, it becomes imperative to consider the privacy attitudes of both care receivers and bystanders, as both user roles are under the system's surveillance [4].

More, the consistency between privacy attitudes collected by researchers and users' privacy behaviors in the real world remains a problem. The existence of the privacy paradox phenomenon [5], indicating a discrepancy between privacy attitudes and behaviors, has been studied extensively in fields such as e-commerce [6], online shopping [7], and social networking sites [8]. However, few studies were conducted in the domain of health monitoring. The presence of the privacy paradox phenomenon suggests that previous studies may have constructed privacy predictive models using datasets derived from inadequate questionnaires, where privacy attitudes were collected instead of privacy behaviors. It indicates that the predictive models based on privacy attitudes may not be sufficient to predict patients' behaviors in real-world. For example, a patient might strongly state in a survey that they value privacy and would never share health data, but then behaviorally grant app permissions for a wellness tracker because they want its social features. Consequently, it becomes crucial to verify the occurrence of this phenomenon and assess the degree to which patients' privacy behaviors diverge from their privacy attitudes.

While previous studies have explored the privacy paradox phenomenon, which highlights the disparity between privacy attitudes and actual behaviors, some investigations have approached this by contrasting general privacy attitudes with situation-specific privacy attitudes [9,10]. It is partly because of the difficulty to collect privacy behaviors directly. These studies revealed that general privacy concerns are not context-specific and may be superseded by situational factors, such as those associated with particular websites or online entities when it comes to online privacy. Also, experiments were conducted to compare the difference between general attitudes and situation-specific ones.

Given the challenges associated with collecting privacy behaviors in real-life health monitoring environments, we decided to test the privacy paradox by comparing general privacy attitudes and situation-specific privacy attitudes as well, instead of privacy behaviors. In the meantime, recognizing the enhanced capacity of virtual reality (VR) to simulate real-world scenarios compared to conventional online questionnaires, which was regarded as one closer measurement to test behaviors in real-world [11], we compared the situation-specific privacy attitudes in questionnaires and the ones in VR platforms.

In this paper, we present the results of two experiments aimed at exploring the potential existence of the privacy paradox phenomenon in health monitoring. While acknowledging the influence of multiple individuals (e.g., care receivers and bystanders) in monitoring environments, our experiments focus on one-person scenarios, assuming participants as the sole occupants of their private homes who will receive health services.

The main contributions of this paper include: (1) introduction of a virtual reality platform, providing the immersion and presence that can better replicate real-life scenarios, and therefore users' behaviors within the virtual environment better represent their real-life behaviors compared to texts; (2) comparison of participants' general privacy attitudes and situation-specific privacy attitudes in both questionnaires and VR; (3) comparison of participants' situation-specific privacy attitudes between questionnaires and VR platforms; (4) providing insights of healthcare privacy settings.

2 Related Works

The term "privacy paradox" emerged at the beginning of the century when Acquisti and Grossklags [12] conducted an experiment, revealing the paradoxical nature of individuals' online disclosure of personal information [13]. A seminal study in 2007 by Norberg et al. further tested the privacy paradox phenomenon, highlighting the disparity between privacy attitudes and behaviors [14,15]. Over the past decades, numerous studies have delved into this phenomenon. In 2017, Spyros Kokolakis et al. [5] conducted a comprehensive literature survey, exploring the existence of the information privacy paradox and elucidating the dichotomy between privacy attitudes and behaviors. Their review encompassed studies from diverse fields, including social networking sites (SNSs), e-commerce, smartphone applications, online shopping, entertainment, finance, location data, personal information trade, and more. Simultaneously, Susanne and Menno [15] undertook a systematic review in the same year, examining 35 theories contributing to the emergence of the privacy paradox phenomenon in online behavior.

In the context of healthcare, the privacy paradox has been investigated using various methods. In 2016, He et al. [16] proposed a conceptual model based on the privacy calculus theory to explore users' adoption of healthcare wearable devices, validating the model through survey data. The post-epidemic era has witnessed a growing trend in research. In 2022, Thomas and Omar [17] specifically focused on the privacy calculus and the privacy paradox in healthcare wearables acceptance, employing a survey-oriented approach to collect data and confirming the presence of the privacy paradox, especially concerning participants' health status.

While most experiments on the privacy paradox have traditionally employed surveys, the VR platform has introduced new dimensions for researchers to assess privacy behaviors. In 2020, Divine et al. [18] highlighted the lack of education and transparency regarding public versus private information on social VR platforms. Their research revealed a striking contrast between the types of information participants shared and chose not to share, demonstrating the existence of the privacy paradox phenomenon. Before their work, minimal research had addressed privacy and self-disclosure in social VR [19].

This paper takes a significant step forward by validating the privacy paradox phenomenon in health monitoring, utilizing the insights provided by the VR platform.

3 Methods

Two studies were conducted to assess participants' general and situation-specific privacy attitudes, with quantitative data collected from both studies (Fig. 1).

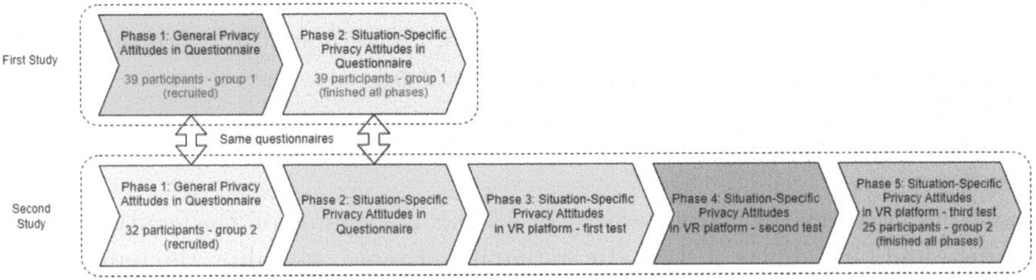

Fig. 1. Phases in Two Studies

The first study, conducted in 2022, comprised two phases and served as a preliminary assessment. It examined participants' general privacy attitudes alongside situation-specific privacy attitudes, offering a comparative analysis. In this study, participants' demographic information was not collected and participants answered the questionnaires anonymously.

To compare general privacy attitudes with situation-specific privacy attitudes in VR, acknowledging that VR results are often more closely aligned with real behaviors than traditional questionnaires [11], we further explored this aspect

Table 1. Setup of Two Studies

	Study 1	Study 2
Year	2022	2023
Phases	Phase 1: General Privacy Attitudes in Questionnaire (1 general scenario provided)	Phase 1: General Privacy Attitudes Questionnaire (1 general scenario provided)
	Phase 2: Situation-Specific Privacy Attitudes in Questionnaire (9 situation-specific scenarios provided)	Phase 2: Situation-Specific Privacy Attitudes in Questionnaire (9 situation-specific scenarios provided)
		Phase 3: Situation-Specific Privacy Attitudes in VR-Test 1 (3 situation-specific scenarios provided)
		Phase 4: Situation-Specific Privacy Attitudes in VR-Test 2 (3 situation-specific scenarios provided)
		Phase 5: Situation-Specific Privacy Attitudes in VR-Test 3 (3 situation-specific scenarios provided)
Demographic Information	Not collected (only contact information was used during the registration)	VR phases - Collected (age, gender, level of education, marital status, professional background)
Region	Not limited	The city where the authors reside
Number of participants	39 finished in total	32 (newly recruited) finished the first two phases, 25 of them finished all phases

in the second study. In this study, we leveraged VR technology, allowing for the collection of additional details such as demographic characteristics, while also restricting the region to the city where the authors reside because participants were required to take tests physically.

The second study, conducted in 2023, was structured into five phases. Due to the significant time lapse between the experiments and the challenge of re-enlisting the same participants, participants were newly recruited. This iteration involved a re-evaluation of participants' general privacy attitudes and situation-specific privacy attitudes before immersing them in VR scenarios to assess their privacy attitudes, resulting in a total of five distinct phases in the second study.

Both studies employed a within-subjects design. Participants were primarily recruited through online social media and the university's advertising channels.

During the recruiting and questionnaires, registration forms and participants' privacy attitudes were gathered using the online questionnaire platform in both studies. In the VR phases of the second study, the application for the Head Mounted Display (HMD) VR platform was seamlessly integrated using Unity Engine. Data collection was carried out using the Oculus Quest 2, equipped with two controllers.

3.1 First Experiment

As depicted in Table 1, the first experiment comprises two phases. During the initial phase, participants' overall privacy attitudes were examined, involving the presentation of a scenario with a general description. Subsequently, in the second phase, participants' situation-specific privacy attitudes were evaluated through nine scenarios (shown in Table 2), each accompanied by detailed descriptions. The examples of scenario descriptions in the two questionnaires are shown in the following sections.

Table 2. Situation-Specific Scenarios

Bedroom	When you are getting dressed, and suddenly have a heart attack
	When you are sitting by the bed, and suddenly get a heavy cough
	When you are making the bed, and suddenly hurt in a slip/ stumble-and-fall accident
Bathroom	When you are taking a shower, and suddenly hurt in a slip/ stumble-and-fall accident
	When you are washing hands, and suddenly suffer a syncope
	When you are washing hands, and suddenly facial weakness is detected
Living room	When you are talking with your friends, and barely noticeable tremor is detected
	When you are processing personal finance, and suddenly suffer a sharp injury
	When you are putting things in place, and suddenly hurt in a slip/ stumble-and-fall accident

Elements of the Scenarios. In both phases, the scenarios incorporated a combination of three elements: place, activity, and medical incident. However, the presentation of scenarios in the two phases differed. In the initial phase, participants were provided with element degrees rather than specific details. For example, an illustration scenario was presented as follows: "When you are doing sensitive activities in a private place in your home, and suddenly encounter a medical emergency." In this example, the privacy level of the place is categorized as private, the privacy level of the activity as sensitive, and the urgency level of the medical incident as urgent.

During the second phase, participants were tasked with individually scaling the privacy level of the place, the privacy level of the activity, and the urgency level of the incident. Their selections aided in mapping the scenario, enabling comparison to the scenario in the first phase through the application of appropriate mapping rules.

Each scenario was accompanied by five questions. Despite the differences in the scenarios between the two phases, the five questions associated with each scenario remained consistent. The general scenario with its questions and an example of situation-specific scenarios with its questions are shown in Table 3. And a complete list of questions are shown in Appendix A.1.

Table 3. Five Questions in Each Scenario

Scenario Description	General Privacy Attitudes Questionnaire: When you are doing sensitive activities in a private place in your home, and suddenly encounter a medical emergency	Situation-Specific Privacy Attitudes Questionnaire: When you are getting dressed in the bedroom, and suddenly have a heart attack
Q1	The person you want to inform	The person you want to inform
Q2	How you would like the event to be recorded	How you would like the event to be recorded
Q3	How you would like the event to be reported	How you would like the event to be reported
Q4	Data type included when reporting	Data type included when reporting
Q5	What to report	What to report

Options of Likert Scale Selection. The utilization of Likert-type rating scales is integral in psychological research. Most Likert scales typically encompass four to seven categories, and previous research findings suggest that 7-point scales tend to exhibit higher reliability compared to other options [20]. However, no definitive conclusion has been reached regarding the impact of varying the number of options on the Likert scale [21].

Additionally, Miller (1956) [22] asserted that the human mind possesses an absolute judgment span capable of distinguishing about seven distinct categories, beyond which it may become impractical [23]. Taking these considerations into account, our study opted for a 7-point Likert scale in the experiment designed to assess participants' situation-specific privacy attitudes. The example setting for place, activity, and incident of a scenario is shown in Table 4.

Scenario Selection. To ascertain the existence of the privacy paradox phenomenon, our objective is to assess the extent to which participants' general privacy attitudes (the first phase) deviate from their situation-specific privacy attitudes (the second phase). To ensure comparability between privacy attitudes in the two phases, we employ mapping rules in the second phase. These rules enable us to identify the scenario among the nine presented scenarios that bear the closest resemblance to the scenario in the first phase. Consequently, the two scenarios in the two phases share similar privacy levels for places, activities, and urgency levels for medical incidents. Correspondingly, responses to these scenarios are anticipated to be similar. Thus, the identification of significant differences in responses reflects the presence of the privacy paradox phenomenon.

As outlined in 3.1, the first-phase scenario provides the degree of each element rather than specific details of place, activity, and incidents. The exemplary scenario is thereby assigned the highest privacy levels for place and activity, as well as the most urgent level ([Privacy level of the location: 7, Privacy level of the activity: 7, Urgency level of the medical incident: 7]). The assignment is made based on the description of the scenario ("private", "sensitive", "medical emergency").

To visualize the disparity between general and situation-specific privacy attitudes, the distances between participants' answers across the two phases are measured. An illustrative example below demonstrates how the distance is calculated. Assuming a participant selects [A, B, A, A, C] as answers in the first-phase scenario and [A, B, B, A, C] in the second-phase test, with one differing answer, the distance between these two scenarios is one (Hamming distance).

Once participants are asked to set the privacy level of the location, activity, and urgency of the event of each scenario (varying from zero to seven), we selected a scenario among nine situation-specific scenarios to compare between the results of phases 1 and 2 based on their own settings. The selection and calculation were based on the Euclidean similarity measure, previously applied in human behavior analysis within spatially constrained contexts, to compute the similarity of each attribute of the activity respectively [24]. In cases where the results of Euclidean distances are equal, priority is given to the scenario with a higher location privacy level. This preference is based on the assumption that certain activities and incidents occur only if the location is known.

Table 4. Example setting for each place, activity, and incident in the first experiment

Description	Level (Scale: 1–7)
Privacy level of the place (Bathroom)	6
Privacy level of the activity (Taking a shower)	7
Privacy level of the activity (Washing hands)	5
Urgency level of the event (Hurt in a slip/stumble-and-fall accident)	5
Urgency level of the event (Suffer a syncope)	6
Urgency level of the event (Facial weakness is detected)	4

3.2 Second Experiment

As illustrated in Table 1, both the scenarios and questions in the first and second phases mirror those employed in the first experiment. However, apart from that, in the rest three phases, we introduced VR-based tests. While the same scenarios were utilized in the second phase, all scenarios were simulated through the VR platform. Each scenario involved a virtual agent avatar engaging in an activity and facing an incident in a corresponding room. The VR environment was designed to simulate a modern, furnished smart home living room to achieve a high degree of functional realism, where the tasks and decisions were authentic. The interaction paradigm was based on direct, natural manipulation using VR motion controllers. Participants could pick up, examine, and place objects in the 3D space, mimicking real-world actions. To illustrate, they were guided to a female/male avatar based on the demographic information that they provided at the beginning of the VR phases. After that, each participant was asked to observe the scenario and imagine that they were the avatar encountering the scenario. The five questions (shown in Table 3), identical to those in the questionnaire, are seamlessly integrated into the scenario. Participants are tasked with implementing sensors (the sensors are listed in Q4 in Appendix A.1) in the room and configuring the settings of the monitoring system. To place a sensor, participants would first select it from the table. The selected sensor would then appear as a handheld 3D model in their virtual hand.

Figures 2 and 3 present two example scenarios designed by a participant. In Fig. 2, the participant places an image sensor on the wall, allowing continuous monitoring in the bedroom, and positions a safety alarm on the bedside table, enabling him to press the button in case of an accident. In Fig. 3, the participant considers activities in the bathroom highly sensitive and decides not to install any sensors in it.

Fig. 2. Scenario 1 in Bedroom

Fig. 3. Scenario 6 in Bathroom

In this phase of recruitment, newly enlisted participants are tasked with directly selecting three scenarios representing the highest privacy level, medium privacy level, and lowest privacy level from the pool of nine scenarios during the registration process. This approach diverges from the methodology in the first experiment, where participants mapped the closest scenario based on the 7-point Likert scale.

Consequently, the VR experiment comprises three tests in total, each featuring scenarios at the highest, medium, and lowest privacy levels. This design ensures the comparability of results across each VR test over time. To test participants' privacy awareness change, we introduce a minimum one-week gap between each phase of the second experiment, which allows us to monitor changes by analyzing the collected quantitative data.

3.3 Ethical Considerations

The research project was notified by the research data organization in the authors' resident country. A consent form and an information letter were distributed to the participants before they took part in the project. Everyone was informed of the background of the research in the information letter. They were notified in the information letter that participation in the project was voluntary, and they could withdraw their consent at any time without giving a reason. The procession of their personal data would follow what had been stated in the consent form.

4 Results

4.1 Results of the First Experiment

In the first experiment, a total of 39 participants completed both phases. The distribution of participants, based on the Hamming distances between their answers across the five items (ranging from zero to five), is depicted in Fig. 4. The Hamming distance, which measures the number of positions at which corresponding answers differ, serves as a direct metric to quantify the attitude-behavior discrepancy central to the privacy paradox.

To establish a threshold for significant discrepancy, we adopted a criterion of three or more differing answers ($\geq 3/5$). This threshold is justified as it indicates that the inconsistency is systemic and exceeds half of the measured items, thereby moving beyond sporadic variations and representing a fundamental divergence between professed privacy attitudes and actual behavioral intentions.

Notably, 28 participants (71.79% of the cohort) demonstrated Hamming distances equal to or exceeding this significant threshold of 3. This preponderance of participants exhibiting substantial discrepancies provides clear empirical evidence that the privacy paradox was markedly observed within the study sample, underscoring a prevalent misalignment between cognitive privacy concerns and intended behavioral responses.

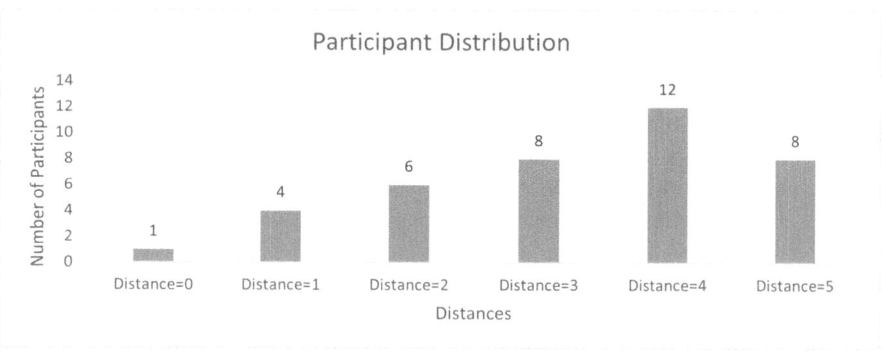

Fig. 4. Participant Distribution of the First Experiment

4.2 Results of the Second Experiment

In the second experiment, a total of 32 participants finished the first two phases, with 25 out of them finished all phases. The demographic information of the participants show finished all phases are shown in Table 5.

Table 5. Demographic Information of Study 2

Demographics	Description	Number	Percentage
Age	Under 20	1	4.00%
	20–50	24	96.00%
Gender	Female	5	20.00%
	Male	20	80.00%
Education	Under College Level	2	8.00%
	College Level	2	8.00%
	Graduation Level	21	84.00%
Marriage	Married	7	28.00%
	Never Married	18	72.00%
Professional Background	Science and Engineering	13	52.00%
	Business and Administration	1	4.00%
	Information and Communication Technology	10	40.00%
	Other	1	4.00%

To be specific, Fig. 5 illustrates the example symbols and detailed descriptions for each phase in the second study. In Phase 1, the questionnaire encompasses a general scenario (referred to as "G"), and participants' responses to this scenario are denoted as G_Ai (where i = 1, 2, ..., 5). Similarly, participants' responses to the nine situation-specific scenarios in the questionnaire are represented as Qi_Aj (where i = 1, 2, ..., 9; j = 1, 2, ..., 5), and their responses to corresponding scenarios in VR are represented as VRi_Aj (where i = 1, 2, ..., 9; j = 1, 2, ..., 5). Notably, the scenario descriptions for Qi (where i = 1, 2, ..., 9) and VRi (where i = 1, 2, ..., 9) are identical. Consequently, when comparing participants' answers to two different scenarios, the distances will also vary from 0 to 5. For example, the distance between G_Ai = A, B, C, C, D and Q1_Ai = A, B, B, C, C is 2, because the third and fifth answers are different.

The study is divided into five phases, each conducted at distinct time points. Noteworthy is that to facilitate comparison of participants' responses to situation-specific scenarios in both the questionnaire and VR, Phase 2 is segmented into three virtual time points (Time Point 2.1, 2.2, 2.3), although it was tested at a single time. Each time point includes one most private scenario, one medium private scenario, and one least private scenario.

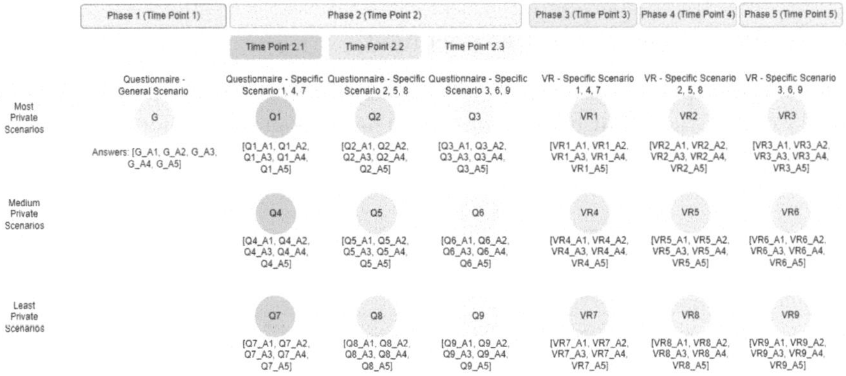

Fig. 5. Example Symbols and Detailed Descriptions for Each Phase in the Second Study

General Privacy Attitudes Versus Situation-Specific Privacy Attitudes in Questionnaire. As outlined in the preceding section, unlike the comparison methodology utilized in the initial two phases, which employed mapping rules, participants were tasked with autonomously selecting the three most private scenarios during the registration process. Consequently, each chosen scenario underwent individual comparison with the responses provided in the general privacy attitudes phase.

Figure 6 presents an overview of the distance distribution for all participants, encompassing results from each of these individual comparisons. For instance, in the case of the first participant, the discrepancy between their answers to the general scenario and the first situation-specific scenario is 4. Similarly, the difference between their answers to the general scenario and the second situation-specific scenario is 1, while the disparity between their answers to the general scenario and the third situation-specific scenario is 4.

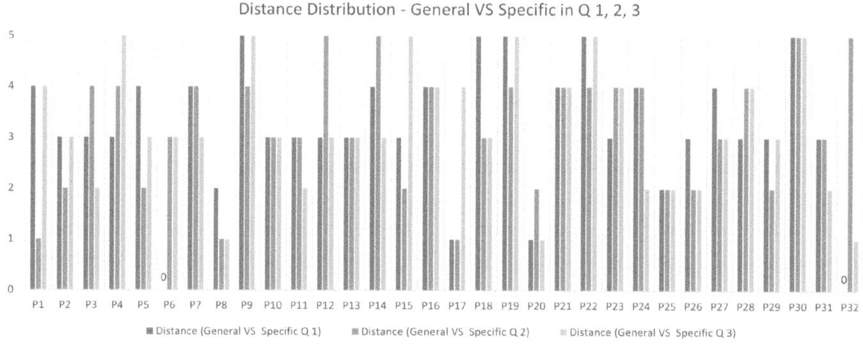

Fig. 6. Overview of Distance Distribution – General Privacy Attitudes (Time Point 1) VS Situation-Specific Privacy Attitudes Towards Most Private Scenario 1 (Time Point 2.1), Most Private Scenario 2 (Time Point 2.2), and Most Private Scenario 3 (Time Point 2.3) in Questionnaire

The figure reveals that, overall, among all scenarios selected by each participant, 16 participants (50.00%) out of 32 exhibited significant and consistent differences between the first and second phases (all distances equal to or more than 3). A significant privacy paradox phenomenon is observed among these participants.

To statistically validate that these observed differences transcend random fluctuations, we conducted one-sample t-tests comparing the Hamming distances against the theoretical random chance level of 2.5. This threshold of 2.5 represents the expected value of differing answers out of 5 items if responses were completely random, calculated as $5 \times 0.5 = 2.5$, where 0.5 represents the probability of random disagreement on any binary comparison.

The statistical analysis revealed that Hamming distances across all three time points significantly exceeded this random baseline: General VS Specific Q1: $M = 3.28$, $SD = 1.27$, $t(31) = 3.47$, $p < .001$; General VS Specific Q2: $M = 3.25$, $SD = 1.21$, $t(31) = 3.51$, $p < .001$; General VS Specific Q3: $M = 3.31$, $SD = 1.24$, $t(31) = 3.70$, $p < .001$. These highly significant results (all p-values $< .001$) provide robust statistical evidence that the observed attitude-behavior discrepancies represent systematic patterns rather than random variations, thereby strongly supporting the presence of the privacy paradox phenomenon in our experimental context.

General Privacy Attitudes Versus Situation-Specific Privacy Attitudes in VR. After that, we compared participants' privacy attitudes to the three most private scenarios in the VR phases with their answers provided in the general privacy attitudes phase.

Figure 7 provides an overview of the distance distribution for all participants, encompassing results from all such individual comparisons. As 25 out of the 32 registered participants finished all VR tests, we barely display the distances from these 25 participants in the figure.

The figure reveals that, overall, among all scenarios selected by each participant, 13 participants (52.00%) out of 25 exhibited significant and consistent differences between the first and second phases (all distances equal to or more than 3). A significant privacy paradox phenomenon is observed among these participants.

The statistical analysis of one-sample t-tests revealed that the Hamming distances across all three time points in the VR platform were significantly greater than the random threshold: General VS VR1: $M = 3.32$, $SD = 1.25$, $t(24) = 3.28$, $p = .0015$; General VS VR2: $M = 3.28$, $SD = 1.31$, $t(24) = 2.98$, $p = .0032$; General VS VR3: $M = 3.36$, $SD = 1.22$, $t(24) = 3.52$, $p = .0009$.

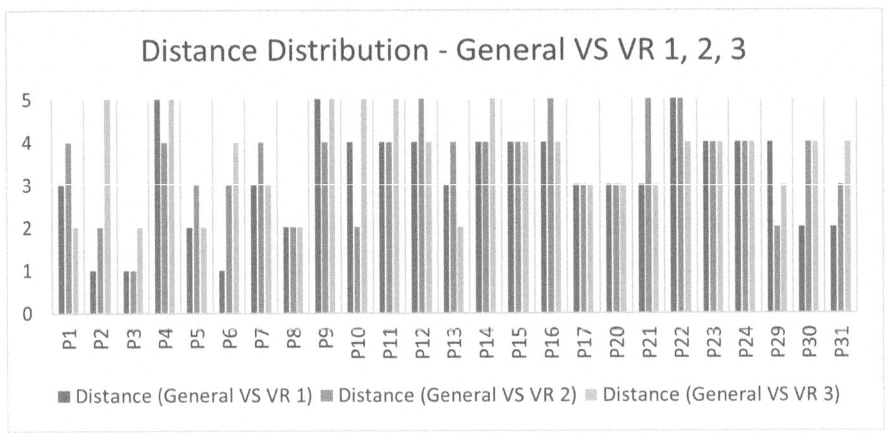

Fig. 7. Overview of Distance Distribution – General Privacy Attitudes (Time Point 1) VS Situation-Specific Privacy Attitudes Towards Most Private Scenario 1 (Time Point 3), Most Private Scenario 2 (Time Point 4), and Most Private Scenario 3 (Time Point 5) in VR

Situation-Specific Privacy Attitudes Versus Situation-Specific Privacy Attitudes in VR. In examining disparities between participants' situation-specific privacy attitudes and their situation-specific privacy attitudes in the VR platform, we compared responses to all scenarios (45 in total). Figure 8 depicts the count of varying answers for each participant.

A notable 22 participants (88.00%) provided more than 20 out of 45 different answers between the situation-specific questionnaire and their situation-specific attitudes in VR. Additionally, 6 participants (24.00%) demonstrated even more pronounced differences (more than 30 out of 45 different answers).

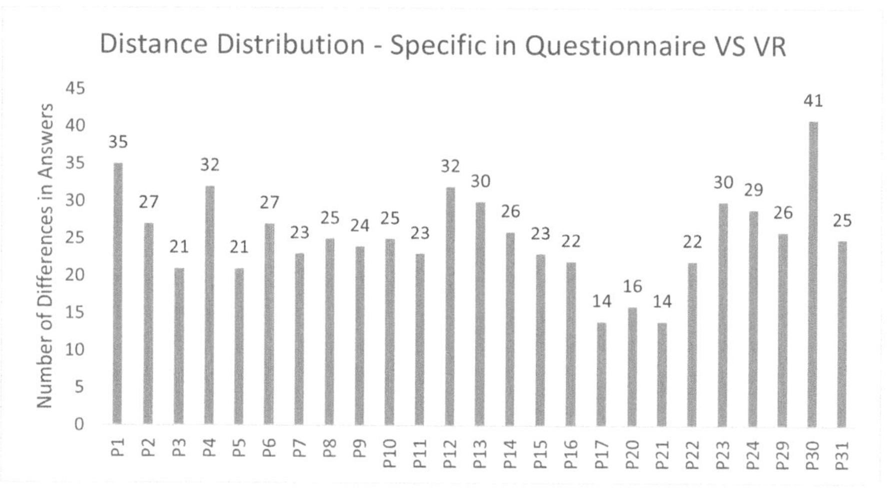

Fig. 8. Distance Distribution of Situation-Specific Privacy Attitudes in Questionnaire VS Situation-Specific Privacy Attitudes in VR

5 Discussion

In this section, we discuss the findings from the results. After that, limitations and future works are discussed.

5.1 Findings

This paper presents two studies conducted to explore the privacy paradox phenomenon in health monitoring. The results of the studies have reflected two findings: (1) Privacy paradox phenomenon exists and it was observed among most of the participants; (2) Participants' privacy attitudes exhibited variability across all phases.

Finding 1: Privacy Paradox Phenomenon Exists. The first study involved 39 participants, all of whom completed both the general privacy attitudes questionnaire (first phase) and the situation-specific privacy attitudes questionnaire (second phase). Notably, the privacy paradox phenomenon was observed in 28 (71.79%) participants.

In the second study, 32 participants completed the first phase and second, with the significant privacy paradox phenomenon observed in 16 (50.00%) of them. Of these, 25 successfully completed the remaining three VR tests (the third phase to the fifth phase), while 7 did not complete all phases. Among those who completed all VR tests, the significant privacy paradox phenomenon was observed in 13 (52.00%) participants. This indicates good convergent validity [27] of the methods within the same group of participants.

The comparative analysis of the first and second phases in both studies revealed a prevalent privacy paradox phenomenon among the majority of participants, with discrepancies in their answers equaling or exceeding 3 (totaling 5 answers). We also noted disparities between participants' privacy attitudes as reported in the questionnaire and within the VR platform, with 88% of participants showing significant divergence (equal to or exceeding 20 out of 45 answers).

In general, building upon our previous findings from the questionnaire-based measures, the analysis within the immersive VR environment reveals an even more pronounced privacy paradox. The mean Hamming distances between situation-specific privacy attitudes in the VR platform were consistently higher across all three time points compared to the questionnaire (VR: M = 3.28 to 3.36; Questionnaire: M = 3.25 to 3.31). This subtle yet consistent elevation in the VR platform suggests that the immersive and perceptually realistic nature of the virtual environment may amplify the divergence between what users profess to care about and how they actually behave.

Finding 2: Participants' Privacy Attitudes Exhibited Variability Across All Phases. According to Fig. 3.1, in our research, the variability of participants' privacy attitudes is mainly considered from the following aspects: the method of data collection, time (or evolution of privacy attitudes), scenarios, and the randomness of human privacy thinking [25]. As it is difficult to estimate the randomness of human thinking, we focus on the former three aspects.

The Method of Data Collection. Ideally, the variability of the method of data collection can be measured by the data collected from the questionnaire session and the VR session. Correspondingly, Figs. 9 and 10 present boxplots illustrating participant distribution when testing privacy attitudes via questionnaire and virtual reality (VR). The figures indicate that overall, when assessing attitudes through VR, more participants demonstrated larger variations compared to the questionnaire, suggesting that methodological differences may influence the variability of privacy attitudes. The figures also reflected good test-retest reliability of both methods [26].

Time (or Evolution of Privacy Attitudes). Upon comparing the magnitude of privacy attitude variability over time within each method, the distributions of Dg-q1 (Q1/25th Percentile = 3.00, Q2/50th Percentile = 3.00, Q3/75th Percentile = 4.00), Dg-q2 (Q1/25th Percentile = 2.00, Q2/50th Percentile = 3.00, Q3/75th Percentile = 4.00), and Dg-q3 (Q1/25th Percentile = 2.00, Q2/50th Percentile = 3.00, Q3/75th Percentile = 4.00) in Fig. 9 show that more participants tended to provide stable responses with the questionnaire at three virtual time points.

Conversely, the distributions of Dg-vr1 (Q1/25th Percentile = 2.00, Q2/50th Percentile = 3.00, Q3/75th Percentile = 4.00), Dg-vr2 (Q1/25th Percentile = 3.00, Q2/50th Percentile = 4.00, Q3/75th Percentile = 4.00), and Dg-vr3 (Q1/25th Percentile = 3.00, Q2/50th Percentile = 4.00, Q3/75th Percentile =

4.00) in Fig. 10 indicate that more participants exhibited greater variability over time in VR.

These findings within each method suggest that longer time intervals (at least one-week gap in VR) may contribute to increased variability.

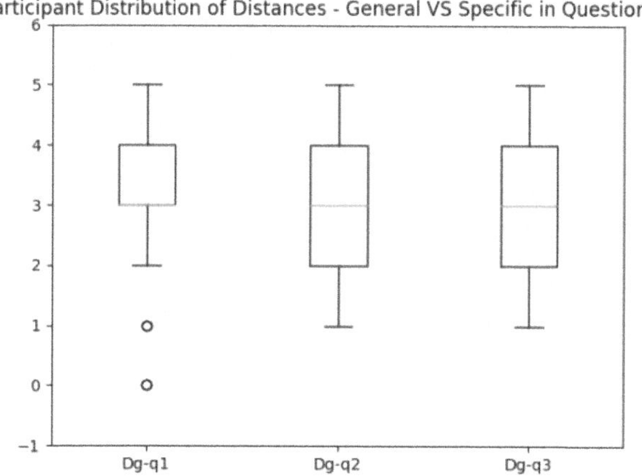

Fig. 9. Participant Distribution - General Attitudes VS Specific Attitudes for Most Private Scenarios in Questionnaire (Distances Between Time Point 1 and 2.1, Time Point 1 and 2.2, Time Point 1 and 2.3)

Scenarios. When analyzing the variability caused by scenarios, we calculate the variability across scenarios at the same privacy level (intra-level distances) and the variability across scenarios at different privacy levels (inter-level distances) in the questionnaire instead of VR, because the test is finished at once, which eliminates the variability caused by the time. Figure 11 shows that more participants have given answers with smaller distances among intra-level scenarios than inter-level scenarios. The results support the fact that participants tend to give stable privacy attitudes to scenarios within the same private level.

5.2 Limitations and Future Works

The study has several limitations. Firstly, in the second experiment, participant recruitment through online social media predominantly drew researchers located on campus due to the requirement for all data to be collected in the same environmental conditions. This geographical limitation introduces potential biases, as the majority of recruited researchers possess technical backgrounds and likely exhibit higher privacy awareness. Secondly, the VR platform offers limited avatar options, featuring one female and one male avatar upon entry. This restricted choice may not adequately address participants' diverse preferences related to health conditions, age, body shape, or other physical features, potentially impacting the sense of immersion and the overall data obtained during the

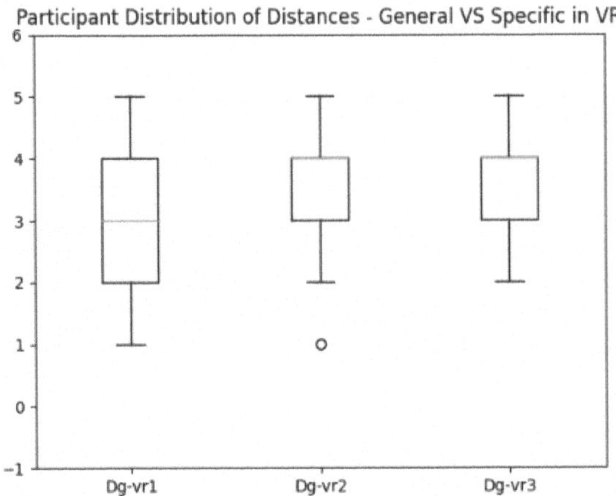

Fig. 10. Participant Distribution - General Attitudes VS Specific Attitudes for Most Private Scenarios in VR (Distances Between Time Point 1 and 3, Time Point 1 and 4, Time Point 1 and 5)

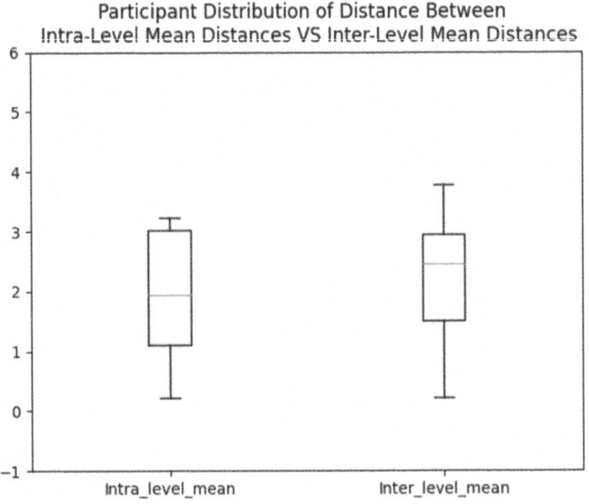

Fig. 11. Participant Distribution - (Intra-Level VS Inter-Level) Mean Distances of Specific Attitudes in Situation-Specific Privacy Attitude Questionnaire

experiment. Thirdly, the sample size in the second study may not be sufficient to encompass participants from diverse backgrounds.

Fourthly, a potential confounding effect arises from the fixed order of the tests, wherein the questionnaire was always administered prior to the tests in the VR environment. While this order follows the logical sequence of attitude (stated attitudes) preceding behavior (situation-specific privacy attitudes), it introduces the possibility that the observed discrepancies could be influenced by temporal factors such as learning or fatigue effects, rather than being solely attributable to the privacy paradox itself.

Considering the mentioned limitations, future efforts will focus on collecting data from various regions nationally or globally (e.g., Asia, America), refining the VR platform to better accommodate participants' specific needs and health conditions, and expanding participant recruitment to ensure gender balance and diversity. More female participants will be invited. Furthermore, to conclusively rule out order effects, future studies will adopt a counterbalanced design where the sequence of the questionnaire and VR tasks is randomized across participants.

6 Conclusion

This paper presents the findings of two studies conducted to examine the presence of the privacy paradox phenomenon. Though several studies have already been done and the phenomenon has been validated in different domains, our study particularly focused on the context of health monitoring environments. The first study was conducted in 2022, containing 2 phases, and the second study was conducted in 2023, containing 5 phases, with three extra VR tests included. Further, we tested and validated if different instruments will lead participants to give different privacy attitudes by comparing the results collected from the questionnaire and VR platform. Last but not least, we explored other variables which resulted in participants' inconsistencies in their answers during the study.

The comparison results from both studies' first and second phases reveal that a majority of participants exhibit the privacy paradox phenomenon, as the distances between their answers are significantly different (equal to or greater than 3 out of 5 answers in total). The comparison results between participants' general privacy attitudes and their situation-specific privacy attitudes in both the questionnaire and the VR platform also underscore this phenomenon. During the VR tests, a subset of participants exhibited notably high inconsistency in their answers, contrasting with the overall stability observed in the remaining participants. Four aspects which could impact their privacy attitudes across different phases were put forward by us, including the method of data collection, time (or evolution of privacy attitudes), scenarios, and the randomness of human privacy thinking.

The findings indicate that for more accurate construction of privacy predictive models, incorporating situation specific privacy attitudes assessed through either questionnaires or VR is preferable to relying on general privacy attitudes. However, given that certain participants in the VR group exhibited significant inconsistency over time, further investigation is needed to determine whether their privacy attitudes will converge over a longer period. Future research will also delve into expanding participant recruitment and conducting studies in diverse regions to validate the results.

Based on the findings, we recommend that researchers carefully balance efficacy and accuracy when selecting methods to collect privacy attitudes and developing privacy predictive models. While distributing questionnaires may yield larger datasets, the accuracy of the models may be relatively lower compared to using privacy attitudes collected via VR platforms.

In addition, healthcare providers should carefully assess the specific contexts or scenarios presented when participants make privacy decisions. If the scenarios are vague, participants may provide inaccurate privacy attitudes, necessitating updates to the model or a real-time discussion between healthcare providers and receivers to ensure accuracy and mutual understanding (Table 6).

A Appendix

A.1 Five Questions in Each Scenario

Table 6. Privacy Attitudes Parameters

Person (Q1) - Multiple Answers Available	(1) Care service provider
	(2) A person I am familiar with
	(3) Myself
How to be recorded (Q2)	(1) Continuously recording
	(2) Automatically recording when the incident is detected (event-triggered)
	(3) Manually recording (human-triggered) - voice command
	(4) Manually recording (human-triggered) – press the button
	(5) No recording at all (not able to send recording data when informing people, but a text message or a call still works)
How to report (Q3) - Multiple Answers Available	(1) I'd like the person I want to inform to remotely monitor me 24 h 7 days whenever they like
	(2) The system should report the event automatically after recording the incident
	(3) Manually report (human-triggered) – voice command
	(4) Manually report (human-triggered) – press the button
Data type included when reporting (Q4) - Multiple Answers Available	(1) Video
	(2) Image
	(3) Audio
	(4) I would like the technologist to decide it for me
	(5) None of the above (Text-only)
What to report (Q5)	(1) Raw recording data
	(2) Privacy-enhanced recording data
	(3) Text message describing the event
	(4) Text message calling for human aids immediately but no description of the event

References

1. Guhr, N., Werth, O., Blacha, P.P.H., Breitner, M.H.: Privacy concerns in the smart home context. SN Appl. Sci. **2**(2), 247 (2020). https://doi.org/10.1007/s42452-020-2025-8
2. Carmody, J., Shringarpure, S., Van de Venter, G.: AI and privacy concerns: a smart meter case study. J. Inf. Commun. Ethics Soc. **19**(4), 492–505 (2021). https://doi.org/10.1108/JICES-04-2021-0042, publisher: Emerald Publishing Limited
3. Malkin, N., Deatrick, J., Tong, A., Wijesekera, P., Egelman, S., Wagner, D.: Privacy attitudes of smart speaker users. Proc. Priv. Enhancing Technol. **2019**, 250–271 (2019). https://doi.org/10.2478/popets-2019-0068
4. Albayaydh, W.S., Flechais, I.: Exploring bystanders' privacy concerns with smart homes in Jordan. In: Proceedings of the 2022 CHI Conference on Human Factors in Computing Systems. CHI '22, Association for Computing Machinery, New York, NY, USA (2022). https://doi.org/10.1145/3491102.3502097
5. Kokolakis, S.: Privacy attitudes and privacy behaviour: a review of current research on the privacy paradox phenomenon. Comput. Secur. **64**, 122–134 (2017). https://doi.org/10.1016/j.cose.2015.07.002, https://www.sciencedirect.com/science/article/pii/S0167404815001017
6. Acquisti, A., Grossklags, J.: Privacy and rationality in individual decision making. IEEE Secur. Privacy **3**(1), 26–33 (2005). https://doi.org/10.1109/MSP.2005.22
7. Beresford, A.R., Kübler, D., Preibusch, S.: Unwillingness to pay for privacy: a field experiment. Econ. Lett. **117**(1), 25–27 (2012). https://doi.org/https://doi.org/10.1016/j.econlet.2012.04.077, https://www.sciencedirect.com/science/article/pii/S0165176512002182
8. Lee, H., Park, H., Kim, J.: Why do people share their context information on social network services? A qualitative study and an experimental study on users' behavior of balancing perceived benefit and risk. Int. J. Hum.-Comput. Stud. **71**(9), 862–877 (2013). https://doi.org/https://doi.org/10.1016/j.ijhcs.2013.01.005, https://www.sciencedirect.com/science/article/pii/S107158191300044X, social Networks and Ubiquitous Interactions
9. Kehr, F., Kowatsch, T., Wentzel, D., Fleisch, E.: Blissfully ignorant: the effects of general privacy concerns, general institutional trust, and affect in the privacy calculus. Inf. Syst. J. **25** (2015). https://doi.org/10.1111/isj.12062
10. Li, H., Sarathy, R., Xu, H.: The role of affect and cognition on online consumers' decision to disclose personal information to unfamiliar online vendors. Decis. Support Syst. **51**(3), 434–445 (2011). https://doi.org/10.1016/j.dss.2011.01.017, https://www.sciencedirect.com/ science/article/pii/S0167923611000467
11. Hepperle, D., Wölfel, M.: Similarities and differences between immersive virtual reality, real world, and computer screens: a systematic scoping review in human behavior studies. Multimodal Technol. Interact. **7**(6) (2023). https://doi.org/10.3390/mti7060056, https://www.mdpi.com/2414-4088/7/6/56
12. Acquisti, A., Grossklags, J.: Losses, gains, and hyperbolic discounting: An experimental approach to information security attitudes and behavior (2003)
13. Dienlin, T., Masur, P.K., Trepte, S.: A longitudinal analysis of the privacy paradox (2019). https://doi.org/10.31235/osf.io/fm4h7
14. Norberg, P., Horne, D., Horne, D.: The privacy paradox: personal information disclosure intentions versus behaviors. J. Consumer Affairs **41**, 100–126 (2007). https://doi.org/10.1111/j.1745-6606.2006.00070.x

15. Barth, S., de Jong, M.D.: The privacy paradox – investigating discrepancies between expressed privacy concerns and actual online behavior – a systematic literature review. Telematics Inform. **34**(7), 1038–1058 (2017). https://doi.org/https://doi.org/10.1016/j.tele.2017.04.013, https://www.sciencedirect.com/science/article/pii/S0736585317302022
16. Li, H., Wu, J., Gao, Y., Shi, Y.: Examining individuals' adoption of healthcare wearable devices: an empirical study from privacy calculus perspective. Int. J. Med. Inform. **88**, 8–17 (2016). https://doi.org/https://doi.org/10.1016/j.ijmedinf.2015.12.010, https://www.sciencedirect. com/science/article/pii/S1386505615300770
17. Jernejcic, T., El-Gayar, O.: The role of the privacy calculus and the privacy paradox in the acceptance of wearables for health and wellbeing. AIS Trans. Hum. Comput. Interact. **14**(4), 490–522 (2022). https://www.proquest.com/scholarly-journals/role-privacy-calculusparadox-acceptance/docview/2759874391/se-2, copyright - Copyright Association for Information Systems Dec 2022; Last updated - 2023-11-18
18. Maloney, D., Zamanifard, S., Freeman, G.: Anonymity vs. familiarity: self-disclosure and privacy in social virtual reality. In: Proceedings of the 26th ACM Symposium on Virtual Reality Software and Technology. VRST '20, Association for Computing Machinery, New York, NY, USA (2020). https://doi.org/10.1145/3385956.3418967
19. Lin, J., Cronje, J., Wienrich, C., Pauli, P., Latoschik, M.: Visual indicators representing avatars' authenticity in social virtual reality and their impacts on perceived trustworthiness. IEEE Trans. Vis. Comput. Graph. **29**(11), 4589–4599 (2023). https://doi.org/10.1109/TVCG.2023.3320234
20. Wakita, T., Ueshima, N., Noguchi, H.: Psychological distance between categories in the Likert scale: comparing different numbers of options. Educ. Psychol. Measur. **72**(4), 533–546 (2012). https://doi.org/10.1177/0013164411431162, place: US Publisher: Sage Publications
21. Simms, L.J., Zelazny, K., Williams, T.F., Bernstein, L.: Does the number of response options matter? Psychometric perspectives using personality questionnaire data. Psychol. Assess. **31**(4), 557–566 (2019). https://doi.org/10.1037/pas0000648, place: US Publisher: American Psychological Association
22. Miller, G.A.: The magical number seven, plus or minus two: some limits on our capacity for processing information. Psychol. Rev. **63**(2), 81–97 (1956). https://doi.org/10.1037/h0043158, place: US Publisher: American Psychological Association
23. Taherdoost, H.: What is the best response scale for survey and questionnaire design; review of different lengths of rating scale/attitude scale/likert scale, pp. 1–10 (2019)
24. Joh, C.H., Arentze, T., Timmermans, H.: Pattern recognition in complex activity travel patterns: comparison of Euclidean distance, signal-processing theoretical, and multidimensional sequence alignment methods. Transp. Res. Rec. **1752**(1), 16–22 (2001)
25. Gerber, N., Gerber, P., Volkamer, M.: Explaining the privacy paradox: a systematic review of literature investigating privacy attitude and behavior. Comput. Secur. **77**, 226–261 (2018). https://doi.org/https://doi.org/10.1016/j.cose.2018.04.002, https://www.sciencedirect.com/science/article/pii/S0167404818303031
26. Polit, D.F.: Getting serious about test-retest reliability: a critique of retest research and some recommendations. Qual. Life Res. **23**, 1713–1720 (2014)
27. Carlson, K.D., Herdman, A.O.: Understanding the impact of convergent validity on research results. Organ. Res. Methods **15**(1), 17–32 (2012)

Decoding Privacy Threats in Mobile Applications: A Multi-layer Analysis of Encrypted Traffic and Server Interactions

Ahmed Mohamed Saad Emam Saad(✉)

Queen's University, Kingston, ON K7L 2N8, Canada
a.saad@queensu.ca

Abstract. Mobile applications increasingly handle sensitive user data, requiring compliance with laws such as China's Personal Information Protection Law (PIPL). With pervasive encryption, traditional payload inspection is infeasible. We introduce a multi-dimensional risk assessment framework that detects potential privacy violations using Transport Layer Security (TLS) flow-level features. At its core is the Contextual Violation Risk (CVR), a novel metric powered by Natural Language Inference (NLI) and reasoning-optimized Large Language Models (LLMs). CVR captures semantic mismatches between an application's declared purpose and its actual server communications (e.g., a health app connecting to data-broker domains). The risk model integrates three complementary dimensions: Data Asymmetry Risk (DAR) for volume-based anomalies, Burst Transfer Risk (BTR) for temporal irregularities, and CVR for semantic compliance. Together, these enable classification of applications by privacy risk profile and potential regulatory concern. Applied to 350 Chinese mobile applications, the framework identified 31 (8.9%) with elevated risk profiles. Validation through stratified expert review of an average of 545 connection flows per application achieved 100% agreement. Weight assignments (CVR 40%, DAR 35%, BTR 25%) were derived from systematic analysis of 142 PIPL enforcement cases, ensuring alignment with regulatory priorities. The results demonstrate the feasibility of automated privacy risk assessment for encrypted mobile traffic and provide a foundation for scalable regulatory compliance monitoring.

Keywords: Privacy compliance auditing · Encrypted traffic analysis · Contextual risk detection · Mobile application privacy assessment · Automated regulatory compliance · Large language models

1 Introduction

In recent years, the exponential growth of mobile applications has significantly transformed the way individuals access services and share information globally

W. Li et al. (Eds.): EISA 2025, CCIS 2897, pp. 119–141, 2026.
https://doi.org/10.1007/978-3-032-21177-4_7

[31]. Mobile applications (Apps), such as banking applications, handle various types of sensitive personal data [14,18,26]. Concurrently, concerns over privacy, data protection, and sovereignty have intensified, prompting regulators worldwide to enact stringent regulations to safeguard personal information [2,12,23]. Prominent examples include the European Union's General Data Protection Regulation (GDPR) [16], the California Consumer Privacy Act (CCPA) [9], and China's Personal Information Protection Law (PIPL) [25]. These frameworks universally emphasize robust user data protection, stringent requirements for cross-border data transfers, and strict compliance mechanisms for organizations handling personal data.

Among these regulatory frameworks, China's PIPL stands out not only due to its stringent requirements, but also because of the sheer scale and complexity of China's mobile application landscape [30]. China hosts the largest mobile user base globally, making its market uniquely susceptible to privacy risks due to the enormous volume and diversity of applications [34]. PIPL Article 40 [25] specifically mandates that critical information infrastructure operators (CIIOs), including applications from sensitive sectors, must strictly localize data within Chinese territory and undergo rigorous security assessments before conducting any cross-border data transfer [17].

Despite these regulatory frameworks and increasing global scrutiny, systematic methods for assessing privacy risks at scale in mobile applications remain largely underexplored [15]. In particular, those involving cross-border encrypted traffic and semantic inconsistencies between the application's declared functionality, actual functionality, and the destinations of its encrypted data flows [5,15]. Current privacy compliance methodologies primarily target explicit data leaks, or rely heavily on manual audits, simplistic rule-based detection, and often missing context-sensitive privacy violations [10,36,40]. Thus, there is a pressing need for advanced and automated frameworks tailored specifically for mobile applications ecosystems. Such frameworks should integrate sophisticated flow-level network analytics with semantic, context-aware compliance assessments, enabling precise evaluation of encrypted mobile applications traffic against the aforementioned regulatory standards.

In response to this gap, this paper introduces a novel and comprehensive framework that integrates multi-layered, Transport Layer Security (TLS) flow-level network traffic analysis with advanced semantic evaluation techniques powered by state-of-the-art Natural Language Inference (NLI) and Large Language Models (LLMs). Our approach unfolds in three distinct stages. First, we conduct an extensive network traffic analysis leveraging NFStream [4] for robust extraction of Layer-7 metadata, capturing fine-grained application-level behaviors and traffic flows. Next, we apply a zero-shot NLI model, `DeBERTa-v3-large-mnli-fever-anli-ling-wanli` [19], to systematically categorize applications based solely on their names and textual descriptions. Finally, we employ a specialized reasoning-optimized LLM, `QwQ` [32], to perform in-depth semantic compliance assessments. Specifically, this LLM evaluates the appropriateness of application data flows, examining server-domain connections against the application's declared category and functional description. Our initial manual validations of this semantic inspection method achieved 100% accuracy, highlighting its reliability.

The key contributions of our research are threefold:

- ⋆ A comprehensive and automated privacy assessment pipeline merging traditional network traffic metrics (e.g., data asymmetry, burstiness) with advanced semantic compliance evaluations.
- ⋆ The introduction of a novel metric, Contextual Violation Rate (CVR), quantifying semantic inconsistencies, significantly enhancing risk evaluation.
- ⋆ An extensive empirical evaluation of 350 popular Chinese mobile applications, uncovering critical compliance risks, revealing notable compliance violations across sensitive sectors.

The remainder of this paper is structured as follows: Sect. 2 reviews relevant regulatory frameworks and existing approaches to compliance assessment. Section 3 details our methodological framework, including data collection, semantic categorization using advanced language models, and the multi-dimensional risk-scoring mechanism. Section 4 presents our empirical findings, highlighting detected compliance issues and insights from semantic analysis. Section 5 summarizes the key contributions and findings. Finally, Sect. 6 discusses the broader regulatory implications of our work, outlines key limitations of the current framework, and proposes directions for future research and deployment.

2 Related Work

Privacy regulations like the EU's GDPR [16], California's CCPA [9], and China's PIPL [25] mandate stringent requirements for personal data management, cross-border transfers, and sensitive information handling. China's PIPL explicitly requires CIIOs and handlers of sensitive personal data to store data domestically and undergo security assessments before data export [24,25]. Ensuring compliance at scale within mobile application ecosystems remains challenging [40,41].

Network traffic analysis traditionally relied on detecting explicit data leaks and cleartext transmissions [7,27]. With widespread TLS encryption, recent studies explore flow-level analytics using statistical characteristics—payload entropy, flow asymmetry, packet timing—to identify anomalous activities [6,27]. However, these approaches suffer from false positives due to limited contextual awareness and inability to distinguish benign high-volume flows from genuine privacy threats.

Machine learning techniques enhance automated privacy risk assessments through supervised and unsupervised models that classify traffic types, identify anomalous flows, and detect privacy-sensitive behaviors [3,22,28,29,37]. LLMs such as `Debertav3` [19] and `Qwen` [1] demonstrate potential to augment rule-based methods by capturing semantic discrepancies that evade traditional detection.

Recent research emphasizes context-aware approaches that interpret semantic coherence between application descriptions, functionality, and encrypted data destinations [11]. State-of-the-art frameworks leverage NLI models like `DeBERTa-v3-large-mnli` for application categorization and reasoning models like `QwQ` for semantic compliance assessments [21,32], enabling automated identification of subtle violations.

Despite progress, critical gaps persist. Existing methodologies lack comprehensive integration between flow-level statistical analyses and semantic contextual assessments, limiting effectiveness in detecting nuanced violations within encrypted traffic. Additionally, insufficient focus exists on systematically evaluating compliance under China's PIPL, particularly for critical infrastructure and sensitive data categories. Our work addresses these limitations through a holistic automated privacy risk framework that integrates robust flow-level analytics, advanced semantic evaluations powered by NLIs and LLMs, and actionable guidelines for regulatory compliance at scale.

3 Methodology

This research presents a comprehensive, automated framework for privacy risk assessment in mobile applications. Moreover, this framework seamlessly integrates advanced flow-level network analytics with semantic, context-aware compliance evaluations. Our methodology unfolds through three interconnected stages: (1) Network Traffic Analysis for robust extraction of Layer-7 metadata and encrypted flow characterization, (2) Application Categorization via NLI using state-of-the-art zero-shot NLI models to systematically classify applications based on their declared functionality, and (3) Semantic Contextual Compliance Assessment leveraging reasoning-optimized LLMs to detect mismatches between declared purposes and actual server communications.

This multi-dimensional approach ensures both statistical rigor in traffic pattern analysis and semantic accuracy in compliance violation detection, enabling scalable privacy auditing of encrypted mobile application traffic.

3.1 Data Collection and Feature Extraction

Dataset Description. To systematically identify and quantify privacy risks in mobile applications, we used a large-scale mobile traffic dataset containing biflow records from real-world Chinese mobile applications. This dataset, described in [38], was selected for its comprehensive coverage and detailed app-level annotations. After reaching out to multiple research groups, this dataset was the only one for which the authors were able to share an anonymized version suitable for privacy-compliant research.

The dataset contains traffic from 350 Android applications. Each application contributes at least 100 MB of traffic, totaling over 611 GB of labeled TCP traffic and an average of 832,558 TCP biflows per app. Traffic was captured under diverse network conditions (WiFi: 85%, 4G: 14.6%), reflecting realistic usage scenarios. Collection was performed using Netlog [35], a self-developed tool based on Android's VPNService API that captures raw network traffic while precisely mapping flows to applications via unique identifier (UID) association. The dataset underwent anonymization aligned with CAIDA guidelines [8], where IP addresses were randomly mapped to ensure user privacy.

3.2 Network Traffic Analysis with Layer-7 Visibility

Flow-level features were extracted using NFStream, a versatile network traffic analyzer offering both statistical and Layer-7 visibility. Despite widespread TLS encryption, privacy-relevant metadata remains observable: DNS queries preceding encrypted connections reveal destination domains, and most mobile applications have not implemented Encrypted Client Hello (ECH), leaving Server Name Indication (SNI) fields visible during TLS handshakes.

The extraction process yielded comprehensive metrics such as *source-to-destination bytes*, *destination-to-source bytes*, *packet inter-arrival times*, *packet counts*, *TCP flag usage*, and critically, *application-level metadata* including *application names* and *requested server domains* extracted from DNS queries and SNI fields for each encrypted TLS flow. The temporal correlation between DNS resolution requests and subsequent encrypted TLS connections enables precise mapping of application behavior to specific external services, even when payload content remains encrypted. We isolated TLS flows specifically due to their prevalence in privacy-sensitive data transfers and their retention of analyzable metadata despite encryption protocols.

3.3 Flow Attribution and Application Labeling

Application attribution was performed using the text (`.txt`) label files provided with each pcap trace. These label files contained timestamped entries with flow directionality and associated app names, in the format: `<timestamp>, <app name>, <protocol>, <src_ip>:<src_port> <dst_ip>:<dst_port>`.

We parsed these entries to extract `(src_ip, src_port, dst_ip, dst_port)` keys and matched them to flow records extracted using NFStream. Application names were primarily in Chinese; therefore, we enriched the dataset using `APPList`, a metadata file providing English translations and application descriptions. Manual corrections were applied for outliers or mismatches.

Each flow was labeled with both Chinese and English app names to provide multilingual cross-reference.

3.4 Application Categorization via NLI

For accurate categorization of CIIO mobile applications, we utilized the `DeBERTa-v3-large-mnli` model, a state-of-the-art zero-shot NLI model. By analyzing each application's name and description, this model assigned each application to one of seven predefined categories (Finance, Health, Government,

Telecommunications, Transportation, Education, or Others) based on CIIO categories identified in prior studies [20,33]. Six of these categories (all except "Others") correspond to sensitive domains highlighted in the literature and are subject to strict compliance requirements under China's PIPL Article 40. Manual verification of category assignments indicated 100% accuracy. Figure 1 visualizes this categorization process, illustrating the input features, model prediction, and verification outcomes.

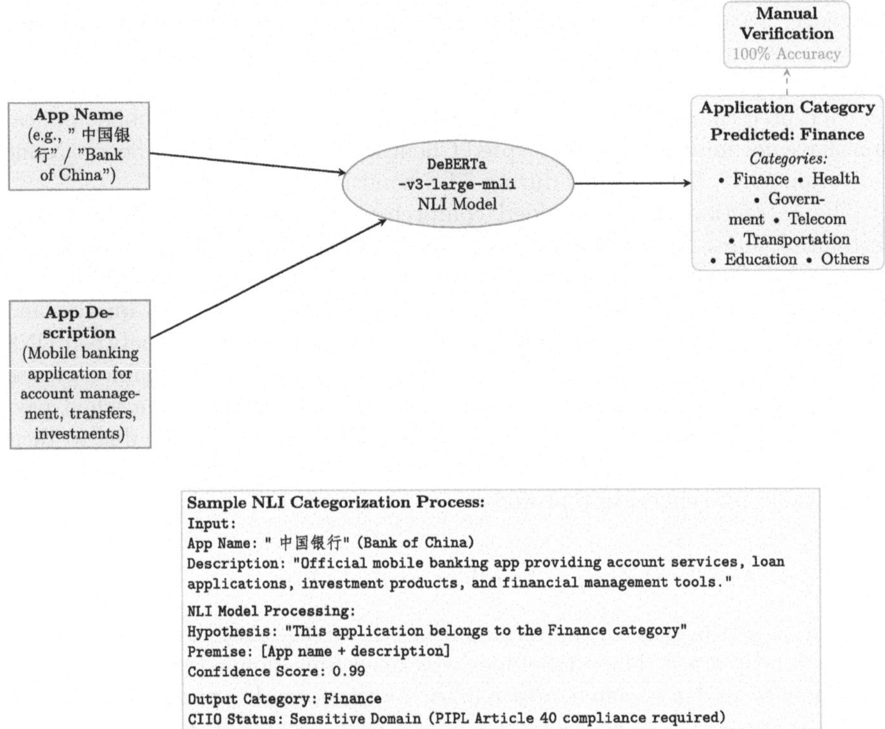

Fig. 1. Application categorization via zero-shot NLI model. The `DeBERTa-v3-large-mnli` model analyzes application names and descriptions to assign applications to one of seven predefined CIIO categories. Manual verification confirmed 100% categorization accuracy across all evaluated applications.

3.5 Semantic Contextual Compliance via LLM

To assess semantic compliance of data flows, we employed the `QwQ` LLM, optimized for reasoning tasks. The model shown in Fig. 2 analyzes whether the encrypted data flows from applications were contextually appropriate based on application categories, server domains, and intended functionality. This step provided semantic validation of compliance, identifying flows potentially violating privacy regulations. The semantic audit was manually verified on a small subset

(545 flows per app) to check correctness. Initial manual verification indicated a 100% accuracy rate for semantic mismatch detection.

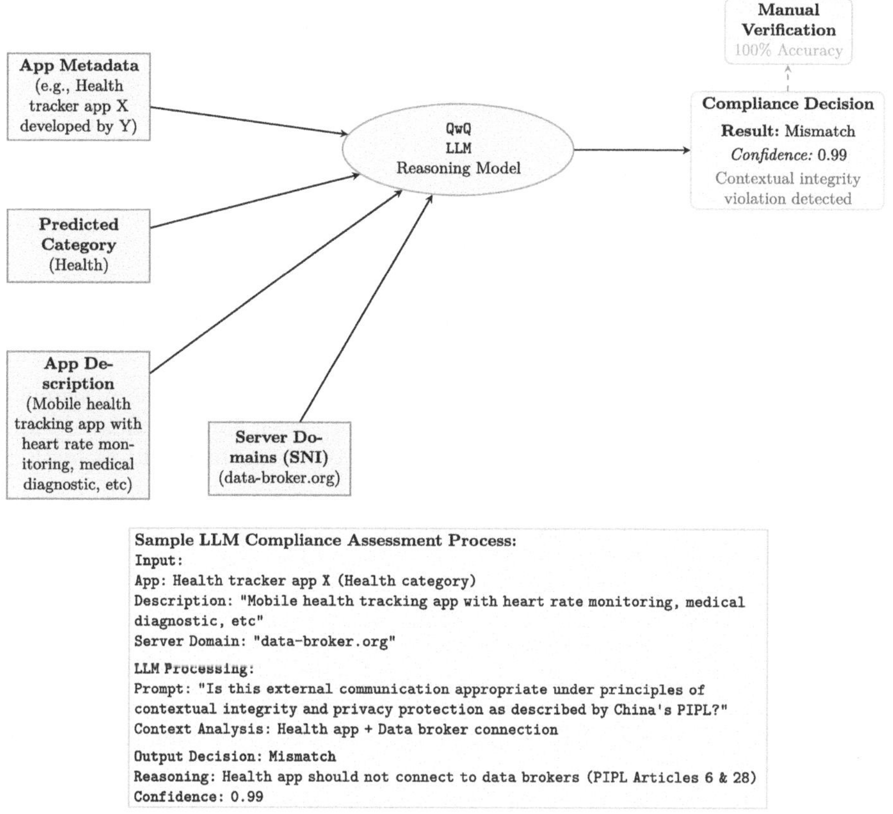

Fig. 2. Semantic contextual compliance verification using LLM. The QwQ model analyzes app metadata, predicted category, description, and server domains to detect mismatches between stated functionality and observed network behavior. A sample assessment process demonstrates the validation workflow with manual verification confirming 100% accuracy.

3.6 Risk Scoring System

Privacy risks were quantified through a multi-dimensional framework that addresses the fundamental challenge of comprehensive privacy compliance assessment. While semantic analysis can detect purpose violations, purely semantic approaches cannot capture the full spectrum of privacy risks present in encrypted mobile traffic. Therefore, our framework employs three complementary risk dimensions derived from flow-level traffic analysis (for detailed flow traffic features, refer to Table 7): semantic consistency assessment, volume-based anomaly detection, and temporal pattern analysis.

Contextual Violation Risk (CVR): Semantic Dimension. Contextual Violation Risk addresses the primary concern of purpose limitation compliance by quantifying semantic inconsistencies between declared and observed data collection purposes. This metric leverages our LLM-based semantic analysis to detect cases where applications access services inconsistent with their stated functionality.

The per-flow CVR score is computed as shown in Eq. (1) :

$$\mathrm{CVR}_i = \sigma\left(\lambda \cdot c_i \cdot \left[\mathbb{I}(d \not\models f_i) + 0.5\,\mathbb{I}(f_i = \emptyset)\right]\right) \tag{1}$$

where:

- ⋆ d = declared data purpose (App metadata)
- ⋆ f_i = inferred flow purpose (LLM analysis for flow i)
- ⋆ λ = violation severity factor (0.8 for severe, 0.5 for moderate violations)
- ⋆ c_i = LLM confidence score for flow i, normalized to $[0, 1]$

Here, $\mathbb{I}(\cdot)$ is an indicator function, and $\sigma(x) = 1/(1 + e^{-x})$ is a sigmoid normalization function mapping the output to $[0, 1]$. Each flow is evaluated individually based on its inferred purpose and the confidence of the LLM in that inference.

For applications with multiple flows, the final app-level CVR score is obtained by averaging the flow-level CVR values as shown in Eq. (2):

$$\mathrm{CVR}_{\mathrm{app}} = \frac{1}{|\mathcal{F}|}\sum_{i=1}^{|\mathcal{F}|} \mathrm{CVR}_i \tag{2}$$

where $\mathcal{F}$ is the set of flows associated with the application. This aggregation ensures that applications exhibiting frequent inconsistencies accumulate a higher overall risk score.

Figure 2 illustrates the semantic verification pipeline. App metadata, declared categories, descriptions, and detected server domains are provided as context to the LLM, which outputs both a binary decision (match or mismatch) and a confidence score.

Based on the computed app-level CVR values, applications are categorized into three audit tiers:

- ⋆ **Low Risk (Compliant)**: $\mathrm{CVR}_{\mathrm{app}} < 0.4$—No significant inconsistencies detected.
- ⋆ **Moderate Risk (Borderline)**: $0.4 \leq \mathrm{CVR}_{\mathrm{app}} < 0.6$—Requires policy review or clarification in user disclosures.
- ⋆ **High Risk (Potential Non-Compliance)**: $\mathrm{CVR}_{\mathrm{app}} \geq 0.6$—Indicates substantial semantic inconsistencies that may warrant regulatory scrutiny.

Threshold Justification: The CVR threshold was selected based on empirical analysis of the risk score distributions across the dataset, setting the compliant threshold at the lower 40th percentile and the high-risk threshold at the upper 60th percentile. High CVR values signal semantic inconsistencies but do not by themselves confirm legal violations.

Data Asymmetry Risk (DAR): Volume-Based Dimension. While CVR effectively detects semantic violations, applications may exhibit privacy risks through abnormal data flow patterns even when maintaining semantic consistency. Data Asymmetry Risk, shown in Eq. (3), addresses this gap by modeling potential covert exfiltration through upload and download imbalance analysis.

$$DAR = \frac{\log\left(1+\sum_{i=1}^{n} B_{\mathrm{ul}}^{(i)}\right)}{\log\left(1+\sum_{i=1}^{n} B_{\mathrm{dl}}^{(i)}\right)+\epsilon}, \quad \epsilon = 10^{-6} \tag{3}$$

where $B_{\mathrm{ul}}^{(i)}$ and $B_{\mathrm{dl}}^{(i)}$ denote the bytes uploaded and downloaded in flow i. The logarithmic transformation mitigates disparities in traffic magnitude, while the ratio highlights asymmetric data transfers. Values greater than 1 signal predominantly upload-oriented flows, marking potential exfiltration risk. The smoothing constant ϵ ensures numerical stability and prevents division by zero.

Burst Transfer Risk (BTR): Temporal Dimension. Beyond semantic consistency and volume analysis, privacy violations often manifest through distinctive temporal patterns that indicate automated or stealth data collection behaviors. Burst Transfer Risk, shown in Eq. (4) quantifies abnormal temporal patterns in data transmissions.

$$\mathrm{BTR} = \frac{1}{n}\sum_{i=1}^{n}\left(\frac{\sigma_{\Delta t}^{(i)}}{\mu_{\Delta t}^{(i)}} \times \frac{P_{\mathrm{ul}}^{(i)}}{P_{\mathrm{total}}^{(i)}}\right) \tag{4}$$

where $\sigma_{\Delta t}^{(i)}$ and $\mu_{\Delta t}^{(i)}$ represent the standard deviation and mean of packet timing intervals for flow i, respectively. The first term measures temporal burstiness, while $P_{\mathrm{ul}}^{(i)}/P_{\mathrm{total}}^{(i)}$ weights this by the proportion of upload traffic. This design ensures that highly bursty flows dominated by uploads are assigned higher risk scores. Values close to zero suggest regular timing and balanced traffic; values approaching or exceeding one indicate highly bursty, upload-heavy behavior characteristic of automated exfiltration.

Multi-dimensional Risk Integration. The three metrics operate synergistically to provide comprehensive privacy risk assessment:

- ⋆ **CVR** captures semantic violations where declared purposes conflict with observed server communications
- ⋆ **DAR** identifies volume-based anomalies that may indicate excessive data collection or covert exfiltration
- ⋆ **BTR** detects temporal patterns characteristic of automated or stealth data transfers

This layered approach ensures that privacy risks are detected across multiple behavioral dimensions. Applications exhibiting high scores across multiple dimensions warrant prioritized regulatory attention, while single-dimension anomalies may indicate specific compliance issues requiring targeted investigation.

3.7 Risk Weight Justification

Determining optimal weights for the three risk dimensions presents a fundamental challenge in multi-dimensional privacy risk assessment: how can we balance semantic violations (CVR), volume anomalies (DAR), and temporal patterns (BTR) in a way that reflects regulatory priorities while maintaining practical utility? We established weight assignments through regulatory enforcement analysis, manual validation of semantic detection, and theoretical risk assessment.

Regulatory Foundation: PIPL Enforcement Pattern Analysis. The primary justification for weight assignment derives from analyzing actual regulatory enforcement patterns. We systematically reviewed 142 PIPL enforcement case summaries [39], examining which specific PIPL articles were cited in violation findings.

PIPL Article-to-Risk Dimension Mapping: Our analysis revealed clear correspondence between PIPL enforcement patterns and our risk dimensions:

Our analysis revealed clear correspondence between PIPL enforcement patterns and our risk dimensions, with CVR (semantic violations) accounting for 46% of enforcement citations, DAR (volume anomalies) for 38%, and BTR (temporal patterns) for 16% of citations.

Based on these enforcement frequencies, initial regulatory-aligned weights were derived using the following Eq. (5):

$$w_i = \frac{\text{Citations}_i}{\sum \text{Citations}} \tag{5}$$

This yielded $w_{\text{CVR}} = 0.46$, $w_{\text{DAR}} = 0.38$, and $w_{\text{BTR}} = 0.16$.

Validation and Weight Adjustment. To validate the most innovative component of our framework, we conducted manual verification of CVR semantic analysis across a representative subset of applications. Domain experts manually inspected connection flows from each application using a statistically determined sample size (average of 545 connections per application, range: 43–664 based on population size) calculated for 99% confidence with ±5% margin of error. The experts evaluated whether the LLM-based semantic assessment correctly identified mismatches. The CVR component achieved 100% accuracy in semantic mismatch detection across all manually verified flows, providing strong empirical support for CVR's central role in the framework.

The sample size $\mathcal{F}'$ for each application was determined using Cochran's formula with finite population correction [13] as shown in Eq. (6):

$$\mathcal{F}' = \frac{\mathcal{F}'_0}{1 + \frac{(\mathcal{F}'_0 - 1)}{F}} \tag{6}$$

where $\mathcal{F}'_0 = \frac{Z^2 \cdot p \cdot (1-p)}{e^2}$ represents the initial sample size for an infinite population, $Z = 2.576$ is the critical value for 99% confidence level, $p = 0.5$ represents maximum variability, $e = 0.05$ is the margin of error, and F is the total number of connections for each application.

While regulatory citation frequency provides legal grounding, the final weights were adjusted to account for detection capability, violation severity, and practical enforcement considerations. Final weights: CVR 40%, DAR 35%, BTR 25%.

Removing any dimension would ignore substantial portions of regulatory enforcement patterns: DAR and BTR together account for 54% of PIPL citation frequency, representing critical violation types not addressable through semantic analysis alone.

Final Weight Assignment: DAR (35%), BTR (25%), CVR (40%). The final configuration balances multiple objectives: CVR receives highest priority (40%) reflecting both its validated detection accuracy and regulatory emphasis on purpose limitation. DAR maintains substantial weight (35%) acknowledging data minimization's importance in privacy regulation. BTR receives enhanced weight (25%) recognizing its unique contribution to detecting behavioral violations that complement semantic analysis.

3.8 Risk Aggregation and Normalization

Risk dimensions are normalized and aggregated using a weighted scoring function that aligns with PIPL compliance priorities as shown in Eq. (7):

$$\begin{aligned} \hat{\mathbf{r}} &= \frac{\mathbf{r} - \min(\mathbf{r})}{\max(\mathbf{r}) - \min(\mathbf{r})} \quad \textit{(Min-Max normalization)} \\ R_{\text{total}} &= 0.35\,\widehat{\text{DAR}} + 0.25\,\widehat{\text{BTR}} + 0.40\,\widehat{\text{CVR}} \end{aligned} \tag{7}$$

where $\mathbf{r} = [\text{DAR}, \text{BTR}, \text{CVR}]$ is the raw risk vector, and $\hat{\mathbf{r}}$ denotes its normalized form. The resulting aggregate score R_{total} serves as the primary compliance risk indicator, with higher values suggesting a greater likelihood of regulatory violations. The weighting scheme prioritizes contextual compliance (i.e., CVR), in accordance with PIPL Article 17, while also incorporating directional asymmetry (i.e., DAR) and traffic burstiness (i.e., BTR) at lower influence.

3.9 Compliance Decision Model

The final compliance status of each application is represented by the binary variable $S \in \{\text{Compliant}, \text{Non-Compliant}\}$, determined by aggregating normalized risk scores and evaluating them against regulation-informed thresholds. The compliance decision logic is detailed in **Algorithm** 1, which takes as input the processed flow set $\mathcal{F}'$ and a predefined weight vector $\mathbf{w} = [0.35, 0.25, 0.40]$.

Algorithm 1. PIPL Compliance Assessment

Require: Processed flows $\mathcal{F}'$, weights $\mathbf{w} = [0.35, 0.25, 0.40]$
Ensure: $S \in \{\text{Compliant}, \text{Non-Compliant}\}$
Compute risk scores [DAR, BTR, CVR] via Eqs. (1)–(3)
Normalize risk vector: $\hat{\mathbf{r}} \leftarrow \text{MinMax}(\mathbf{r})$
Aggregate weighted risk: $R_{\text{total}} \leftarrow \mathbf{w} \cdot \hat{\mathbf{r}}^{\top}$
Scan for sensitive terms to set flag S_{sens}
if $R_{\text{total}} < 0.4$ **and** $\neg S_{\text{sens}}$ **then**
    return Compliant ▷ Minimal risk, no sensitive data exposure
else
    return Non-Compliant ▷ Elevated risk or sensitive data detected
end if

The compliance status S indicates whether an application meets baseline regulatory expectations under PIPL principles. An application is labeled *Compliant* if it demonstrates low aggregated risk ($R_{\text{total}} < 0.4$) and does not trigger sensitive content alerts ($S_{\text{sens}} = \text{False}$). Otherwise, it is flagged as *Non-Compliant*, suggesting the need for further regulatory review.

Design Rationale: The dual evaluation via R_{total} and S_{sens} targets two distinct but complementary risks. R_{total} captures behavioral anomalies (e.g., asymmetric uploads, bursty transfers, semantic mismatches), while S_{sens} serves as a direct lexical scan for known sensitive categories such as health, finance, etc. This two-pronged approach reduces reliance on any single feature and mitigates blind spots where semantic inference (i.e., CVR) might miss sensitive flows not disclosed in app metadata.

The weight vector $\mathbf{w} = [0.35, 0.25, 0.40]$ reflects the relative importance of DAR, BTR, and CVR based on their empirical variance observed across a pilot subset of the dataset. CVR is assigned the highest weight (0.40) to emphasize semantic inconsistencies as a critical compliance signal under purpose limitation principles. The decision threshold (0.4) was calibrated through preliminary distribution analysis, selecting a conservative cutoff that captures the upper quartile of aggregated risk scores in a held-out validation set.

3.10 Validation Mechanisms

To further enhance the reliability of compliance decisions, we introduce two post-hoc validation mechanisms that address session-level integrity and semantic content consistency.

Connection Integrity Check. The first safeguard examines the proportion of TCP reset packets within each flow. A session is flagged as anomalous if more than 15% of packets are connection resets, indicating potential data exfiltration disruptions or evasion attempts. The formal definition is given in Eq. (8).

$$\mathbb{I}_{\text{reset}} = \left[\frac{\sum P_{\text{RST}}}{\sum P_{\text{total}}} > 0.15\right] \quad \textit{(TCP-level anomaly detection)} \tag{8}$$

Semantic Consistency Audit. The second mechanism audits sensitive-purpose violations by scanning content against a dictionary of protected categories. This is used to populate the S_{sens} flag, referenced in Algorithm 1. The binary flag is computed as defined in Eq. (9).

$$\begin{aligned} S_{\text{sens}} &= \exists t \in T : t \downarrow \mathcal{C}_{\text{sens}} \neq \emptyset \\ \mathcal{C}_{\text{sens}} &= \{\text{health, financial, etc.}\} \end{aligned} \tag{9}$$

4 Case Study and Results

4.1 Case Study

We applied our framework to 350 Chinese mobile applications as an exploratory analysis to demonstrate the methodology's capability for privacy risk assessment. The dataset included:

- ⋆ **9,640,418 TLS flows** collected from 224 volunteers, recruited to collect the traffic of designated Apps.
- ⋆ **Server metadata** derived from SNI and DNS reverse lookups.
- ⋆ **App category labels** inferred using NLI as described in methodology section.

4.2 Risk Tier Distribution

Risk-based segmentation of the aggregated score R_{total} grouped applications into four tiers: Low, Moderate, High, and Critical. Table 1 summarizes the tier distribution across all 350 applications.

Table 1. Distribution of Applications Across Risk Tiers

Risk Tier	Risk Score Range	App Count (%)
Critical	[0.80, 1.00]	0 (0.0%)
High	[0.60, 0.80)	1 (0.3%)
Moderate	[0.40, 0.60)	30 (8.6%)
Low	[0.00, 0.40)	319 (91.1%)

4.3 Privacy Risk Assessment Results

Our framework identified *31 applications (8.9%)* with elevated privacy risk profiles requiring potential regulatory attention, while *319 applications (91.1%)* demonstrated low-risk behavioral patterns. The distribution indicates that the majority of analyzed applications exhibit relatively compliant network behavior patterns.
High-Risk Applications: One application (Tencent Weiyun) was classified as high-risk, exhibiting concerning patterns across multiple risk dimensions that warrant immediate regulatory review.
Moderate-Risk Applications: Thirty applications demonstrated moderate risk profiles, primarily driven by specific behavioral anomalies or semantic inconsistencies that require further investigation. These include prominent applications across various categories such as financial services (ICBC, PingAn Bank), education platforms (MOOC, XueXiTong), and entertainment services (Bilibili, iQiyi Reader).

4.4 Category-Level Analysis

Analysis across application categories revealed varied risk patterns, suggesting that privacy compliance challenges differ substantially by application domain. Rather than universal non-compliance patterns, the framework identified specific applications within each category that exhibit concerning behaviors, indicating targeted rather than systematic compliance issues.

Notable Findings:

- ⋆ Financial applications: showed mixed results, with some major institutions (ICBC, PingAn Bank) flagged for moderate risk
- ⋆ Educational platforms: demonstrated elevated CVR scores, suggesting potential semantic mismatches in data handling practices
- ⋆ Entertainment and media applications: frequently exhibited volume-based anomalies indicative of extensive data collection practices

The complete list of all studied applications, along with their assigned risk tiers, is provided in Tables 2, 3, 4, 5 and 6 in the Appendix for full transparency and reproducibility.

5 Conclusion

This paper presented a novel multi-dimensional framework for automated privacy risk assessment of mobile applications under China's PIPL. The framework introduces three complementary risk dimensions: CVR for semantic compliance assessment, DAR for volume-based anomaly detection, and BTR for temporal pattern analysis. Our exploratory application to 350 Chinese mobile applications revealed that 31 applications (8.9%) exhibited elevated privacy risk profiles warranting potential regulatory attention. Expert-based stratified validation of 545 connection flows per application confirmed 100% accuracy in detecting semantic mismatches between applications' declared purposes and their observed server communications. This semantic analysis capability addresses a critical gap in privacy compliance assessment for encrypted mobile traffic.

Key technical contributions include: (1) automated semantic compliance verification using LLM-based analysis of encrypted traffic metadata, (2) multi-dimensional risk quantification combining regulatory priorities with behavioral analysis, and (3) scalable assessment methodology applicable to large mobile application ecosystems. The framework's weight assignment (CVR: 40%, DAR: 35%, BTR: 25%) was grounded in systematic analysis of 142 PIPL enforcement cases, ensuring alignment with regulatory priorities while maintaining comprehensive risk coverage. The framework demonstrates that meaningful privacy risk assessment of encrypted mobile traffic is feasible through analysis of observable metadata patterns and semantic consistency evaluation. This research establishes the feasibility of scalable, automated privacy risk assessment as a practical tool for regulatory compliance monitoring in the era of encrypted mobile communications, providing a foundation for policy-aware auditing under stringent data protection regulations.

6 Discussion, Limitations and Future Work

The multi-dimensional framework presented in this work addresses a fundamental challenge in privacy regulation enforcement: how to assess compliance in an era where mobile applications predominantly use encrypted communications. By combining semantic analysis of observable metadata with statistical behavioral assessment, the framework bridges the gap between technical network analysis and regulatory requirements.

Several important limitations constrain the current framework's applicability and scope. For example, our analysis was confined to Chinese Android applications, limiting broader applicability to other regions and platforms. The framework's effectiveness across different regulatory environments and mobile ecosystems remains to be validated. While the CVR component achieved validated accuracy through manual verification, the exploratory nature of the overall analysis limits definitive compliance determinations. Risk scores indicate potential compliance concerns rather than definitive legal violations, requiring case-by-case regulatory review for formal enforcement actions.

For future work, several research directions would enhance the framework's capabilities and applicability. For example, extending coverage to iOS applications and cross-border traffic datasets would better reflect global privacy risk landscapes and validate the framework's generalizability across different mobile ecosystems. Future extensions could incorporate TLS fingerprinting, encrypted SNI (ESNI) analysis, or zero-knowledge inference methods to better handle obfuscated or anonymized flows as encryption technologies evolve. In addition, incorporating geolocation-aware risk assessments through appropriate datasets would enable full deployment of jurisdictional compliance features under PIPL Article 38 and similar cross-border transfer regulations.

The convergence of these research directions would establish automated privacy risk assessment as a mature capability supporting regulatory enforcement in the global mobile application ecosystem.

Appendix

Table 2. Applications with Low Risk (Part 1)

App Name	Risk Tier
360clouddisk (360安全云盘)	Low
360 Mobile Phone Assistant (360手机助手)	Low
360 Cleaning master (360清理大师)	Low
58com (58同城)	Low
Blued (Blued)	Low
CC live (CC直播)	Low
Dropbox (Dropbox)	Low
LOFTER (LOFTER)	Low
QQ (QQ)	Low
QQPim (QQ同步助手)	Low
QQ Browser (QQ浏览器)	Low
UC browser (UC浏览器)	Low
WPS Office (WPS office)	Low
Wifi master key (WiFi万能钥匙)	Low
1tian (甜相机)	Low
cmc securities (中信证券)	Low
PICC (中国人保)	Low
abcchina (中国农业银行)	Low
CCB (中国建设银行)	Low
China Mobile (中国移动)	Low
China galaxy stock (中国银河证券)	Low
Bank of China (中国银行)	Low
Maidanba (买单吧)	Low
Unionpay (云闪付)	Low
Huzhu Document (互助文档)	Low
traffic management 12123 (交管12123)	Low
Bankcomm (交通银行)	Low
Qie FM (企鹅FM)	Low
zybang (作业帮)	Low
JieDaiBao (借贷宝)	Low
Fenqile (分期乐)	Low
citiccard mobilebank (动卡空间)	Low
Huawei app market (华为应用市场)	Low
Huawei wear (华为穿戴)	Low

Table 3. Applications with Low Risk (Part 2)

App Name	Risk Tier
GongYin RongeLian (工银融e联)	Low
PingAn carowner (平安好车主)	Low
PingAn PuHui (平安普惠)	Low
PingAn Stock (平安证券)	Low
PingAn life insurance (平安金管家)	Low
GF securities YiTaoJin (广发易淘金)	Low
Wechat (微信)	Low
KuaiDuiZuoYe (快对作业)	Low
KuaiYa (快牙)	Low
YueDong sport (悦动圈)	Low
DongCheDi (懂车帝)	Low
360mobilesafe (手机卫士)	Low
Mobile Phone Business hall (手机营业厅)	Low
ppdai loan (拍拍贷借款)	Low
CMB (招商银行)	Low
wacai365 (挖财记账)	Low
Mybus (掌上公交)	Low
Sougou browser2 (搜狗搜索)	Low
Sougou browser1 (搜狗浏览器)	Low
Sougou Input (搜狗输入法)	Low
Alipay (支付宝)	Low
Douyu Live (斗鱼直播)	Low
so young (新氧医美)	Low
WuYou trip (无忧行)	Low
YiChe (易车)	Low
inke live (映客)	Low
Zhixue (智学网)	Low
Zhixing train ticket (智行火车票)	Low
CaoCao (曹操出行)	Low
Youdao translator (有道翻译官)	Low
umoney (有钱花)	Low
Laifenqi (来分期)	Low
autohome (汽车之家)	Low
Bitauto Autoprice (汽车报价大全)	Low
YangCongXueYuan (原洋葱数学 洋葱学院)	Low
Explorer (浏览器)	Low
ZhangLe (涨乐财富通)	Low
DiDi Driver (滴滴车主)	Low
CM Security (猎豹安全)	Low

Table 4. Applications with Low Risk (Part 3)

App Name	Risk Tier
Clean Master (猎豹清理大师)	Low
9fbank wanka (玖富万卡)	Low
Guazi (瓜子二手车)	Low
China Telecom (电信营业厅)	Low
Baidu (百度)	Low
BaiciZhan (百词斩)	Low
Guiderank (盖得排行)	Low
zhidao (知到)	Low
Shenzhouzuche (神州租车)	Low
HuiShengHuo (移动惠生活)	Low
Mi Home (米家)	Low
WangShangGuoWang (网上国网)	Low
eloancn (翼龙贷财富)	Low
KaoYanBang (考研帮)	Low
Umetrip (航旅纵横)	Low
Huajiao Live (花椒直播)	Low
DuoShan (多闪)	Low
Eastmoney Fund (天天基金)	Low
CPIC APP (太平洋保险)	Low
CBOX (央视影音)	Low
Quark (夸克)	Low
Xuebajun (学霸君)	Low
AnYiHua (安逸花)	Low
YiRen finance (宜人财富)	Low
YiRenDai (宜人贷借款)	Low
Xiaobanlong (小伴龙-儿童早教)	Low
Yuankousuan (小猿口算)	Low
Yuansouti (小猿搜题)	Low
Xiaomi health (小米运动)	Low
yeemiao (小豆苗)	Low
TongHuaShun (同花顺)	Low
cmccmap (和地图)	Low
Hellobike (哈出行)	Low
HaiLaidian (嗨来电)	Low
Yiqianbao (壹钱包)	Low

Table 5. Applications with Low Risk (Part 4)

App Name	Risk Tier
Wandoujia (豌豆荚)	Low
Huolala (货拉拉-拉货搬家)	Low
Huochebang (货车帮司机)	Low
CheLaiLe (车来了)	Low
Chelun wzsearch (车轮违章查询)	Low
software store (软件商店)	Low
Yunmanman (运满满司机)	Low
TuNiu (途牛旅游)	Low
Postal savings bank of China (邮储银行)	Low
JinTaiYang (金太阳)	Low
Shoujiduoduo (铃声多多)	Low
galaxy futures (银河期货开户交易)	Low
YangGuangHui (阳光惠生活)	Low
SuiShouJi (随手记)	Low
vbill plus (随行付Plus)	Low
XueQiu (雪球股票)	Low
Xiangcao video (香草视频)	Low
MaFengWo1 (马蜂窝旅游)	Low
JiaKaoBaoDian (驾考宝典)	Low
ovital (奥维互动地图)	Low
Mamanet2 (妈妈网孕育-怀孕育儿)	Low
XueXiQiangGuo (学习强国)	Low
Huya Live (虎牙直播)	Low
MaFengWo2 (蚂蜂窝自由行)	Low
Chubao Phone (触宝电话)	Low
CaiNiao (菜鸟裹裹)	Low
ezviz Video (萤石云视频)	Low
HMS Core (HMS Core)	Low
Keep (Keep)	Low
360 loan (360借条-贷款分期借款)	Low
Suning finance (苏宁金融)	Low

Table 6. Applications with Risk Tier ≥ Moderate and Non-Compliance Status

App Name	Risk Tier
Tencent Weiyun (腾讯微云)	High
MOOC in Chinese Universities (中国大学)	Moderate
ICBC (中国工商银行)	Moderate
Cloudhub (云之家)	Moderate
Bilibili Comic (哔哩哔哩漫画)	Moderate
XueXiTong (学习通)	Moderate
Safety Education Platform (安全教育平台)	Moderate
Android Market (安卓市场)	Moderate
Jellipop Match (宾果消消)	Moderate
PingAnBank (平安口袋银行)	Moderate
DangDang (当当)	Moderate
YingShiDaQuan (影视大全)	Moderate
Wukong Finance (悟空理财)	Moderate
Sohu News (搜狐新闻)	Moderate
Mobike (摩拜单车)	Moderate
Youyuan (有缘网)	Moderate
LiuLiShuo (流利说-英语)	Moderate
Crows Zero (热血高校)	Moderate
iQiyi Reader (爱奇艺阅读)	Moderate
FengDu Reader (疯读小说)	Moderate
Baidu Mobile Assistance (百度手机助手)	Moderate
Tangdou (糖豆)	Moderate
Meituan Takeout (美团外卖)	Moderate
PP Sports (PP体育)	Moderate
Tencent News (腾讯新闻)	Moderate
Auto Clicker (自动点击器)	Moderate
ZhuiShuShenQi (追书神器免费版)	Moderate
Jinshan Ciba (金山词霸)	Moderate
Eleme-star (饿了么星选)	Moderate
MaShang Finance (马上金融)	Moderate
GaoTieGuanJia (高铁管家)	Moderate

Table 7. Risk Dimensions and Associated Flow-Level Features

Category	Feature(s)	Rationale
Directionality	src2dst_bytes, dst2src_bytes, exfiltration_ratio	Detect asymmetric flows that may indicate data exfiltration
Volume	bidirectional_bytes, src2dst_packets, dst2src_packets	Helps quantify the overall scale of data transmission
Duration	bidirectional_duration_ms, src2dst_duration_ms, dst2src_duration_ms	Short, high-volume flows may reflect stealthy or automated transfers
Temporal	src2dst_mean_piat_ms, dst2src_mean_piat_ms, bidirectional_mean_piat_ms	Irregular or bursty patterns may reveal non-human-initiated activity
Ports	src_port, dst_port	Can help detect non-standard use of TLS or proxy tunneling
Application Layer	requested_server_name, user_agent, content_type	Offers semantic context on app behavior and communication targets
Geolocation Info	dst_ip, destination_country, flagged_non_chinese	Critical for identifying cross-border data flows and compliance risks
TCP Flags	src2dst_syn_packets, dst2src_ack_packets, etc.	Useful for spotting handshake anomalies or protocol misuse
App Metadata	application_name, app_name_chinese, description	Assists in correlating low-level behavior with app purpose
Statistical Measures	src2dst_stddev_ps, bidirectional_stddev_ps	High variance can indicate obfuscation or bot-like behavior

References

1. Yang, A., et al.: Qwen2.5 technical report. arXiv preprint arXiv:2412.15115 (2024)
2. Alamri, H., Maple, C., Mohamad, S., Epiphaniou, G.: Do the right thing: a privacy policy adherence analysis of over two million apps in apple iOS app store. Sensors **22**(22), 8964 (2022)
3. Anderson, B., McGrew, D.: Machine learning for encrypted malware traffic classification: accounting for noisy labels and non-stationarity. In: Proceedings of the 23rd ACM SIGKDD International Conference on Knowledge Discovery and Data Mining, pp. 1723–1732 (2017)
4. Aouini, Z., Pekar, A.: NFStream: a flexible network data analysis framework. Comput. Netw. **204**, 108719 (2022)
5. Apple Inc.: App store review guidelines (2024). https://developer.apple.com/app-store/review/guidelines/. Accessed 26 Apr 2025
6. Azab, A., Khasawneh, M., Alrabaee, S., Choo, K.K.R., Sarsour, M.: Network traffic classification: techniques, datasets, and challenges. Digit. Commun. Netw. **10**(3), 676–692 (2024)
7. Bremler-Barr, A., Harchol, Y., Hay, D., Koral, Y.: Deep packet inspection as a service. In: Proceedings of the 10th ACM International on Conference on emerging Networking Experiments and Technologies, pp. 271–282 (2014)
8. CAIDA Project: Anonymization techniques and policies (nd). https://www.caida.org/projects/impact/anonymization/. Accessed 15 Mar 2025
9. California Department of Justice: California consumer privacy act (CCPA). https://www.oag.ca.gov/privacy/ccpa. Accessed 15 Jan 2023

10. Chandra, S., Wondabio, L.S.: Developing audit manual design for audit of small and medium-sized entities and applying data sharing in cloud to increase audit efficiency. In: ICE-BEES 2021: Proceedings of the 4th International Conference on Economics, Business and Economic Education Science, ICE-BEES 2021, Semarang, Indonesia, 27–28 July 2021, p. 42. European Alliance for Innovation (2022)
11. Chen, J., Huang, C., Han, J.: VioDroid-Finder: automated evaluation of compliance and consistency for android apps. Empir. Softw. Eng. **29**(3), 64 (2024)
12. Cinar, A.C., Kara, T.B.: The current state and future of mobile security in the light of the recent mobile security threat reports. Multimedia Tools Appl. **82**(13), 20269–20281 (2023)
13. Cochran, W.G.: Sampling Techniques. Wiley (1977)
14. Ebrahimi, F., Tushev, M., Mahmoud, A.: Mobile app privacy in software engineering research: a systematic mapping study. Inf. Softw. Technol. **133**, 106466 (2021)
15. Enck, W., et al.: TaintDroid: an information-flow tracking system for realtime privacy monitoring on smartphones. ACM Trans. Comput. Syst. (TOCS) **32**(2), 1–29 (2014)
16. European Union: General data protection regulation (GDPR) (2016). https://www.gdpr-info.eu/. Accessed 15 Jan 2024
17. Gibson, Dunn & Crutcher LLP: China passes the personal information protection law, to take effect on November 1 (2021). https://www.gibsondunn.com/china-passes-the-personal-information-protection-law-to-take-effect-on-november-1/?pdf=display. Accessed 26 Apr 2025
18. Harborth, D., Pape, S.: Investigating privacy concerns related to mobile augmented reality apps-a vignette based online experiment. Comput. Hum. Behav. **122**, 106833 (2021)
19. He, P., Gao, J., Chen, W.: DeBERTaV3: improving deBERTa using electra-style pre-training with gradient-disentangled embedding sharing. arXiv preprint arXiv:2111.09543 (2021)
20. Herrera, L.C., Maennel, O.: A comprehensive instrument for identifying critical information infrastructure services. Int. J. Crit. Infrastruct. Prot. **25**, 50–61 (2019)
21. Laurer, M., van Atteveldt, W., Salleras Casas, A., Welbers, K.: Less annotating, more classifying – addressing the data scarcity issue of supervised machine learning with deep transfer learning and BERT - NLI (2022). https://osf.io/74b8k, preprint, Open Science Framework
22. Lotfollahi, M., Jafari Siavoshani, M., Shirali Hossein Zade, R., Saberian, M.: Deep packet: a novel approach for encrypted traffic classification using deep learning. Soft Comput. **24**(3), 1999–2012 (2020)
23. Naji, J., Latif, S., Maslat, F.: Current security issues and vulnerabilities associated with mobile application. In: Alshamrani, S.S. (ed.) Impact of Mobile Services on Business Development and E-Commerce, pp. 102–120. IGI Global (2024). https://www.igi-global.com/chapter/current-security-issues-and-vulnerabilities-associated-with-mobile-application/374391
24. National People's Congress: Data security law of the People's Republic of China (2021). https://digichina.stanford.edu/work/translation-data-security-law-of-the-peoples-republic-of-china/. Accessed 11 July 2022
25. National People's Congress: Personal information protection law (PIPL) (2021). http://en.npc.gov.cn.cdurl.cn/2021-12/29/c_694559.htm. Adopted 20 Aug 2021. English version updated December 29, 2021

26. Nema, P., Anthonysamy, P., Taft, N., Peddinti, S.T.: Analyzing user perspectives on mobile app privacy at scale. In: Proceedings of the 44th International Conference on Software Engineering, pp. 112–124 (2022)
27. Papadogiannaki, E., Ioannidis, S.: A survey on encrypted network traffic analysis applications, techniques, and countermeasures. ACM Comput. Surv. (CSUR) **54**(6), 1–35 (2021)
28. Ren, J., et al.: Bug fixes, improvements,... and privacy leaks. In: The 25th Annual Network and Distributed System Security Symposium (NDSS 2018) (2018)
29. Ren, J., Rao, A., Lindorfer, M., Legout, A., Choffnes, D.: Recon: revealing and controlling PII leaks in mobile network traffic. In: Proceedings of the 14th Annual International Conference on Mobile Systems, Applications, and Services, pp. 361–374 (2016)
30. Roe, D.: What you need to know about China's personal information protection law (2021). https://www.cmswire.com/customer-experience/what-you-need-to-know-about-chinas-personal-information-protection-law/. Accessed 26 Apr 2025
31. Stocchi, L., Pourazad, N., Michaelidou, N., Tanusondjaja, A., Harrigan, P.: Marketing research on mobile apps: past, present and future. J. Acad. Market. Sci., 1–31 (2022)
32. Team, Q.: QWQ-32B: embracing the power of reinforcement learning (2025). https://qwenlm.github.io/blog/qwq-32b/
33. Viira, T.: Lessons Learned: Critical Information Infrastructure Protection: How to Protect Critical Information Infrastructure. IT Governance Ltd (2018)
34. Wang, H., et al.: Beyond google play: a large-scale comparative study of Chinese android app markets. In: Proceedings of the Internet Measurement Conference 2018, pp. 293–307 (2018)
35. Wang, X., Chen, S., Su, J.: Real network traffic collection and deep learning for mobile app identification. Wirel. Commun. Mob. Comput. **2020**(1), 4707909 (2020)
36. Xia, M., Gong, L., Lyu, Y., Qi, Z., Liu, X.: Effective real-time android application auditing. In: 2015 IEEE Symposium on Security and Privacy, pp. 899–914. IEEE (2015)
37. Zang, J., Dummit, K., Graves, J., Lisker, P., Sweeney, L.: Who knows what about me? A survey of behind the scenes personal data sharing to third parties by mobile apps. Technol. Sci. (2015103001) (2015). https://techscience.org/a/2015103001/. Accessed 29 Oct
38. Zhao, S., Chen, S., Wang, F., Wei, Z., Zhong, J., Liang, J.: A large-scale mobile traffic dataset for mobile application identification. Comput. J. **67**(4), 1501–1513 (2024)
39. Zhou, M.M., Qu, Z., Wan, J., Wen, B., Yao, Y., Lu, Z.: Understanding Chinese internet users' perceptions of, and online platforms' compliance with, the personal information protection law (PIPL). Proc. ACM Hum.-Comput. Interact. **8**(CSCW1), 1–26 (2024)
40. Zimmeck, S., et al.: Maps: scaling privacy compliance analysis to a million apps. In: Proceedings on Privacy Enhancing Technologies (2019)
41. Zimmeck, S., et al.: Automated analysis of privacy requirements for mobile apps. In: NDSS, vol. 2, pp. 1 4 (2017)

Efficient Deduplication over Encrypted Data Under Flexible Access Control

Xiaofeng Jia[1] and Songnian Zhang[2](✉)

[1] Zhejiang University, Hangzhou 310058, China
[2] Xidian University, Xi'an 710071, China
zhangsongnian@xidian.edu.cn

Abstract. Data deduplication is an effective technique for eliminating redundancy in outsourced data, thereby reducing both storage consumption and communication overhead. Existing encrypted deduplication schemes typically support secure cloud storage and sharing with certain privacy guarantees, but they often fall short in large-scale deployments and rarely achieve, at the same time, flexible access control and robustness against duplicate-faking and ownership-faking attacks. In this work, we propose an efficient encrypted deduplication scheme with fine-grained access control. Our design combines symmetric encryption with a novel tag-generation mechanism to ensure data confidentiality and high performance, while allowing data owners to specify individualized authorization policies. Rigorous security analysis shows that the proposed scheme preserves data privacy and integrity and is secure against both duplicate-faking and ownership-faking attacks. Extensive experiments further demonstrate its practicality: compared with Yang et al.'s scheme, our construction achieves up to 327× higher computational efficiency, reduces communication cost by a factor of 2.962, and lowers storage overhead by a factor of 1.002 for 100 KB files.

Keywords: Efficient data deduplication · Flexible access control · Duplicate fake attack · Ownership fake attack

1 Introduction

With the accelerating digitalization of society and continuous advances in network throughput, outsourcing data to the cloud has become a dominant storage paradigm, driving explosive growth in cloud-resident datasets. For example, EDGE DELTA projects that global digital data will reach 200 ZB by 2025 [6]. Meanwhile, duplicate content is ubiquitous: the duplication ratio for general Internet files is estimated to be around 50–60%, and can be even higher in specific environments—approximately 70–80% in development shares and 80–95% in virtualization libraries. In this context, data deduplication, which enables storage providers to eliminate redundant data blocks, has been widely deployed to reduce storage and bandwidth costs [5]. To safeguard data privacy, however, data

W. Li et al. (Eds.): EISA 2025, CCIS 2897, pp. 142–162, 2026.
https://doi.org/10.1007/978-3-032-21177-4_8

owners typically encrypt files with distinct cryptographic keys before outsourcing them. This practice transforms identical plaintexts into unrelated ciphertexts, undermining straightforward deduplication and making redundancy elimination over encrypted data significantly more challenging. As a result, how to efficiently perform secure deduplication directly on outsourced ciphertexts remains a challenging and actively studied problem.

To address the above challenges, a variety of schemes have been proposed. However, existing approaches still fail to simultaneously satisfy security, flexible access control, and efficiency requirements in real-world deployments. On the one hand, many schemes [7,8,11,14,16,18,21,29] assume semi-honest data owners who follow the prescribed protocol and do not launch active attacks such as duplicate-faking [25] or ownership-faking [28]. On the other hand, works that explicitly consider malicious behavior [25,28] typically address only one class of attacks, rather than providing simultaneous protection against both. Moreover, with respect to flexible access policies, practical deployments require (i) inter-deduplication across users and administrative domains without key conversion, and (ii) inter-user access policies that support multiple access modes. For instance, schemes such as [26–28] employ bilinear pairings to enable the cloud server to check whether ciphertexts generated under different public keys are consistent, but this technique imposes a substantial performance penalty. In addition, the scheme by Yang et al. [26] supports inter-deduplication only between two domains, which limits its applicability in more complex multi-domain environments. Finally, to the best of our knowledge, few existing solutions maintain high computational efficiency for both intra-domain and inter-domain deduplication at big-data scale.

To address these issues, we propose a new secure deduplication scheme with flexible access control. Our main contributions are as follows:

- *Efficient deduplication over encrypted data with flexible access control.* We design an efficient scheme tailored for high-throughput deduplication over large-scale encrypted cloud data (e.g., 64 MB files). In particular, our construction leverages symmetric encryption algorithms such as AES [10] to optimize encryption and decryption performance, and employs Bloom filters [12] to efficiently test whether a data item already exists in the outsourced dataset. For flexible access control, each data owner can register multiple logical IDs and associate distinct data-access policies with each ID, enabling fine-grained and individualized authorization.
- *Robustness against duplicate-faking and ownership-faking attacks.* Our scheme is explicitly designed to resist both duplicate-faking and ownership-faking attacks mounted by malicious data owners. Before performing deduplication, the cloud server verifies the consistency between the tag and the corresponding ciphertext, thereby preventing duplicate-faking attacks. To thwart ownership-faking attacks, the cloud server allows a data owner to download a stored ciphertext only if they can provide a reliable and valid tag associated with that ciphertext.

- *Security analysis and empirical evaluation.* We provide a rigorous security analysis showing that the proposed scheme guarantees data confidentiality and integrity while remaining secure against both duplicate-faking and ownership-faking attacks. Furthermore, extensive experimental results demonstrate that our scheme significantly outperforms Yang et al.'s scheme [26]: for 100 KB files, it achieves up to 327× higher computational efficiency, reduces communication cost by a factor of 2.962, and lowers storage overhead by a factor of 1.002.

The remainder of this paper is organized as follows. Section 2 introduces the system model, threat model, and design goals. Section 3 reviews the necessary preliminaries. Section 4 presents the proposed scheme, and Sects. 5 and 6 provide the security analysis and performance evaluation, respectively. Section 7 discusses related work. Finally, Sect. 8 concludes the paper.

2 Models and Design Goals

This section specifies the system model, formalizes the threat model, and states the design goals that our scheme is intended to achieve.

2.1 System Model

As illustrated in Fig. 1, we consider a secure data-deduplication system consisting of a storage server (SS), a functionality server (FS), and multiple data owners $\mathcal{D} = \{\mathrm{DO}_1, \mathrm{DO}_2, \ldots, \mathrm{DO}_n\}$. In this setting, each data owner DO_μ $(1 \leq \mu \leq n)$ outsources its data to the SS for personal or organizational use. The SS, in cooperation with the FS, performs both intra-domain and inter-domain deduplication over the outsourced data to reduce storage and bandwidth consumption. We next detail the roles of these entities.

- *Storage server* (SS). The storage server SS provides storage services for the data owners in $\mathcal{D}$ and is responsible for eliminating redundant data items so that only a single physical copy of each distinct item is maintained, thereby improving storage efficiency.
- *Functionality server* (FS). The functionality server FS maintains and enforces access-control policies on behalf of the data owners in $\mathcal{D}$ and collaborates with the SS to implement data deduplication. FS also acts as a registration authority: when a data owner $\mathrm{DO} \in \mathcal{D}$ wishes to use the storage service, she or he must first register with FS, which then issues the necessary credentials to enable secure data storage and deduplication.
- *Data owners* $\mathcal{D} = \{\mathrm{DO}_1, \ldots, \mathrm{DO}_n\}$. Each data owner DO_μ $(1 \leq \mu \leq n)$ incrementally uploads data to the SS. For simplicity, we assume that each upload consists of a single message m. To ensure data confidentiality, DO_μ encrypts m under her or his secret key before transmitting it to the SS; consequently, the SS stores ciphertexts that may be encrypted under different keys.

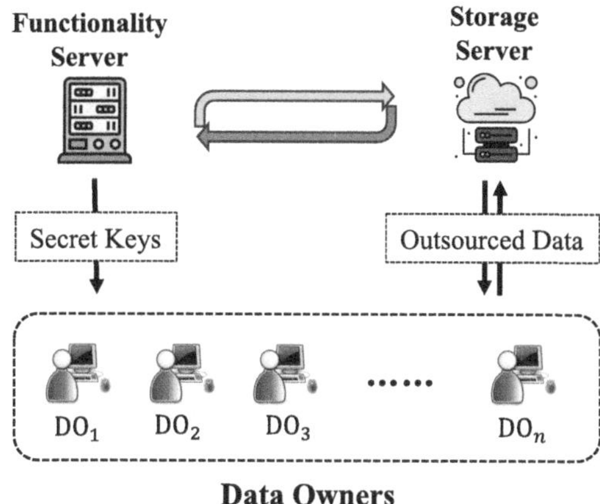

Fig. 1. System model under consideration.

2.2 Threat Model

In our threat model, the functionality server (FS) is assumed to be fully trusted and always behaves honestly. In contrast, the storage server (SS) and the data owners $\mathcal{D}$ may be malicious and can launch active attacks. In particular, a malicious SS may modify stored messages, return stale or incorrect content, or reorder and delete items so as to influence deduplication outcomes. Likewise, a malicious data owner DO $\subset \mathcal{D}$ may upload mismatched tag ciphertext pairs to the SS or attempt to access data without proper authorization. Unless otherwise stated, we assume that there is no collusion among any parties; this is reasonable in regulated environments where detected collusive behavior would incur substantial legal and reputational penalties [23].

2.3 Design Goals

Based on the above threat model, our scheme is designed to achieve the following goals:

- *Privacy.* Although the storage server SS can observe outsourced ciphertexts and the corresponding tags sent by data owners, it must not be able to recover the underlying plaintexts from these ciphertexts.
- *Resistance to duplicate-faking and ownership-faking attacks.* The scheme must prevent both types of attacks launched by malicious data owners. In a duplicate-faking attack [25], an adversarial data owner uploads mismatched tag–ciphertext pairs to the SS in order to trigger the deletion of another owner's data item during deduplication; thus, preventing such behavior is critical. In an ownership-faking attack [28], a data owner attempts to convince the SS that she or he owns a particular message by submitting a forged tag. Our design provides protection against both duplicate-faking and ownership-faking attacks within a single framework.

- *Data integrity.* Since only one physical copy of each data item is stored on the SS, that unique copy may be altered due to hardware failures or other faults. The scheme must therefore guarantee integrity, enabling data owners to verify whether the data they download have been modified.
- *Availability and flexible access control.* To reduce storage and management overhead, the scheme performs deduplication both within and across different data owners (i.e., intra- and inter-deduplication). In addition, it must support flexible access control, allowing a data owner to delegate or authorize data access to other data owners as needed.
- *Efficiency.* Efficiency is essential for practical deployment [15]. The scheme should minimize computational, communication, and storage overhead in order to remain suitable for real-world large-scale cloud environments.

3 Building Blocks

In this section, we review two key primitives, the Bloom filter (BF) and the block cipher AES, which serve as fundamental building blocks of our scheme.

3.1 Bloom Filter

The Bloom filter (BF) is a probabilistic data structure that represents a set as a fixed-length bit array and supports membership queries, answering whether an element is definitely not in the set or may belong to it [12]. Owing to its computational and storage efficiency, Bloom-filter techniques have been widely used in cloud data deduplication systems [9,24,28]. Typically, a Bloom filter is manipulated via three algorithms $\Pi_{\mathtt{BF}} = \{\mathtt{BF.Setup}(), \mathtt{BF.Insert}(), \mathtt{BF.Check}()\}$.

- $\mathtt{BF.Setup}(\lambda, \ell, \eta)$. Given a security parameter λ, the number of hash functions ℓ, and the Bloom-filter length η, this algorithm initializes the data structure as follows:
  - **Step 1**. Choose ℓ hash functions $\{h_i(\cdot) \mid i \in [1, \ell]\}$ for the Bloom filter, each mapping an element to an index in $\{0, \ldots, \eta - 1\}$.
  - **Step 2**. Allocate a bit array BF of length η and initialize it to all zeros, i.e., set $\mathtt{BF}[j] = 0$ for all $j \in [0, \eta - 1]$.

  The algorithm outputs the initialized Bloom filter BF (and the associated hash functions).
- $\mathtt{BF.Insert}(\mathtt{BF}, W)$. Given a Bloom filter BF and a set of messages W, this algorithm inserts each message $w \in W$ into BF by setting

$$\mathtt{BF}[h_i(w)] \leftarrow 1 \quad \text{for all } i \in [1, \ell].$$

  Finally, it outputs the updated Bloom filter BF, which now represents the set W.
- $\mathtt{BF.Check}(w', \mathtt{BF})$. Given a message w' and a Bloom filter BF representing a set W, this algorithm determines whether $w' \in W$ by checking the bits at positions $h_i(w')$ for all $i \in [1, \ell]$. If all corresponding bits in BF are 1, it outputs that w' is (possibly) in W; otherwise, it outputs that $w' \notin W$.

3.2 AES

To ensure the confidentiality of outsourced data, we use the Advanced Encryption Standard (AES) [10] as the underlying symmetric-key encryption primitive. In our setting, AES is modeled by the following three algorithms $\Pi_{\texttt{AES}} = \{\texttt{AES.KeyGen}(), \texttt{AES.Enc}(), \texttt{AES.Dec}()\}$:

- AES.KeyGen(λ): given a security parameter λ, this algorithm outputs a secret key sk.
- AES.Enc(sk, m): given a secret key sk and a message m, this algorithm outputs a ciphertext $C(m)$.
- AES.Dec($sk, C(m)$): given a secret key sk and a ciphertext $C(m)$, this algorithm recovers and outputs the corresponding plaintext message m.

We require the usual correctness property, i.e., for any key sk output by AES.KeyGen and any message m, it holds that $\texttt{AES.Dec}(sk, \texttt{AES.Enc}(sk, m)) = m$.

4 The Proposed Scheme

In this section, we present the proposed secure deduplication scheme. We first describe the system architecture, which supports three data-access policy types: *owner type*, *group type*, and *public type*. We then outline the scheme, which is structured into five phases: key management, data deduplication, data upload, data download, and dispute resolution.

4.1 System Architecture

As noted earlier, in our architecture each data owner DO_μ (with $\mu \in \{1, \ldots, n\}$) may be assigned multiple logical identifiers, e.g., $(\text{ID}_{\mu 1}, \text{ID}_{\mu 2}, \ldots)$, according to her or his needs. As shown in Fig. 2, each identifier ID_j (with $j \in \{1, \ldots, N\}$) is associated with a specific group G_j. Even when multiple identifiers belong to the same data owner, they are treated as independent principals; in particular, privileges granted to one identifier neither propagate to nor depend on those of another. We designate G_0 as the *public group*, meaning that every registered identifier is automatically included in G_0. For simplicity of exposition, we assume that each data owner DO_μ belongs to exactly one non-public group G_j in addition to G_0 and thus holds a single non-public identifier $\text{ID}_{\mu j}$.

Within this architecture, a data owner DO_μ with identifier $\text{ID}_{\mu j}$ (where $1 \leq \mu \leq n$ and $1 \leq j \leq N$), belonging to groups G_0 and G_j, holds three distinct keys—usk_μ, gsk_j, and psk_0—all issued by the functionality server FS. These keys authorize access to *owner-type*, *group-type*, and *public-type* files, respectively, as illustrated in Fig. 3. Specifically, usk_μ is the per-owner secret key of DO_μ and is used to encrypt individually owned sensitive data. In contrast, gsk_j is the group secret key for G_j ($1 \leq j \leq N$), shared by all data owners in G_j and thereby enabling inter-deduplication and authorized access over files uploaded by group members. Finally, each registered data owner DO_μ shares a public-group secret key psk_0, which supports deduplication and access control across all registered data owners.

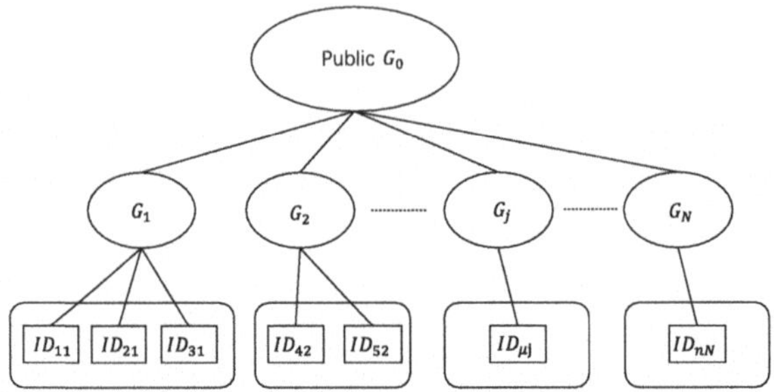

Fig. 2. System architecture under consideration.

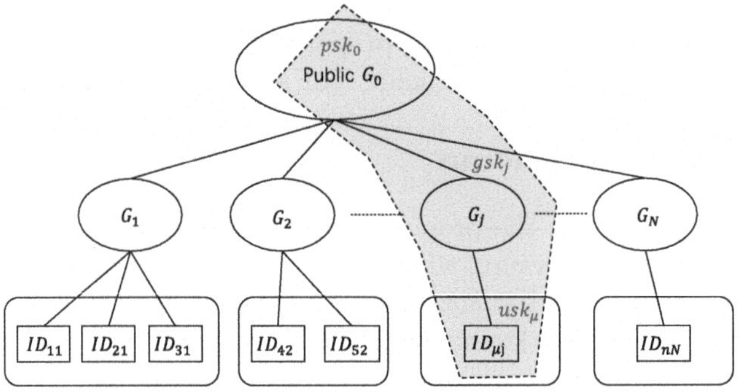

Fig. 3. Key management under consideration.

4.2 Key Management

In the key management phase, the functionality server FS first invokes $\texttt{BF.Setup}(\lambda, \ell, \eta)$ to generate the hash family $\{h_i(\cdot)\}_{i=1}^{\ell}$ and instantiates a cryptographic hash function $H(\cdot) : \{0,1\}^* \to \{0,1\}^{256}$ (e.g., SHA-256). It then runs $\texttt{AES.KeyGen}(\lambda)$ to obtain a master secret key $msk \in \{0,1\}^{256}$. Based on these primitives, FS finally derives the key triple (usk, gsk, psk) as follows:

$$\begin{aligned} usk &= H(msk||001), \\ gsk &= H(msk||010), \\ psk &= H(msk||100). \end{aligned}$$

For the storage server SS, it initializes a database to store ciphertexts uploaded by data owners. To avoid races caused by concurrent uploads, SS maintains two lists of Bloom-filter bit arrays: $\texttt{HBF} = \{\texttt{HBF}_j \mid j \in \{0, \ldots, N\}\}$ and $\texttt{TBF} = \{\texttt{TBF}_j \mid j \in \{0, \ldots, N\}\}$. Specifically, $\texttt{HBF}_j$ denotes the history Bloom filter for group G_j, which records the set of data uploaded *before* a fixed cutoff time (e.g., 00:00:00 each day). In contrast, $\texttt{TBF}_j$ denotes the temporary Bloom filter for group G_j, which tracks the set of data uploaded *within* the current daily window (e.g., from 00:00:00 to 23:59:59). When the current time passes the designated cutoff, SS merges $\texttt{TBF}_j$ into $\texttt{HBF}_j$ (e.g., via bitwise OR) and reinitializes $\texttt{TBF}_j$ for the next window. Finally, HBF is stored in a *public* directory on SS so that every registered data owner can download it, whereas TBF resides in a *private* directory and is accessible only to SS.

Next, the data owner DO_μ registers with the functionality server FS by providing her or his identifier $\text{ID}_{\mu j}$ and the corresponding group index j (i.e., group G_j). Upon successful registration, FS computes and issues DO_μ's key triple (usk_μ, gsk_j, psk_0) as follows:

$$usk_\mu = H(usk||\text{ID}_{\mu j}||v), gsk_j = H(gsk||G_j||v), psk_0 = H(psk||G_0||v).$$

The version parameter v in the above equations is initialized to 1 and is updated as needed (e.g., upon system upgrades). Finally, the functionality server FS returns (usk_μ, gsk_j, psk_0) to DO_μ.

4.3 Data Deduplication

This phase consists of two sub-phases: *offline data deduplication* and *online data deduplication*. The former is performed by the data owner DO_μ, while the latter is carried out by the storage server SS. By offloading preliminary checks to the client side, this division of labor substantially reduces the workload on SS and improves the overall efficiency of the system.

Offline Data Deduplication. As mentioned earlier, our scheme supports three data-authorization types: *owner type*, *group type*, and *public type*. Owner-type authorization is used to store an individual owner's sensitive files, to which no other users have access. The other two authorization types correspond to a non-public group G_j (with $j \in \{1, \ldots, N\}$) and to the public group G_0, respectively. Data owners within the same group can thus perform inter-deduplication on their outsourced group files. Consequently, the offline deduplication procedure differs slightly for these three types; we outline the generic steps below. When a data owner DO_μ intends to upload a message m to SS, she or he proceeds as follows:

- **Step 1.** Compute the plain tag $\text{PTag}(m) = H(m)$ and check whether $\text{PTag}(m)$ has already been stored locally. If so, no further action is required and the procedure terminates; otherwise, proceed to Step 2.
- **Step 2.** Perform deduplication checks for group G_j and the public group G_0 as follows:
  - *Action 1.* Download $\texttt{HBF}_j \in \texttt{HBF}$ and $\texttt{HBF}_0 \in \texttt{HBF}$ from the public directory of SS.
  - *Action 2.* Compute the check tag $\text{CTag}_j(m) = H\big(H(m) \,\|\, gsk_j \,\|\, 0\big)$ and test whether all positions $\texttt{HBF}_j[h_i(\text{CTag}_j(m))]$ are set to 1 for all $i \in \{1, \ldots, \ell\}$. If this condition holds, store $\text{PTag}(m)$ locally and terminate; otherwise, proceed to *Action 3*.

- *Action 3.* Compute the check tag $\mathrm{CTag}_0(m) = H\big(H(m) \,\|\, psk_0 \,\|\, 0\big)$ and test whether all positions $\mathtt{HBF}_0[h_i(\mathrm{CTag}_0(m))]$ are set to 1 for all $i \in \{1, \ldots, \ell\}$. If this condition holds, store $\mathrm{PTag}(m)$ locally and terminate; otherwise, proceed to the online data deduplication phase.

Online Data Deduplication. If a data owner DO_μ with $(\mathrm{ID}_{\mu j}, G_j, G_0)$ determines during the offline phase that the message m has not yet been stored, she or he sends the check tags $(\mathrm{CTag}_j(m), \mathrm{CTag}_0(m))$ to the storage server SS. Upon receiving these tags, SS performs *online data deduplication* using steps analogous to the offline checks; the key difference is that SS, rather than DO_μ, now executes the membership tests against $\mathtt{TBF}_j$ and $\mathtt{TBF}_0$. For example, SS verifies whether all positions $\mathtt{TBF}_j[h_i(\mathrm{CTag}_j(m))]$ are set to 1 for all $i \in \{1, \ldots, \ell\}$ to decide whether m already appears in the temporary storage of group G_j. If SS finds a copy of m, it returns an "Existence" notification to DO_μ and takes no further action; otherwise, it returns an "Inexistence" notification.

4.4 Data Upload

If DO_μ receives an "Existence" notification from SS, she or he takes no further action. Otherwise, DO_μ proceeds to encrypt the message m. Specifically, DO_μ first generates a secret key k by invoking $\mathtt{AES.KeyGen}(\lambda)$ and then computes the ciphertext $C(m) = \mathtt{AES.Enc}(k, m)$. The subsequent steps performed by DO_μ depend slightly on the chosen authorization type (owner, group, or public).

- **Owner type**. If the authorization type of message m is classified as *owner type*, the data owner DO_μ, the storage server SS, and the functionality server FS proceed as follows:
  - *Step 1.* DO_μ first computes the search tag $\mathrm{STag}_\mu(m)$ and the key tag $\mathrm{KTag}_\mu(m)$ as follows:

$$\mathrm{STag}_\mu(m) = H(H(m)||usk_\mu||1), \mathrm{KTag}_\mu(m) = H(H(m)||usk_\mu||2).$$

    Then, DO_μ encrypts the secret key k by running $\mathtt{AES.Enc}(\mathrm{KTag}_\mu(m), k)$ to obtain $C(k)$, and computes the verification tag $\mathrm{VTag}_\mu(m)$ as

$$\mathrm{VTag}_\mu(m) = H\big(\mathrm{STag}_\mu(m) \,\|\, usk_\mu \,\|\, H(C(m))\big).$$

    Finally, DO_μ sends $(\mathrm{ID}_{\mu j}, \mathrm{STag}_\mu(m), \mathrm{VTag}_\mu(m), C(m), C(k))$ to SS.
  - *Step 2.* Upon receiving the message from DO_μ, the storage server SS computes $H(C(m))$ and forwards $(\mathrm{ID}_{\mu j}, \mathrm{STag}_\mu(m), \mathrm{VTag}_\mu(m), H(C(m)))$ to FS.
  - *Step 3.* Upon receiving the message from SS, the functionality server FS computes usk_μ from $\mathrm{ID}_{\mu j}$ as

$$usk_\mu = H(usk \,\|\, \mathrm{ID}_{\mu j} \,\|\, v).$$

FS then verifies whether the following equation holds:

$$\mathrm{VTag}_\mu(m) \stackrel{?}{=} H\big(\mathrm{STag}_\mu(m) \,\|\, usk_\mu \,\|\, H(C(m))\big).$$

If the equation holds, FS takes no further action and SS stores $(\mathrm{ID}_{\mu j}, \mathrm{STag}_\mu(m), \mathrm{VTag}_\mu(m), C(m), C(k))$ in its database. Otherwise, FS informs SS of the inconsistency, and SS discards the received data from DO_μ.

- **Group type**. If the authorization type of message m is classified as *group type*, DO_μ, SS, and FS proceed as follows:
  - *Step 1.* DO_μ first computes the check tag $\mathrm{CTag}_j(m)$, the search tag $\mathrm{STag}_j(m)$, and the key tag $\mathrm{KTag}_j(m)$ as

$$\begin{aligned}\mathrm{CTag}_j(m) &= H\big(H(m) \,\|\, gsk_j \,\|\, 0\big),\\ \mathrm{STag}_j(m) &= H\big(H(m) \,\|\, gsk_j \,\|\, 1\big),\\ \mathrm{KTag}_j(m) &= H\big(H(m) \,\|\, gsk_j \,\|\, 2\big).\end{aligned}$$

  Then, DO_μ encrypts the secret key k by running $\texttt{AES.Enc}(\mathrm{KTag}_j(m), k)$ to obtain $C(k)$ and computes the verification tag $\mathrm{VTag}_j(m)$ as

$$para = \mathrm{CTag}_j(m) \,\|\, \mathrm{STag}_j(m), \mathrm{VTag}_j(m) = H\big(para \,\|\, gsk_j \,\|\, H(C(m))\big).$$

  Finally, DO_μ sends $(\mathrm{ID}_{\mu j}, G_j, \mathrm{CTag}_j(m), \mathrm{STag}_j(m), \mathrm{VTag}_j(m), C(m), C(k))$ to SS.
  - *Step 2.* Upon receiving the message from DO_μ, SS computes $H(C(m))$ and forwards $(\mathrm{ID}_{\mu j}, G_j, \mathrm{CTag}_j(m), \mathrm{STag}_j(m), \mathrm{VTag}_j(m), H(C(m)))$ to FS.
  - *Step 3.* Upon receiving the message from SS, FS computes gsk_j from G_j as $gsk_j = H\big(gsk \,\|\, G_j \,\|\, v\big)$. FS then sets $para = \mathrm{CTag}_j(m) \,\|\, \mathrm{STag}_j(m)$ and verifies whether the following equation holds:

$$\mathrm{VTag}_j(m) \stackrel{?}{=} H\big(para \,\|\, gsk_j \,\|\, H(C(m))\big).$$

  If the equation holds, FS takes no further action. In this case, SS stores $(\mathrm{ID}_{\mu j}, G_j, \mathrm{CTag}_j(m), \mathrm{STag}_j(m), \mathrm{VTag}_j(m), C(m), C(k))$ in its database and inserts $\mathrm{CTag}_j(m)$ into $\texttt{TBF}_j$ by setting

$$\texttt{TBF}_j[h_i(\mathrm{CTag}_j(m))] \leftarrow 1, \quad \forall i \in [1, \ell].$$

  Otherwise, FS informs SS of the inconsistency, and SS discards the outsourced data.
- **Public type**. If the authorization type of message m is classified as *public type*, DO_μ, SS, and FS proceed analogously to the *group type* case. The main difference is that DO_μ uses the public-group key psk_0 to generate the tags $(\mathrm{CTag}_0(m), \mathrm{STag}_0(m), \mathrm{KTag}_0(m), \mathrm{VTag}_0(m))$, and FS performs the tag–ciphertext consistency check based on psk_0 (rather than gsk_j). For brevity, we omit the full description here.

Finally, SS will merge TBF into HBF at a specific time point, such as 00:00:00 each day, and reinitialize TBF using the following equations:

$$(\texttt{HBF}_j[i] = \texttt{HBF}_j[i] \vee \texttt{TBF}_j[i]) \wedge (\texttt{TBF}_j[i] = 0).$$

where $j \in [1, N]$, and $i \in [1, \eta]$.

Corollary 1 (Correctness of Tag–Ciphertext Consistency). As described above, when a message m is not found during the deduplication phase, the data owner DO_μ must upload either ($\mathrm{ID}_{\mu j}$, STag(m), VTag(m), $C(m)$, $C(k)$) or ($\mathrm{ID}_{\mu j}$, G_j, CTag(m), STag(m), VTag(m), $C(m)$, $C(k)$) to SS, depending on the authorization type. To mitigate the risk of duplicate-faking attacks, FS and SS are required to verify that the received tags (STag(m), VTag(m)) or (CTag(m), STag(m), VTag(m)) and the ciphertext $C(m)$ are all derived from the same underlying message m, thereby ensuring tag–ciphertext consistency. To this end, SS computes $H(C(m))$ and forwards either ($\mathrm{ID}_{\mu j}$, STag(m), VTag(m), $H(C(m))$) or ($\mathrm{ID}_{\mu j}$, G_j, CTag(m), STag(m), VTag(m), $H(C(m))$) to FS. FS then performs the tag–ciphertext consistency checks exactly as specified in Step 3 for the *owner type*, *group type*, and *public type*, respectively.

Correctness. The correctness of the tag–ciphertext consistency protocol is straightforward. If the tags (STag(m), VTag(m)) or (CTag(m), STag(m), VTag(m)) and the ciphertext $C(m)$ are generated from the *same* message m, then the verification equations in Step 3 hold by construction. Conversely, if the tags and $C(m)$ are generated from *different* messages, FS will detect this mismatch by checking whether the corresponding verification equation(s) fail, i.e., whether one of the following equations does not hold:

$$\mathrm{VTag}(m) \stackrel{?}{=} H(\mathrm{STag}(m) \,\|\, usk_\mu \,\|\, H(C(m))),$$

$$\mathrm{VTag}(m) \stackrel{?}{=} H(\mathrm{CTag}(m) \,\|\, \mathrm{STag}(m) \,\|\, gsk_j \,\|\, H(C(m))),$$

$$\mathrm{VTag}(m) \stackrel{?}{=} H(\mathrm{CTag}(m) \,\|\, \mathrm{STag}(m) \,\|\, psk_0 \,\|\, H(C(m))).$$

4.5 Data Download

In the data download phase, a data owner DO_μ with ($\mathrm{ID}_{\mu j}$, G_j, G_0) who wishes to download a message m sends (AuType(m), STag(m)) to the storage server SS, where AuType(m) denotes the authorization type of m. SS then searches its storage for a record indexed by STag(m). If a matching record is found, SS returns (STag(m), $C(m)$, $C(k)$) to DO_μ. Upon receipt, DO_μ recovers m according to the authorization type.

Since the steps that DO_μ must perform to recover m and verify data integrity are essentially the same for *owner-type*, *group-type*, and *public-type* messages, we detail only the owner-type case for simplicity. In this case, DO_μ first computes $\mathrm{KTag}_\mu(m) = H\big(H(m) \,\|\, usk_\mu \,\|\, 2\big)$, and uses $\mathrm{KTag}_\mu(m)$ to recover the secret key k by running $\texttt{AES.Dec}\big(\mathrm{KTag}_\mu(m),\, C(k)\big)$. Next, DO_μ recovers m by computing

$m \leftarrow \texttt{AES.Dec}(k, C(m))$, and checks whether the following equation holds:

$$\text{STag}(m) \stackrel{?}{=} H\big(H(m) \,\|\, usk_\mu \,\|\, 1\big).$$

If the equation holds, DO_μ accepts the recovered message m as valid. Otherwise, DO_μ rejects the result and proceeds to the dispute phase.

Since the recovery and integrity-check steps are nearly identical for *owner type*, *group type*, and *public type* messages, we detail the *owner type* case for brevity. In this case, DO_μ first derives $\text{KTag}_\mu(m) = H\big(H(m) \,\|\, usk_\mu \,\|\, 2\big)$, and uses it to recover the encryption key k by running $\texttt{AES.Dec}\big(\text{KTag}_\mu(m), C(k)\big)$. Next, DO_μ decrypts the ciphertext $C(m)$ to obtain m by running $\texttt{AES.Dec}\big(k, C(m)\big)$. Finally, DO_μ verifies integrity by checking $\text{STag}(m) \stackrel{?}{=} H\big(H(m) \,\|\, usk_\mu \,\|\, 1\big)$. If the equality holds, DO_μ accepts the recovered message m; otherwise, DO_μ proceeds to the dispute stage.

4.6 Dispute

If the recovered message m fails the verification in the data download phase, DO_μ proceeds to the dispute phase. In this phase, DO_μ sends $(\text{AuType}(m), \text{STag}(m))$ to the functionality server FS, while the storage server SS forwards its search result $(\text{STag}(m), C(m), C(k))$ to FS. Upon receiving data from both DO_μ and SS, FS executes the same recovery and verification steps as in the data download phase to reconstruct and validate the message m. By doing so, FS can determine whether SS has altered the stored data and whether DO_μ indeed holds the appropriate authorization to access m.

5 Security Analysis

In this section, we present a security analysis of the proposed scheme. In particular, following the design goals specified in Sect. 2.3, we show that our construction guarantees privacy, resists both duplicate-faking and ownership-faking attacks, and ensures data integrity.

5.1 Privacy Analysis

We now show that the proposed scheme guarantees the confidentiality of uploaded data against both the functionality server FS and the storage server SS. For clarity, we focus on the file deduplication process for *owner-type* data; the arguments for *group-type* and *public-type* data are analogous.

To enable deduplication in cooperation with FS and SS, the data owner DO_μ sends the ciphertexts $(C(m), C(k))$ together with the corresponding tags $(\text{STag}_\mu(m), \text{VTag}_\mu(m))$ to SS. Since $C(m)$ and $C(k)$ are produced using the block cipher AES, their confidentiality follows from the security of AES. Moreover, for SS to recover m solely from the tags $(\text{STag}_\mu(m), \text{VTag}_\mu(m))$, it would need to invert the underlying one-way hash function, which is computationally infeasible.

Regarding the functionality server FS, although it is modeled as *trusted*, we still aim to prevent FS from learning the outsourced data. In our scheme, FS assigns the keys (usk_μ, gsk_j, psk_0) to each registered data owner DO_μ in group G_j. However, as described in Sect. 4.3, DO_μ locally samples a random element $k \in \{0,1\}^{256}$ as the symmetric key to encrypt m into its ciphertext $C(m)$. The key k is then encrypted under $\text{KTag}_\mu(m) = H\big(H(m) \,\|\, usk_\mu \,\|\, 2\big)$. Since FS has no access to $H(m)$, the security of the hash function ensures that FS cannot derive $\text{KTag}_\mu(m)$ and thus cannot decrypt $C(k)$, nor consequently $C(m)$. Therefore, the proposed scheme preserves data confidentiality against both SS and FS for owner-type files.

5.2 Duplicate Fake Attack Resilience

Duplicate fake attacks occur when a malicious data owner DO_μ, associated with $(\text{ID}_\mu, G_j, G_0)$, attempts to deduplicate a correct data item by constructing a fake tag. In this case, we require the functionality server FS to perform a tag-ciphertext consistency check.

Specifically, if DO_μ sends mismatched tag-ciphertext data, such as $(\text{STag}_\mu(m'), \text{VTag}_\mu(m'), C(m), C(k))$, to the storage server SS. Afterward, SS computes $H(C(m))$ and forwards $(\text{STag}_\mu(m'), \text{VTag}_\mu(m'), H(C(m)))$ to FS. FS then retrieves usk_μ and computes $\text{VTag}_\mu(m) = H(\text{STag}_\mu(m') \,\|\, usk_\mu \,\|\, H(C(m)))$ according to the scheme. Clearly, FS can easily determine that the calculated tag does not match the received tag, i.e., $\text{VTag}_\mu(m') \neq \text{VTag}_\mu(m)$. As a result, our proposed scheme can effectively resist duplicate fake attacks.

5.3 Ownership Fake Attack Resilience

We now analyze ownership-faking attacks launched by malicious data owners. We distinguish two cases: (i) a data owner DO_μ with $(\text{ID}_{\mu j}, G_j, G_0)$ does not possess the message m but attempts to trigger deduplication for m within her or his group; (ii) a data owner DO_μ with $(\text{ID}_{\mu j}, G_j, G_0)$ tries to download the ciphertext corresponding to m without being authorized to access m.

Case i: DO_μ does not possess the message m. In this scenario, DO_μ cannot correctly compute the parameters ($C(m)$, $\text{STag}_\mu(m)$, $\text{KTag}_\mu(m)$, $C(k)$, $\text{VTag}_\mu(m)$) without the actual message m. Our scheme is designed to handle a large message space, covering files from kilobytes to megabytes. Hence, a malicious owner cannot feasibly enumerate all possible messages in the supported space and compute valid tuples for each candidate. Therefore, with overwhelming probability, DO_μ fails to construct a consistent set of values that passes the tag–ciphertext checks, and the scheme prevents ownership-faking attacks in this case.

Case ii: DO_μ is not authorized to access m. To initiate a download in our scheme, DO_μ must submit the search tag $\text{STag}_\mu(m)$ to SS. This tag is generated via a secure hash function whose input includes $H(m)$. If DO_μ is not authorized to access m, she or he does not know m and thus does not know $H(m)$.

In this setting, a malicious data owner DO_μ cannot forge a valid search tag $\mathrm{STag}_\mu(m)$, which is computed from $H(m)$ and the owner's secret key using the hash function. Consequently, the adversary cannot convince SS or FS that she or he legitimately owns m or obtain the corresponding ciphertext.

In conclusion, the proposed scheme effectively resists ownership-faking attacks from malicious data owners in both cases.

5.4 Data Intergrity

From Sect. 4.5, recall that the data owner DO_μ can detect data tampering by verifying the recovered message. If a malicious SS modifies the stored ciphertext $C(k)$ or $C(m)$, then DO_μ will be unable to correctly recover the originally uploaded message m. In this case, for an owner-type file, DO_μ further checks whether $\mathrm{STag}_\mu(m) \stackrel{?}{=} H\big(H(m) \,\|\, usk_\mu \,\|\, 1\big)$, where m is the message recovered from the downloaded ciphertext $C(m)$. If the equality holds, DO_μ accepts the downloaded file as intact; otherwise, she or he concludes that the stored data have been tampered with. Thus, the scheme enables DO_μ to determine whether data integrity is preserved based on this check.

6 Performance Evaluatioin

In this section, we evaluate the performance of the proposed scheme in terms of computational, communication, and storage overheads. We implemented our scheme in Java on a MacBook Pro equipped with an Apple M1 chip (10-core CPU) and 32 GB of RAM. For comparison, we also implemented Yang et al.'s scheme [26], using type A1 curve parameters for the bilinear pairing. To ensure comparable security levels, both schemes employ AES-256 as the symmetric encryption algorithm and SHA-256 as the hash function. For our scheme, we further fix the number of hash functions in the Bloom filter to $\ell = 20$.

6.1 Computational Costs

For a secure data deduplication scheme in a cloud-storage setting, the deduplication procedure is typically the dominant component affecting the overall efficiency, compared with other operations. We therefore focus on evaluating the computational costs of our scheme and that of Yang et al. [26] with respect to this component. To clearly illustrate the performance, we conduct comprehensive experiments under different parameter settings, varying the file size $|f|$ and the duplication ratio δ.

It is important to note that Yang et al.'s scheme cannot detect a malicious user who uploads a ciphertext and a tag computed from different data, whereas our scheme explicitly includes mechanisms for such detection. Consequently, we evaluate the performance of our scheme under two adversarial models: a *semi-honest* model (for both our scheme and Yang et al.'s scheme) and a *malicious* model (for our scheme only). In particular, in the semi-honest model for our scheme, the functionality server FS and the storage server SS are not required to perform tag–ciphertext consistency checks, while these checks are enabled in the malicious model.

Intra-deduplication. As shown in Fig. 4, we report the execution time of intra-deduplication as a function of the file size $|f|$ and the duplication ratio δ, respectively. In the figures, the label "semi-honest" denotes the performance of each scheme under the semi-honest model, whereas "malicious" denotes the performance of our scheme under the malicious model.

From Fig. 4a, it is clear that our scheme, under both the semi-honest and malicious models, achieves better computational efficiency than Yang et al.'s scheme, especially for small file sizes (e.g., $|f| = 100$ KB). This improvement is mainly because, in Yang et al.'s scheme, the data owner must perform expensive computations in the target group $\mathbb{G}_T$ to generate the secret key, which significantly degrades efficiency. Regarding Fig. 4b, both schemes exhibit improved performance as the duplication ratio increases from 10% to 50%, with our scheme consistently outperforming Yang et al.'s scheme across all settings.

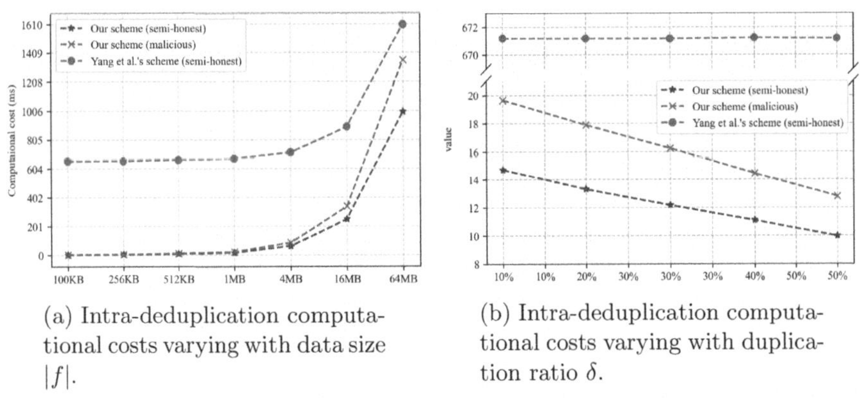

(a) Intra-deduplication computational costs varying with data size $|f|$.

(b) Intra-deduplication computational costs varying with duplication ratio δ.

Fig. 4. Intra-deduplication computational costs: (a) varying with data size $|f|$, setting duplication ratio $\delta = 0$; (b) varying with duplication ratio δ, setting data size $|f| =$ 1 MB.

Inter-deduplication. Similar to Sect. 6.1, we next present the experimental results for inter-deduplication of our scheme and Yang et al.'s scheme under the semi-honest model, together with the performance of our scheme under the malicious model, as shown in Fig. 5. Specifically, Fig. 5a exhibits trends similar to those in Fig. 4a. In particular, the execution time of our scheme under both the semi-honest and malicious models is lower than that of Yang et al.'s scheme under the semi-honest model when the file size $|f|$ ranges from 100 KB to 64 MB.

Regarding Fig. 5b, we observe that the efficiency of our scheme under both models improves as the duplication ratio δ increases from 10% to 50%. The main reason is that, once an identical copy is found on the storage server SS during the deduplication phase, a data owner can skip encrypting the corresponding file. In contrast, the performance of Yang et al.'s scheme degrades as δ increases, because the cloud service provider must perform equality checks between ciphertexts in the target group $\mathbb{G}_T$ to determine whether a file has already been stored, which incurs substantial computational overhead.

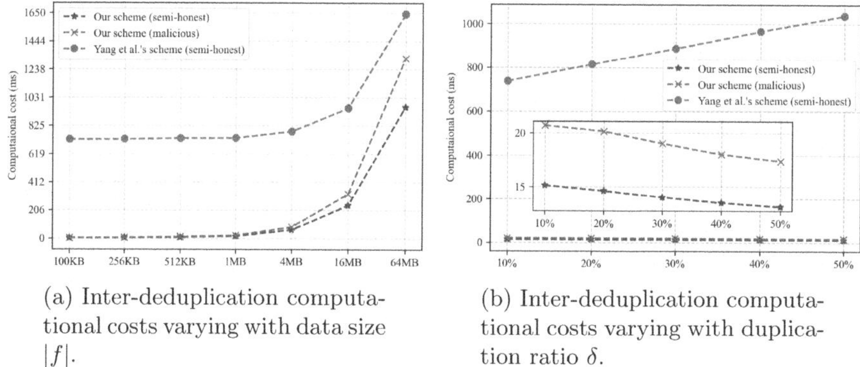

(a) Inter-deduplication computational costs varying with data size $|f|$.

(b) Inter-deduplication computational costs varying with duplication ratio δ.

Fig. 5. Inter-deduplication computational costs: (a) varying with data size $|f|$, setting duplication ratio $\delta = 10\%$; (b) varying with duplication ratio δ, setting data size $|f| = 1\,\text{MB}$.

6.2 Communication Overheads

In this section, we compare the communication overheads of our scheme and Yang et al.'s scheme [26] under the semi-honest model, and also evaluate the communication overheads of our scheme under the malicious model. We observe that the communication overheads of our scheme under the semi-honest and malicious models are nearly identical, and both are significantly lower than those of Yang et al.'s scheme under the semi-honest model. Concretely, the communication overheads of our scheme consist of the following three components:

i) **DO→SS.** This denotes the traffic from the data owner DO to the storage server SS, where DO uploads (CTag(m), STag(m), VTag(m), $C(k)$, $C(m)$). Here, CTag(m) is used only for *group-type* and *public-type* files. The combined length of the first four items is fixed at 1280 bits, while the length of $C(m)$ depends on the size of the message m.

ii) **SS→DO.** This denotes the traffic from SS to DO when the data owner downloads the `TBF` and `HBF` arrays from the public directory on SS. The length of a Bloom-filter array is given by $\eta = \ell \times w \times 1.44$, where $w =$

10^3 is the size of the set stored in the Bloom filter. To further reduce the false-positive rate, we enlarge the Bloom filter by a factor of five, obtaining $\eta = \ell \times w \times 1.44 \times 5$. Note that the communication overhead of SS→DO is independent of the size of the updated message.

iii) **SS→FS.** This denotes the traffic from SS to the functionality server FS, where SS sends (CTag(m), STag(m), VTag(m), $H(C(m))$) to FS. The total length of this data is fixed at 1024 bits. Importantly, this communication is required only under the malicious model, where SS must engage FS to perform tag–ciphertext consistency checks in order to resist duplicate-faking attacks.

In contrast, in Yang et al.'s scheme, the local manager (LM) forwards all messages received from the data owner (DO) to the cloud service provider (CSP), so that the communication overhead on the LM→CSP link is identical to that on the DO→CSP link. Concretely, the DO must send $(\tau^1, \tau^2, C(m))$ toward the CSP, where $\tau^1 \in \mathbb{G}_1$ and $\tau^2 \in \{0,1\}^{128}$. The underlying reason is that the LM is only responsible for performing intra-deduplication and does not store outsourced data; thus, it must forward all deduplicated data to the CSP for long-term storage (Fig. 6).

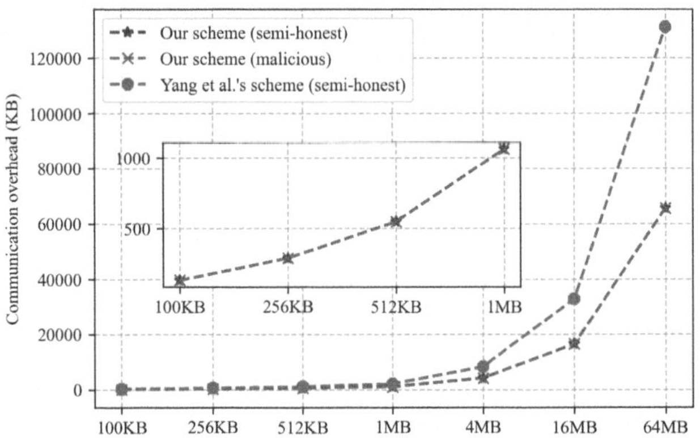

Fig. 6. Communication overheads.

6.3 Storage Overheads

In this section, we compare the storage overhead of our scheme with that of Yang et al.'s scheme [26]. Table 1 reports the storage cost of both schemes as a function of the file size $|f|$ and the duplication ratio δ. We consider a dataset of 10^6 files for a single data owner, where each file has a fixed size. The label "No Dedup" indicates that there is no duplication among the 10^6 files, whereas "10% Dedup" means that $10^6 \times 10\% = 10^5$ files are duplicates; "30% Dedup" and "50% Dedup" are defined analogously.

Since storage consists of two components, the total storage is computed as

$$\text{RES} = 2 \times \eta + \big(|C(m)| + |C(k)| + 3 \times 256\big) \times 10^6 \times (1 - \delta),$$

where the first term accounts for the two Bloom filters (of length η each), and the second term corresponds to the storage of two AES ciphertexts and three SHA-256-based tags for each non-duplicate file. As shown in Table 1, the storage space is dominated by the ciphertext component, and our scheme achieves lower overall storage overhead than Yang et al.'s scheme. Moreover, both schemes benefit from higher duplication ratios δ, as increased deduplication leads to reduced storage consumption.

Table 1. Storage overheads varying with data size $|f|$ and duplication ratio δ.

		100 KB	256 KB	512 KB	1 MB	4 MB
	Plaintext	95.367 GB	244.141 GB	488.281 GB	0.954 TB	3.815 TB
Our scheme	No DeDup	95.565 GB	244.338 GB	488.479 GB	0.954 TB	3.815 TB
	10% DeDup	86.012 GB	219.908 GB	439.634 GB	0.858 TB	3.433 TB
	30% DeDup	66.905 GB	171.047 GB	341.945 GB	0.668 TB	2.670 TB
	50% DeDup	47.799 GB	122.186 GB	244.256 GB	0.477 TB	1.907 TB
Yang et al.'s scheme	No DeDup	95.874 GB	244.647 GB	488.788 GB	0.954 TB	3.815 TB
	10% DeDup	86.287 GB	220.183 GB	439.909 GB	0.859 TB	3.434 TB
	30% DeDup	67.112 GB	171.253 GB	342.152 GB	0.668 TB	2.671 TB
	50% DeDup	47.937 GB	122.324 GB	244.394 GB	0.477 TB	1.908 TB

7 Related Work

Recently, leading cloud storage providers such as Dropbox [1], Google Drive [2], Mozy [3], and SpiderOak [4] have adopted data deduplication as a promising technique to reduce storage space and associated costs. In parallel, researchers have proposed various cryptographic solutions to further advance secure deduplication [21].

Early deduplication systems relied on convergent encryption (CE), which encrypts data using its hash value and a related tag [11,20,22]. However, these constructions lacked a formal security analysis. To address this, Bellare et al. introduced Message-Locked Encryption (MLE) to formalize the security of deduplication-based encryption [8]. Building on this line of work, Koo et al. [21] proposed a secure deduplication scheme with a two-layer architecture, where fog nodes in the first layer perform local deduplication and a cloud server in the second layer assists users with global deduplication. Nevertheless, the use of deterministic, message-dependent symmetric keys [17] entails inherent security limitations [13]. To mitigate these issues, Keelveedhi et al. [17] proposed transforming predictable messages into unpredictable ones. In the same year, Abadi et al. [7] designed a randomized MLE scheme based on bilinear pairings that enables the cloud server to determine whether two randomized ciphertexts encrypt the same message; however, this approach suffers from significant efficiency overhead. Jiang et al. [16] later improved deduplication efficiency by introducing decision-tree techniques in the cloud-storage setting. Subsequently, a number of schemes [14,19,29] further enhanced the functionality and performance of cloud deduplication. A common limitation of all these constructions is that they assume semi-honest data owners. To address malicious behavior by data owners, Yan et al. [25] proposed a proof mechanism to counter ownership-faking attacks. More recently, the schemes in [26,28] employ bilinear pairings to allow the cloud server to verify whether ciphertexts are consistent with their corresponding tags. Unfortunately, these approaches incur substantial computational costs and do not simultaneously protect against both duplicate-faking and ownership-faking attacks. In addition, the scheme of Yang et al. [26] supports inter-deduplication across only two domains, which limits its applicability in more general multi-domain environments.

As discussed above, existing approaches still fail to simultaneously provide strong security, flexible access control, and high efficiency in realistic cloud deployments. This work aims to close this gap.

8 Conclusion

In this paper, we have presented an efficient deduplication scheme over encrypted data with flexible access control. Our construction leverages symmetric encryption to ensure the semantic security of outsourced data while preserving high encryption and decryption performance. In addition, we design a new tag-generation mechanism that enables fine-grained and flexible access control across different users. Rigorous security analyses show that the proposed scheme guarantees data privacy and integrity and is secure against both duplicate-faking and ownership-faking attacks. Finally, extensive experimental results demonstrate that our scheme outperforms that of Yang et al. in terms of computational cost, communication overhead, and storage overhead.

Acknowledgments. This research was supported in part by the National Natural Science Foundation of China under Grant 62402362; in part by China Postdoctoral Science Foundation under Grant 2023M742743.

Disclosure of Interests. The authors have no competing interests to declare that are relevant to the content of this article.

References

1. Dropbox, a file-storage and sharing service. http://www.dropbox.com
2. Google driver. http://drive.google.com

3. Mozy: A file-storage and sharing service. http://mozy.com/
4. Sipderoak. https://spideroak.com/
5. Data deduplication overview (2022). https://learn.microsoft.com/en-us/windows-server/storage/data-deduplication/overview
6. 6 vital data storage statistics you must know (2024). https://edgedelta.com/company/blog/data-storage-statistics
7. Abadi, M., Boneh, D., Mironov, I., Raghunathan, A., Segev, G.: Message-locked encryption for lock-dependent messages. In: Canetti, R., Garay, J.A. (eds.) CRYPTO 2013. LNCS, vol. 8042, pp. 374–391. Springer, Heidelberg (2013). https://doi.org/10.1007/978-3-642-40041-4_21
8. Bellare, M., Keelveedhi, S., Ristenpart, T.: Message-locked encryption and secure deduplication. In: Johansson, T., Nguyen, P.Q. (eds.) EUROCRYPT 2013. LNCS, vol. 7881, pp. 296–312. Springer, Heidelberg (2013). https://doi.org/10.1007/978-3-642-38348-9_18
9. Cheng, G., Guo, D., Luo, L., Xia, J., Gu, S.: LOFS: a lightweight online file storage strategy for effective data deduplication at network edge. IEEE Trans. Parallel Distrib. Syst., 2263–2276 (2022)
10. Daemen, J.: AES proposal: Rijndael (1999)
11. Douceur, J.R., Adya, A., Bolosky, W.J., Simon, D., Theimer, M.: Reclaiming space from duplicate files in a serverless distributed file system. In: International Conference on Distributed Computing Systems, pp. 617–624. IEEE Computer Society (2002)
12. Gionis, A., Indyk, P., Motwani, R.: Similarity search in high dimensions via hashing. In: International Conference on Very Large Data Bases, pp. 518–529 (1999)
13. Harnik, D., Pinkas, B., Shulman-Peleg, A.: Side channels in cloud services: deduplication in cloud storage. IEEE Secur. Priv., 40–47 (2010)
14. Huang, Q., Zhang, Z., Yang, Y.: Privacy-preserving media sharing with scalable access control and secure deduplication in mobile cloud computing. IEEE Trans. Mobile Comput., 1951–1964 (2021)
15. Jiang, S., Jiang, T., Wang, L.: Secure and efficient cloud data deduplication with ownership management. IEEE Trans. Serv. Comput., 1152–1165 (2020)
16. Jiang, T., Chen, X., Wu, Q., Ma, J., Susilo, W., Lou, W.: Secure and efficient cloud data deduplication with randomized tag. IEEE Trans. Inf. Forensics Secur., 532–543 (2017)
17. Keelveedhi, S., Bellare, M., Ristenpart, T.: DupLESS: server-aided encryption for deduplicated storage. In: USENIX Security Symposium, pp. 179–194. USENIX (2013)
18. Koo, D., Hur, J.: Privacy-preserving deduplication of encrypted data with dynamic ownership management in fog computing. Future Gener. Comput. Syst., 739–752 (2018)
19. Liu, J., Asokan, N., Pinkas, B.: Secure deduplication of encrypted data without additional independent servers. In: Ray, I., Li, N., Kruegel, C. (eds.) ACM SIGSAC Conference on Computer and Communications Security, pp. 874–885. ACM (2015)
20. Rahumed, A., Chen, H.C.H., Tang, Y., Lee, P.P.C., Lui, J.C.S.: A secure cloud backup system with assured deletion and version control. In: International Conference on Parallel Processing Workshops. IEEE Computer Society (2011)
21. Shin, Y., Koo, D., Hur, J.: A survey of secure data deduplication schemes for cloud storage systems. ACM Comput. Surv., 74:1–74:38 (2017)
22. Storer, M.W., Greenan, K.M., Long, D.D.E., Miller, E.L.: Secure data deduplication. In: Kim, Y., Yurcik, W. (eds.) Workshop On Storage Security and Survivability, pp. 1–10. ACM (2008)

23. Veugen, T., de Haan, R., Cramer, R., Muller, F.: A framework for secure computations with two non-colluding servers and multiple clients, applied to recommendations. IEEE Trans. Inf. Forensics Secur., 445–457 (2015)
24. Wu, S., et al.: EAD: a collision-free and high performance deduplication scheme for flash storage systems. In: IEEE International Conference on Computer Design, pp. 155–162. IEEE (2020)
25. Yan, Z., Ding, W., Yu, X., Zhu, H., Deng, R.H.: Deduplication on encrypted big data in cloud. IEEE Trans. Big Data, 138–150 (2016)
26. Yang, X., Lu, R., Choo, K.R., Yin, F., Tang, X.: Achieving efficient and privacy-preserving cross-domain big data deduplication in cloud. IEEE Trans. Big Data, 73–84 (2022)
27. Yang, X., Lu, R., Shao, J., Tang, X., Ghorbani, A.A.: Achieving efficient and privacy-preserving multi-domain big data deduplication in cloud. IEEE Trans. Serv. Comput., 1292–1305 (2021)
28. Yang, X., Lu, R., Shao, J., Tang, X., Ghorbani, A.A.: Achieving efficient secure deduplication with user-defined access control in cloud. IEEE Trans. Depend. Secur. Comput., 591–606 (2022)
29. Yuan, H., Chen, X., Li, J., Jiang, T., Wang, J., Deng, R.H.: Secure cloud data deduplication with efficient re-encryption. IEEE Trans. Mobile Comput., 442–456 (2022)

A 2D-ELSCM-Based Chaotic Image Encryption Scheme for Incomplete Fingerprints

Haoyu Sun(✉), Tianran Dong, and Xinyu Zhou

School of Electronic and Information Engineering, Liaoning Technical University, Huludao 125105, Liaoning, China
2298438552@qq.com

Abstract. Biometric authentication in high-security environments such as customs and defense facilities requires strong protection of raw and intermediate data, especially when incomplete fingerprints are involved. Conventional encryption schemes, designed for intact images, often fail to adapt to such degraded samples. To address this issue, we propose an image encryption framework based on the two-dimensional Exponential-Logistic-Sine Chaotic Map (2D-ELSCM). The framework integrates a logarithmic fractional digit-driven scrambling strategy and a bidirectional ciphertext feedback diffusion mechanism, achieving global decorrelation, enhanced avalanche effects, and strict reversibility. Experimental results confirm its strong security, adaptability, and feasibility for protecting biometric privacy

Keywords: 2D-ELSCM chaotic system · Multi-level scrambling · Incomplete fingerprints · Bidirectional ciphertext feedback diffusion

1 Introduction

In high-security environments such as customs, border inspection, and defense industrial zones, stringent requirements are imposed on resource access and personnel identity verification. These tasks are typically accomplished through biometric authentication systems, such as facial or fingerprint recognition. However, the raw and intermediate biometric data generated during authentication, if not adequately protected, are highly vulnerable to attacks during acquisition, transmission, or long-term storage, thereby posing severe privacy and security risks. Most existing biometric encryption schemes are designed for complete images and have not fully considered scenarios involving "incomplete fingerprints," which are common among individuals with disabilities where scars, damage, or partial acquisition lead to missing or degraded ridge patterns. As a result, incomplete fingerprints often exhibit insufficient security under conventional encryption systems and face an elevated risk of privacy leakage. Thus, there is an urgent need for an encryption scheme that can simultaneously ensure high security while adapting to incomplete fingerprint patterns.

W. Li et al. (Eds.): EISA 2025, CCIS 2897, pp. 163–176, 2026.
https://doi.org/10.1007/978-3-032-21177-4_9

To address this challenge, we propose a chaotic image encryption framework specifically designed for incomplete fingerprint protection, following Shannon's classical "permutation–diffusion" paradigm. At the system level, a two-dimensional Exponential–Logistic–Sine Coupled Map (2D-ELSCM) is constructed. Building on the classical Logistic–Sine map, the system incorporates exponential functions, fractional regulation factors, and cross-coupling mechanisms, thereby exhibiting stronger sensitivity to initial conditions. The Lyapunov exponents remain positive across a wide parameter range, with hyperchaotic behavior observed, significantly enhancing unpredictability. By introducing a control parameter k, a scaling factor h, and dual initial values (x_0, y_0), the scheme forms a four-dimensional key space far larger than that of conventional systems, providing effective resistance against brute-force attacks. Analyses based on bifurcation diagrams, Lyapunov exponents, and the 0–1 test confirm the complex dynamics and superior chaotic properties of the proposed 2D-ELSCM.

At the algorithmic level, improvements are introduced in both permutation and diffusion stages. On the permutation side, traditional content-independent methods (e.g., row–column swaps, mapping permutations, or space-filling curve scans) are effective for intact fingerprints but perform poorly on incomplete cases, where local periodic patterns tend to amplify correlations and hinder secure scrambling. To overcome this limitation, we propose a logarithmic fractional-digit driven permutation strategy under the principles of "weak content coupling, strong global coverage, and strict reversibility." Specifically, logarithmic features are extracted from pixel values and used to construct index sequences that guide two-level row–column sorting and a global reordering, thereby reducing the risk of local texture overfitting and enhancing adaptability to incomplete fingerprint distributions.

On the diffusion side, conventional approaches such as plaintext–key XOR or one-way ciphertext feedback (e.g., [1,2]) suffer from limited avalanche effects and single propagation paths, making it difficult for small perturbations to diffuse globally. To address these shortcomings, we design a bidirectional ciphertext-feedback diffusion mechanism with an initialization vector (IV). Starting from the IV, each pixel is XORed with both the chaotic sequence and the ciphertext of its left and upper neighbors, enabling perturbations to propagate along horizontal and vertical paths simultaneously. This enhances the avalanche effect, improves diffusion capability, and preserves strict reversibility, which is essential for secure fingerprint storage.

Experimental evaluations on incomplete fingerprint samples demonstrate that the proposed scheme achieves near-ideal values for key performance indicators: information entropy ($\approx$7.9973), NPCR ($\approx$99.54%), and UACI ($\approx$33.42%). Moreover, ciphertext pixel correlations approach zero, and histograms approximate uniform distributions, further verifying randomness and security. These results confirm that the proposed method effectively conceals incomplete ridge information, provides strong avalanche and reversibility properties, and offers a practical solution for privacy protection of biometric data belonging to individuals with disabilities in high-security applications (Fig. 1).

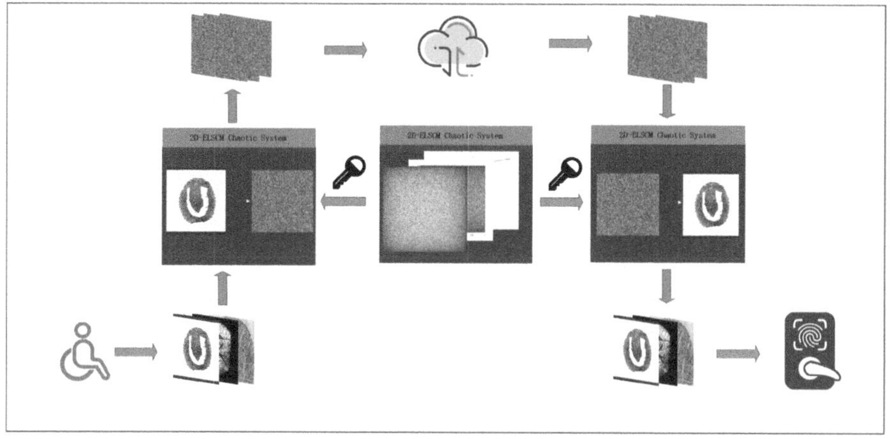

Fig. 1. Application scenario of incomplete fingerprint protection.

2 The 2D Exponential-Logistic-Sine Chaotic Map (2D-ELSCM)

In this section, the 2D-ELSCM with high sensitivity and randomness is proposed. Multiple random tests are performed to assess the stability, chaotic attributes and usability of this chaotic map.

2.1 2D-ELSCM

Chaotic mappings have found widespread application in image encryption due to their simple structure, sensitivity to initial values, and good pseudorandomness. Among these, the Logistic map and Sine map are classic examples of one-dimensional chaotic systems. The logistic chaotic map and the sine chaotic map are defined as:

$$\begin{cases} x_{n+1} = \mu x_n(1 - x_n) & x_n \in (0,1),\ \mu \in (0,4] \\ x_{n+1} = \mu \sin(\pi x_n) & x_n \in (0,1),\ \mu \in (0,1] \end{cases} \tag{1}$$

Here, x_n denotes the state variable at the nth iteration, and μ represents the control parameter.

Although these one-dimensional chaotic maps exhibit good chaotic properties under certain conditions, their structurally simple chaotic sequences often lack uniform distribution and show weak randomness within certain parameter ranges. To address these issues, this paper designs a novel chaotic map. By incorporating exponential functions, fractional scaling factors, and cross-coupling mechanisms between state variables, it merges and extends the two original maps into a two-dimensional system. This effectively enhances the complexity and security of the chaotic system. The system is defined as follows:

$$\begin{cases} x_{j+1} = \sin\left(\frac{25}{h(i)} \times \left(25e^{y_j} k y_j \left(1 - h(i)x_j^2 + 0.3y_j\right)\right)\right) \\ y_{j+1} = \sin\left(\frac{25}{h(i)} \times \left(25e^{x_j} k x_j \left(x_j + h(i)y_j(1 - y_j^2)\right)\right)\right) \end{cases} \tag{2}$$

$x_j, y_j \in (-1, 1)$ represent the iterative state variables of the system; $k \in (0, 1]$ is the control parameter used to adjust the nonlinearity strength of the system; $h(i) \in (0.5, 2]$ is the dynamic scaling factor that can modulate the system behavior at different iterations; and the introduction of exponential terms e^x, e^y significantly enhances the sensitivity and complexity of the system.

2.2 Branch Diagram

Bifurcation diagrams provide a visual representation of how a system's state evolves as control parameters are modified. A well-defined chaotic system exhibits high sensitivity to initial conditions and parameters, displaying markedly different trajectories for adjacent parameter paths. This paper plots bifurcation diagrams for the system under various parameter settings. During plotting, initial conditions were set to $x_0 = 0.2117$ and $y_0 = 0.917$. Each parameter set underwent 500 iterations, with the first 400 iterations discarded to eliminate transient effects. The results from the subsequent 100 iterations were used to plot bifurcation points. When the parameter h is fixed at 0.67 and the control parameter $k \in (0, 1]$, the bifurcation diagram of the system state variable y is shown in the figure; when parameter $k = 0.76$ is fixed and scaling factor $h \in [0.5, 2]$ is varied, the bifurcation diagram of system state variable y is shown in the figure. These images demonstrate its excellent chaotic properties under different parameter conditions (Fig. 2).

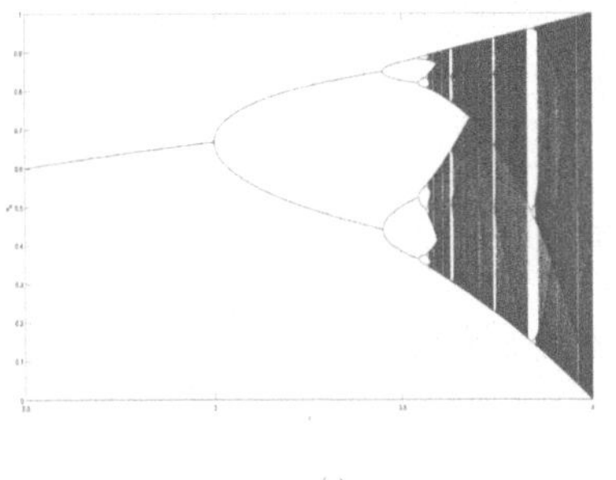

(a)

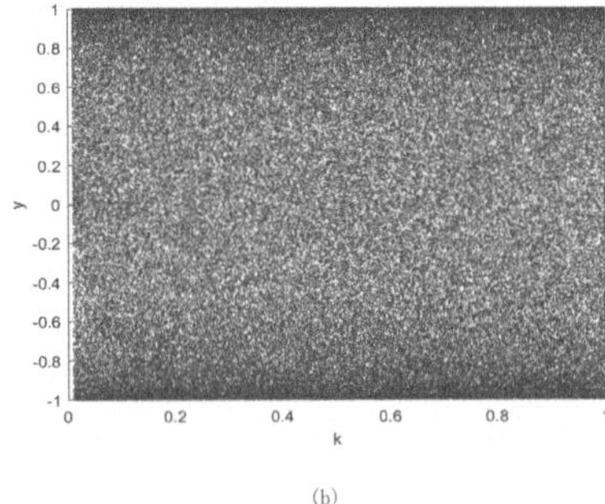

(b)

Fig. 2. Bifurcation diagrams of 2D-ELSCM under representative parameter sweeps.

2.3 Lyapunov Exponent

The Lyapunov exponent is a crucial metric for evaluating the performance of chaotic systems, serving to describe a system's sensitivity to initial conditions. A positive value indicates that the chaotic system exhibits extreme sensitivity to initial conditions. For the two-dimensional coupled chaotic system discussed in this paper, its calculation formula is as follows:

$$\lambda_{\max} = \lim_{N\to\infty} \frac{1}{N} \sum_{k=0}^{N-1} \ln \|J_k v_k\| \tag{3}$$

Here, J_k denotes the Jacobian matrix at the k-th step, and v_k represents the tangent space basis vector. When $\lambda_{\max} > 0$, it indicates that the system exhibits chaotic behavior, with larger values representing stronger chaos. If both Lyapunov exponents of the chaotic system are greater than zero, it demonstrates that the system is in a hyperchaotic state. Compared with regular chaotic behavior, such a hyperchaotic system possesses stronger unpredictability and randomness, as illustrated in the Lyapunov exponent figure (Fig. 5) (Fig. 3).

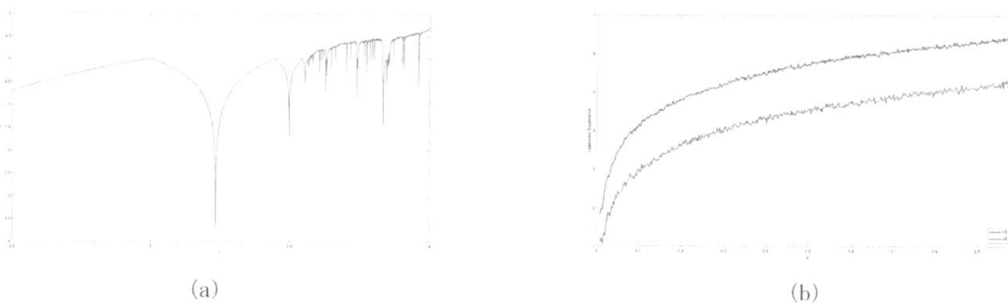

(a) (b)

Fig. 3. Lyapunov exponent

2.4 0–1 Testing

The 0–1 test is a commonly used method for assessing chaotic properties. It involves mapping a time series onto a two-dimensional plane and calculating the mean displacement of trajectories to obtain the growth rate correlation coefficient K. When K approaches 0, the system exhibits regular periodic motion, indicating non-chaotic behavior; when K approaches 1, the system displays irregular Brownian motion, signifying chaotic behavior. The figure displays the 0–1 test results for the 2D-ELSCM. It can be observed that for nearly all parameter values of K that are not zero, the corresponding 0–1 test results approach 1. This indicates that the chaotic system operates in a chaotic state within the studied parameter range, capable of generating highly random sequences (Fig. 4).

$$K_c = \lim_{n\to\infty} \frac{\log M_c(n)}{\log n} \tag{4}$$

Here, K_c denotes the complexity index, n is the scale parameter tending to infinity, $M_c(n)$ represents the counting function at scale n, and log is the logarithmic operation used to measure the growth rate.

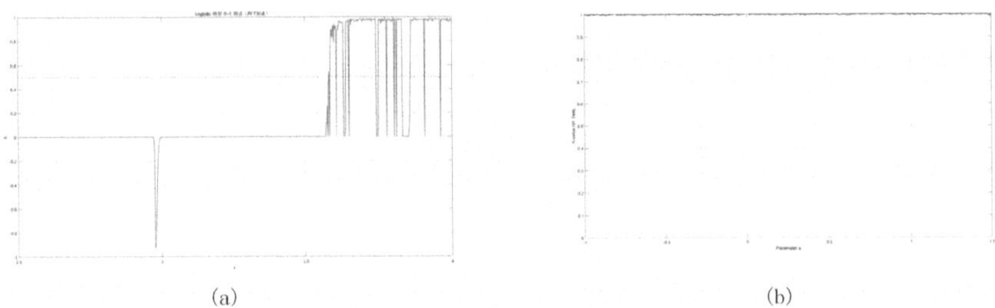

(a) (b)

Fig. 4. Left: representative Lyapunov-exponent evidence of chaos. Right: 0–1 test indicating chaotic behavior across parameter ranges.

3 Encryption Process

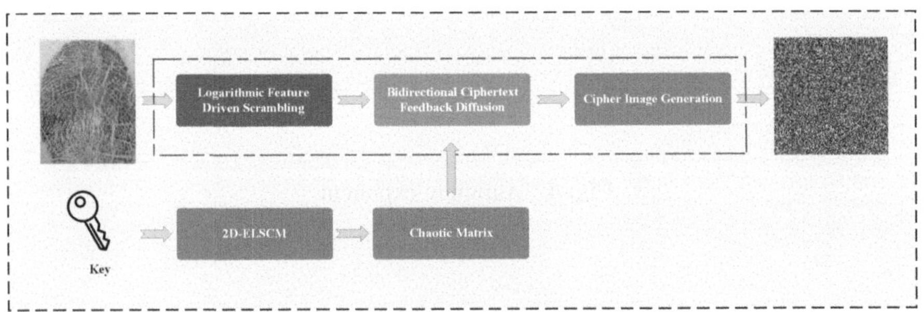

Fig. 5. Overall Encryption Process

3.1 Scrambling Operation

Step 1: Logarithmic Feature Extraction and S_1 Construction. First, input the grayscale image P. For each pixel $P(i, j)$ in the image, this paper performs zero-value preprocessing to avoid data anomalies when subsequently taking the natural logarithm. When a pixel value is 0, this paper defaults it to 1. Next, the natural logarithm is calculated for each pixel, and the fractional part is truncated. To ensure the resulting matrix exhibits well-defined discrete features, the fourth to sixth decimal places of $f(i, j)$ are extracted and concatenated into a three-digit integer, which is then populated into matrix S_1. For example, when pixel value $P(1,1) = 233$, the calculation yields $\ln(233) \approx 5.4510384$. Its fractional part is 0.4510384. Extracting the 4th to 6th digits yields 038, thus $S_1(1,1) = 38$.

$$\begin{cases} L(i,j) = \ln\big(\max(P(i,j),1)\big) \\ S_1(i,j) = \text{digits}(L(i,j),4,6) \end{cases} \tag{5}$$

Step 2: Row-Column Index Sorting. After obtaining matrix S_1, this paper performs sorting operations along both dimensions—rows and columns—to generate an index matrix for subsequent randomization. For the i-th row of matrix S_1, the row vector undergoes ascending sorting. This not only orders the row elements but also sorts the indices recording their original positions. For example, if a row of matrix S_1 contains elements $[866, 588, 984]$, its index sequence is $[1, 2, 3]$. After sorting the row elements to $[588, 866, 984]$, the sorted index sequence becomes $[2, 1, 3]$. Combining row number information with column indices constructs a two-dimensional matrix O for subsequent precise pixel position swapping. Similarly, each column of the S_1 matrix is sorted in ascending order to obtain the column index matrix q_1, which will be used for subsequent column-direction randomization operations.

$$\begin{cases} q(i,:) = \text{sort}\big(S_1(i,:),\, 1\big) \\ O(i,j) = \big(i,\, q(i,j)\big) \quad 1 \le j \le N \\ q_1(:,j) = \text{sort}\big(S_1(:,j),\, 1\big) \quad 1 \le j \le M \end{cases} \tag{6}$$

Step 3: Two-Stage Permutations Generate Intermediate Images. After constructing the row-column indices, this paper performs a secondary permutation on image P using the matrices O and q_1 generated in Step 2, producing the scrambled image C_2. First, the coordinate matrix O is used to swap the positions of elements within pixels. For example, if the element at position $(2,1)$ in matrix O is $(2,2)$, the pixel at position $(2,1)$ in image P is swapped with the pixel at position $(2,2)$. After applying this rule to every point in image P, the scrambled intermediate result matrix C_1 is obtained. At this stage, matrix C_1 only alters the column positions of each pixel. This paper further processes it using matrix q_1. For each column of image C_1, the pixels are rearranged using the corresponding column values of q_1 as vertical indices, thereby changing the row positions of the pixels to produce matrix C_2. For instance, if the first column of C_1 is [233, 16, 25], while the corresponding first column of matrix q_1 has elements [1, 3, 2], then the third element in the first column is placed in the second position of the corresponding column in matrix C_1.

$$\begin{cases} C_1(i,j) = P\big(O_r(i,j),\, O_c(i,j)\big) \\ C_2(:,j) = C_1\big(q_1(:,j),\, j\big) \end{cases} \tag{7}$$

Step 4: Global Reordering to Obtain C_3. After two rounds of randomization through the preceding steps, the pixel positions within image C_2 have been sufficiently disrupted. However, to further enhance the randomization effect and eliminate any residual local features that may persist across the entire image, this paper introduces a global indexing approach. This method reorders all pixels within the entire image, yielding the randomized image C_3. First, this step again extracts the fractional part of each pixel's logarithmic value. However, unlike Step 1, different decimal places are selected this time. This change alters the features relied upon for randomization, differing from local randomization and enhancing the randomness and unpredictability of the final result. The fifth to seventh decimal places are extracted, and the resulting integers are populated into a new matrix S_2. Matrix S_2 is then expanded into a one-dimensional vector using column-major order. This vector is sorted in ascending order, and the one-dimensional vector q_2 records the reordered position of each pixel, forming the final global index. For example, the third element in column-major order occupies the first position in the ascending one-dimensional vector, so the corresponding element at the first position of vector q_2 is 3. Similarly, matrix C_2 is expanded into a vector $v = \mathrm{vec}(C_2)$ using column-major order. This vector is then reordered according to index q_2 and finally rearranged into matrix form to yield matrix C_3, representing the scrambled image. For instance, if the first element of one-dimensional vector q_2 is 3, the third element of the resulting vector v is placed at the first position to generate vector v'.

$$\begin{cases} q_2 = \mathrm{sort}(s, 1) \\ v' = v(q_2) \\ C_3 = \mathrm{reshape}(v', M, N) \end{cases} \tag{8}$$

3.2 Generation of Chaos Sequences

In this paper, based on the selected initial values and parameters, the chaotic system is iterated for $2MN + 101$ times to generate chaotic sequences. The first 100 elements are discarded to eliminate the transient effects caused by the initial iterations. For the remaining $2MN + 1$ elements, where $M \times N$ denotes the size of the image to be encrypted, the subsequent $2MN$ elements generated by the chaotic system are used to construct the chaotic matrices S_3 and S_4. First, the chaotic system generates a one-dimensional chaotic sequence from (x, y), which is defined as follows:

$$\begin{cases} s(t) = \dfrac{x(t) + y(t)}{2} \\ v(t) = \left\lfloor \dfrac{s(t) - \min(s)}{\max(s) - \min(s) + \varepsilon} \times 256 \right\rfloor \end{cases} \tag{9}$$

In this paper, the first MN generated elements are filled into matrix S_3, and the subsequent MN elements are filled into matrix S_4 for the subsequent diffusion operation. The last element is taken as the initialization vector IV, which serves as the starting point for the diffusion of the first pixel.

$$\begin{cases} S_3 \leftarrow v(1{:}MN) \\ S_4 \leftarrow v(MN{+}1{:}2MN) \\ IV \leftarrow v(2MN{+}1) \end{cases} \tag{10}$$

3.3 Diffusion Operation

For the scrambled image, the pixel positions have already been fully randomized, but some plaintext information may still be exposed through the gray-level distribution characteristics. Therefore, this paper designs a diffusion method that combines the chaotic matrix S_4 with the auxiliary matrix L to further enhance the encryption effect. Essentially, this method performs XOR operations between the elements of the chaotic matrix generated by the chaotic system and the scrambled image, while introducing the initialization vector (IV) at the beginning of the diffusion process. This ensures that the diffusion starts from the very first pixel and propagates through the entire image. In this way, even a tiny change in any pixel of the plaintext image can be rapidly magnified and spread across the entire ciphertext image, significantly improving resistance against differential attacks.

Step 1: First, the two-dimensional chaotic system is iterated, and after discarding the initial elements, a sequence is obtained. After normalization and quantization processing, the sequence is reconstructed into chaotic matrices S_3 and S_4, whose sizes are consistent with the image size. Matrix S_3 is used to construct the auxiliary matrix L, while matrix S_4 is directly employed in the diffusion process as a source of randomness or perturbation.

Step 2: For each element of matrix S_3, the 4th to 6th decimal digits of its fractional part are extracted and filled into the matrix L, thereby enhancing the nonlinear complexity during the diffusion process.

$$L(i,j) = \big(\text{digits}(\ln(S_3(i,j)), 4, 6)\big) \bmod 256. \tag{11}$$

For all elements in matrix L, each value is an integer in the range 0 to 255, ensuring that they lie within the same range as pixel gray values, so they can be directly used in XOR operations during the diffusion process.

Step 3: In the diffusion stage, each pixel value is jointly determined by itself, matrix L, matrix S_4, and the values of neighboring pixels. Let the scrambled image be denoted as C_3 and the diffused image as C_4, then the diffusion formula is given by:

$$\text{Prev}(i,j) = \begin{cases} IV & i=1,\ j=1, \\ C_4(i,j-1), & i=1,\ j>1 \\ C_4(i-1,N), & j=1,\ i>1 \\ C_4(i,j-1) \oplus C_4(i-1,j) & i>1,\ j>1. \end{cases} \tag{12}$$

$$C_4(i,j) = C_3(i,j) \oplus L(i,j) \oplus S_4(i,j) \oplus \text{Prev}(i,j). \tag{13}$$

Because XOR is reversible, Eqs. (12)–(13) also specify the inverse diffusion. The bidirectional feedback structure ensures perturbations propagate along both horizontal and vertical directions, strengthening the avalanche effect while preserving reversibility.

4 Simulation Results and Security Analysis

To verify the performance and security of the proposed encryption scheme, several standard analyses were conducted, including keyspace analysis, information entropy, correlation of adjacent pixels, histogram analysis, and resistance to differential attacks.

4.1 Keyspace Analysis

A secure encryption scheme requires a sufficiently large keyspace to resist brute-force attacks. The proposed method relies on multiple parameters and initial conditions (k, h, x_0, y_0) of the 2D-ELSCM chaotic system, forming a four-dimensional keyspace. The effective keyspace size is estimated to be larger than 2^{200}, far exceeding the commonly accepted security bound of 2^{100}, thereby ensuring robustness against exhaustive search.

4.2 Information Entropy

Information entropy measures the randomness of an image [3]. For an 8-bit grayscale image, the entropy $H(m)$ is defined as:

$$H(m) = -\sum_{i=0}^{255} p(m_i) \log_2 p(m_i) \tag{14}$$

Ideally, $H(m) = 8$. In our experiments, the encrypted images yield high entropy values, indicating near-uniform gray-level distributions and strong resistance to statistical attacks. Table 1 reports the results.

Table 1. Information Entropy for Encryption

Image	Entropy
1	7.9974
2	7.9971
3	7.9974
Average	7.9973
[4]	7.9972

4.3 Correlation Analysis

In plain images, adjacent pixels are highly correlated [5]. The correlation coefficient between two adjacent pixels x and y is calculated as:

$$r_{xy} = \frac{\mathrm{cov}(x, y)}{\sqrt{D(x)} \cdot \sqrt{D(y)}} \tag{15}$$

In encrypted images, the correlation coefficients in horizontal, vertical, and diagonal directions are close to zero, demonstrating that the scheme effectively eliminates pixel dependencies (Fig. 6).

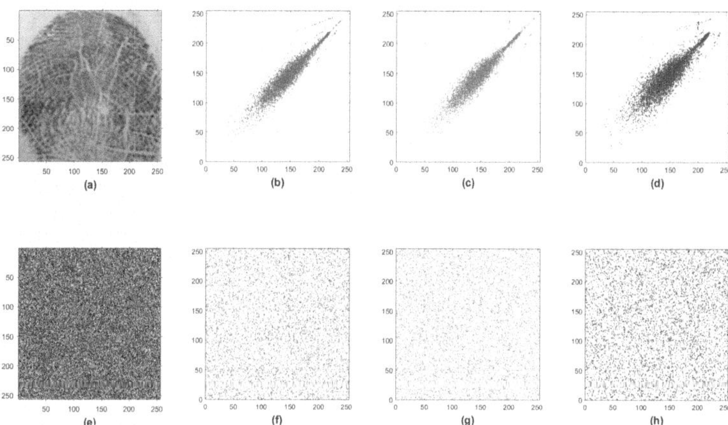

Fig. 6. Correlation analysis: plain versus cipher image scatter plots. Cipher shows near-zero correlation in all directions.

4.4 Histogram Analysis

Histograms of plain images typically reveal non-uniform distributions with visible peaks and valleys, which may leak statistical information. In contrast, the histograms of cipher images generated by our scheme are uniformly distributed, indicating that plaintext features are well concealed (Fig. 7).

4.5 Differential Attack Analysis

The sensitivity to small plaintext changes was evaluated using the Number of Pixels Change Rate (NPCR) [6] and Unified Average Changing Intensity (UACI)

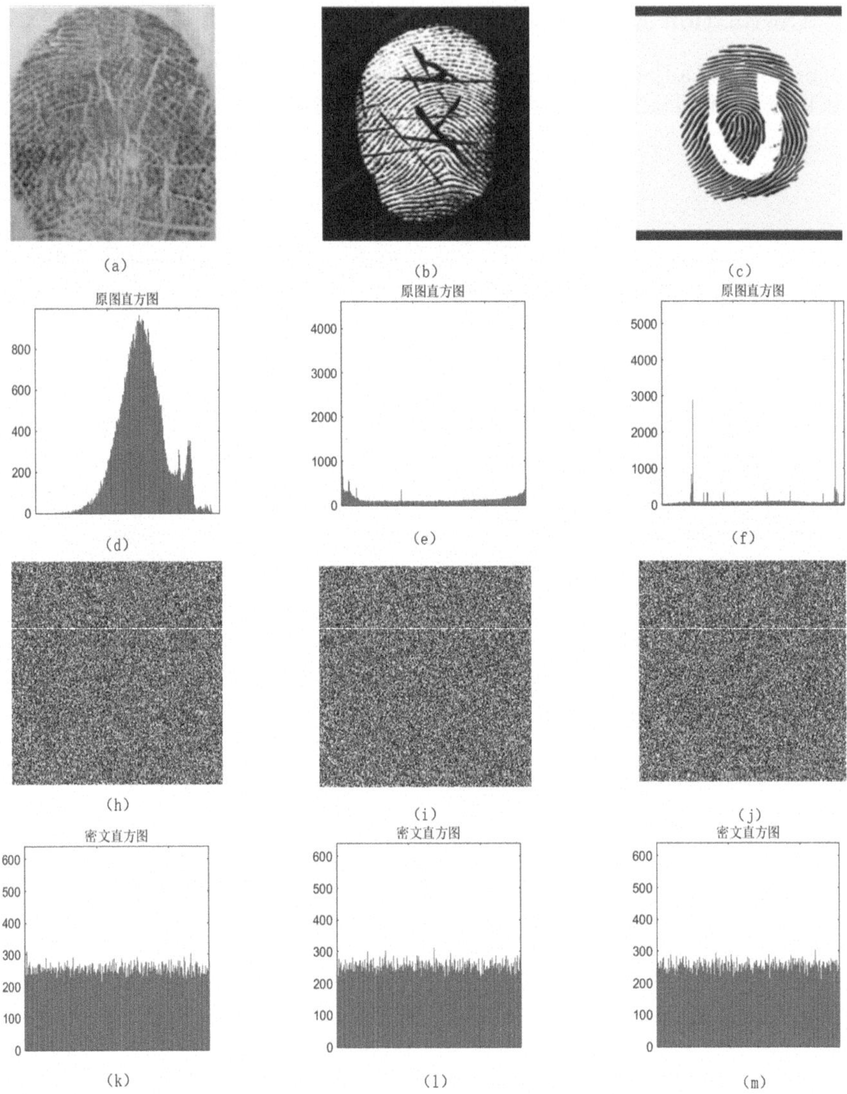

Fig. 7. Histogram comparison: plain (top) vs. cipher (bottom). Cipher histograms approximate uniformity.

[7], defined as:

$$\begin{cases} \text{NPCR} = \dfrac{1}{M \times N} \displaystyle\sum_{i=1}^{M} \sum_{j=1}^{N} D(i,j) \times 100\% \\ \text{UACI} = \dfrac{1}{M \times N} \displaystyle\sum_{i=1}^{M} \sum_{j=1}^{N} \dfrac{|C_1(i,j) - C_2(i,j)|}{255} \times 100\% \end{cases} \tag{16}$$

where $M \times N$ is the image size, C_1 and C_2 are two cipher images differing by one-pixel change in the plaintext, and

$$D(i,j) = \begin{cases} 0, & C_1(i,j) = C_2(i,j) \\ 1, & C_1(i,j) \neq C_2(i,j) \end{cases} \tag{17}$$

Ideally, NPCR $\approx$ 99.6% and UACI $\approx$ 33.5%. The proposed method produces values close to these theoretical benchmarks, confirming strong resistance to differential attacks (Table 2).

Table 2. NPCR and UACI Results

Image	NPCR	UACI
1	99.6078	33.5337
2	99.4003	33.2734
3	99.6017	33.4504
Average	99.5366	33.4192
[8]	99.5651	30.9123

Overall, the results demonstrate that the proposed encryption scheme achieves high entropy, low pixel correlation, uniform histograms, and robustness against statistical and differential attacks, making it a secure and practical solution for incomplete fingerprint protection. References to Figs. 6, 7 and Tables 1, 2 support these claims.

5 Discussion

Compared with traditional encryption schemes optimized for complete fingerprints, the proposed 2D-ELSCM-based method is more suitable for incomplete or degraded samples. Conventional content-independent permutations rely on continuous ridge structures, which often fail when local textures are missing. In contrast, the logarithmic fractional-digit-driven scrambling extracts weakly coupled pixel features rather than ridge continuity, preserving randomness even under partial defects. Meanwhile, the bidirectional ciphertext-feedback diffusion propagates perturbations in both directions, compensating for local incompleteness and maintaining global diffusion. Together, these mechanisms ensure high entropy, low correlation, and robustness against attacks, making the scheme well adapted to incomplete fingerprint protection.

6 Conclusion

In this paper, we presented a chaotic image encryption scheme designed for incomplete fingerprint protection in high-security environments. The proposed framework leverages the two-dimensional Exponential-Logistic-Sine Chaotic Map (2D-ELSCM) to generate high-quality key streams with strong sensitivity, wide chaotic intervals, and an enlarged key space. On this basis, a logarithmic fractional digit-driven scrambling strategy and a bidirectional ciphertext feedback diffusion mechanism were developed to enhance decorrelation, strengthen avalanche effects, and ensure strict reversibility. Experimental analyses confirmed that the scheme achieves strong statistical randomness, high differential sensitivity, and robustness against common attacks, while maintaining pixel-level decryption consistency. These findings demonstrate that the proposed method not only improves the security of fingerprint image encryption but also enhances adaptability to degraded biometric patterns, offering a practical solution for biometric privacy protection in high-security applications.

References

1. Zhang, C., Chen, J., Chen, D.: Cryptanalysis of an image encryption algorithm based on a 2D hyperchaotic map. Entropy **24**(11), 1551 (2022). https://doi.org/10.3390/e24111551
2. Wen, H., Lin, Y., Kang, S., et al.: Secure image encryption algorithm using chaos-based block permutation and weighted bit planes chain diffusion. iScience **27**(1), 108123 (2024). https://doi.org/10.1016/j.isci.2023.108123
3. Lin, H., Wang, C., Cui, L., et al.: Hyperchaotic memristive ring neural network and application in medical image encryption. Nonlinear Dyn. **110**(1), 841–855 (2022)
4. Akkasaligar, P.T., Biradar, S.: Selective medical image encryption using DNA cryptography. Inf. Secur. J. Glob. Perspect. **29**(2), 91–101 (2020)
5. Gafsi, M., Abbassi, N., Hajjaji, M.A., et al.: Improved chaos-based cryptosystem for medical image encryption and decryption. Sci. Program. **2020**, 1–22 (2020)
6. Wu, Y., Noonan, J.P., Agaian, S., et al.: NPCR and UACI randomness tests for image encryption. Cyber J. Multidisc. J. Sci. Technol. J. Sel. Areas Telecommun. **1**(2), 31–38 (2011)
7. Srinivasu, P.N., Norwawi, N., Amiripalli, S.S., et al.: Secured compression for 2D medical images through the manifold and fuzzy trapezoidal correlation function. Gazi Univ. J. Sci. **35**(4), 1372–1391 (2021)
8. Abdelfattah, R.I., Mohamed, H., Nasr, M.E.: Secure image encryption scheme based on DNA and new multi chaotic map. J. Phys. Conf. Ser. **1447**(1), 012053–012065 (2020)

A Blockchain-Based Dynamic Game Incentive Mechanism for Privacy-Preserving Computation

Sicheng Pan, Jiayi Tang, Youqi Li, Cong Zuo(✉), Licheng Wang, Yanli Yuan, and Liehuang Zhu

Beijing Institute of Technology, Beijing 100081, China
zuocong10@gmail.com

Abstract. Privacy-preserving computation has become a critical component in data collaboration, yet existing systems often suffer from high cryptographic overhead and lack effective incentives for honest participation. To address these issues, we propose a blockchain-based dynamic game incentive mechanism for privacy-preserving computation, which uses a combination of rewards and regulatory penalties to incentivize rational participants, who aim to maximize their interests, to remain honest in secure multi-party computation (MPC). Building on this approach, we introduce a Shapley value-based reward distribution mechanism to ensure fair compensation according to each participant's actual contribution. To maintain low on-chain cost while preventing manipulation, we introduce a seed-driven deterministic consensus procedure that enables off-chain Monte Carlo approximation of Shapley values while ensuring on-chain verifiability. The entire incentive and verification process is automated through smart contracts, ensuring transparency, verifiability, and trustless execution. Analysis shows that under rational assumptions, honest computation becomes the dominant strategy, prompting participants to proactively engage in honest computation to maximize their own gains. Our results provide a practical and incentive-compatible framework for fair, efficient, and trustworthy privacy-preserving computation in decentralized environments.

Keywords: Blockchain · Dynamic game theory · Incentive mechanism · Privacy-preserving computation

1 Introduction

Nowadays, data collaboration across organizations has become increasingly essential. However, the coexistence of data silos and privacy concerns severely restricts direct data sharing [12]. Privacy-preserving computation [2,14,15,20], including techniques such as MPC, homomorphic encryption, and federated learning, offers a promising solution for secure data collaboration without compromising individual privacy.

W. Li et al. (Eds.): EISA 2025, CCIS 2897, pp. 177–195, 2026.
https://doi.org/10.1007/978-3-032-21177-4_10

Due to its salient features, such as privacy preservation and verifiable computation, MPC has emerged as a fundamental cryptographic paradigm for collaborative computation without compromising data confidentiality. MPC integrates various cryptographic techniques, including secret sharing, homomorphic encryption, and oblivious transfer, to enable secure joint computation among mutually distrustful parties. However, employing complex cryptographic primitives [5] typically introduces substantial computational overhead. The work of [19] demonstrates that in oblivious transfer-based MPC protocols, the execution time of the oblivious transfer protocol accounts for an exceptionally high proportion of the overall MPC application runtime, reaching up to 96.64%. Therefore, using complex cryptographic primitives greatly affects the efficiency of the MPC protocol. To mitigate these issues, introducing an incentive mechanism that encourages honest behavior and deters malicious actions could reduce the reliance on heavy cryptographic operations.

In this paper, we propose a blockchain-based dynamic game incentive mechanism for MPC that integrates non-cooperative and cooperative game-theoretic principles to ensure rational honesty and fair contribution-based reward allocation. The mechanism employs a deposit–audit strategy to discourage dishonest behavior, while the reward allocation is enhanced through a Shapley value–based scheme computed via an off-chain Monte Carlo approximation algorithm, significantly reducing on-chain computational overhead [1,16]. To ensure that all honest participants derive an identical Shapley value vector despite the off-chain computation, we further introduce a seed-driven deterministic consensus process, enabling verifiable and manipulation-resistant agreement on contribution values. Furthermore, the entire mechanism is implemented through smart contracts deployed on the blockchain, thereby ensuring transparency, auditability, and trustworthiness throughout the process.

Contributions. Based on the above design, this paper addresses the incentive and fairness challenges in blockchain-assisted MPC by combining strategic deterrence with contribution-aware reward allocation. We formally analyze the proposed mechanism under rational participant behavior and demonstrate how it achieves honest participation, fair reward distribution, and practical scalability. The main contributions of this work are summarized as follows:

- We propose a dynamic non-cooperative game–based incentive mechanism for MPC, which guides participants to behave honestly through a combination of rewards and random audit-based penalties.
- We develop a contribution-aware reward distribution scheme based on the Shapley value. Leveraging off-chain Monte Carlo approximation and an on-chain seed-driven deterministic consensus process, the mechanism provides fair, verifiable, and manipulation-resistant compensation according to each participant's marginal contribution.
- We conduct a comprehensive game-theoretic and security analysis, demonstrating that under the honest-majority assumption, the smart contract guarantees consistent contribution assessment, prevents reward manipulation or

under-reporting through automated verification and consensus, and establishes an all-honest Nash equilibrium in repeated MPC tasks.

1.1 Organization

The remainder of this paper is organized as follows. Section 2 reviews related work on incentive mechanisms and game theory. Section 3 presents the system model for the blockchain-based dynamic game incentive mechanism and introduces the underlying model assumptions. Section 4 describes the cryptographic primitives mentioned in this paper. Section 5 presents the design of the incentive mechanism. Section 6 analyzes the proposed incentive mechanism using relevant concepts from game theory and conducts a security analysis. Section 7 concludes the paper and discusses potential future directions.

2 Related Work

Privacy-preserving computation, particularly secure multi-party computation (MPC), has attracted extensive attention in recent years due to its ability to enable collaborative data analysis without revealing private inputs. However, the practical deployment of MPC systems faces two fundamental challenges: how to properly incentivize rational participants to contribute resources and data, and how to model and regulate strategic behaviors that may undermine system correctness and fairness. Existing studies mainly address these challenges from the perspectives of incentive mechanism design and game-theoretic modeling. In this section, we review representative works in these two directions and clarify the limitations that motivate our proposed approach.

2.1 Incentive Mechanisms

Two primary concerns for participants in MPC are resource consumption and the risk of privacy leakage. Designing effective incentive mechanisms is crucial to ensure the participation of a sufficient number of high-quality contributors who are willing to share their data and computing power.

Wang et al. [18] proposed an incentive mechanism to motivate the vehicle [11] to follow the planned route. This mechanism relies on fixed reward structures that cannot accurately reflect each participant's actual contribution. He et al. [7] proposed an incentive mechanism based on game theory for federated learning. This mechanism only considers whether the participants are honest, but does not take into account the participants' contributions to the model training. These incentive mechanisms cannot accurately evaluate the contributions of all participants. A contribution-based reward distribution mechanism is more effective in enhancing participant motivation. Zhang et al. [24] proposed a game-theoretic model that considers participants' trade-offs between privacy protection and incentives. Similarly, Murhekar et al. [13] introduced a fair auction and negotiation incentive mechanism that optimizes participant selection and reward distribution to ensure system sustainability. However, these incentive mechanisms all rely on a central authority, and the system's operation is contingent on that authority remaining secure and trustworthy.

Based on the above limitations, we design a contribution-based incentive mechanism to ensure the accurate evaluation of all participants' contributions. And the entire mechanism is implemented through smart contracts deployed on the blockchain, thereby ensuring transparency, auditability, and trustworthiness throughout the process.

2.2 Game Theory

Game theory provides a powerful framework for analyzing rational behavior in decentralized environments. Its application ranges from peer-to-peer networks [22] to blockchain consensus mechanisms [9], where it is used to model and prevent strategic manipulations.

In non-cooperative models, each player acts independently: equilibrium concepts like Nash [4] or Stackelberg [10] describe stable outcomes where no one can unilaterally improve their payoff. During the audit of differential privacy algorithms, Yang et al. [21] proposed a herd audit Stackelberg game framework, where auditors create a credible accountability threat to algorithm developers by formulating audit strategies, thereby incentivizing them to comply with privacy declarations. Kaluannakkage and Buyya [8] argue that an economic incentive mechanism based on the Stackelberg model can effectively curb free-riding behaviors in federated learning. Dong et al. [3] resolved the verifiability issue of collusion cheating by rational cloud providers in cloud outsourcing computation by designing smart contracts that induce a sequential equilibrium in game theory, while ensuring low cost and high efficiency.

In cooperative models, players may form binding coalitions or share payoffs; concepts such as coalition formation games and the Shapley value then characterize how groups form and how gains are allocated. Sun et al. [17] innovatively model the federated learning process as a sequential cooperative game and employ the Shapley value as the core game-theoretic concept to measure client contributions, thereby systematically addressing three key challenges of federated learning: model robustness, communication costs, and computational costs. He et al. [6] design a Shapley value-based incentive mechanism for collaborative edge computing. It encourages cooperation among rational service providers by inducing optimal offloading strategies, substantially improving system performance and ensuring fair revenue distribution while addressing privacy concerns through aggregating profit functions.

Previous works have largely confined their analyses to a single type of game, focusing either on non-cooperative games to ensure individual rationality or on cooperative games to achieve collective fairness. In contrast, this study integrates insights from both game types to simultaneously ensure participant honesty and fairness in reward allocation.

3 System Model and Assumption

To facilitate a rigorous analysis of the proposed incentive mechanism, we first formalize the system architecture and clarify the underlying assumptions. This section abstracts the key entities involved in the MPC process, their interactions, and the role of blockchain-based smart contracts in enforcing incentives and regulating strategic behaviors. By explicitly stating the system model and assumptions, we establish a clear analytical foundation for the subsequent game-theoretic formulation and mechanism design.

3.1 System Model

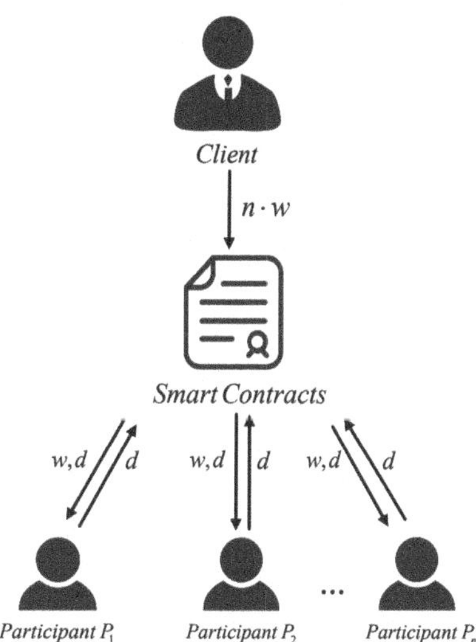

Fig. 1. System model of the incentive mechanism involving the client, smart contracts, and participants

In this paper, we designed a blockchain-based dynamic game incentive mechanism for MPC. Our system facilitates the seamless execution of MPC tasks between clients and computing participants. As shown in Fig. 1 (the variables will be described in Subsect. 5.1), the system consists of three primary entities:

- **Client:** Client C initiates a MPC task by defining the function task to be computed, the number of participants, the total reward, and the deadlines for each stage of the computation.
- **Participants:** A set of n participants $P_1, P_2, \ldots, P_n$ jointly perform the MPC protocol. Each participant holds a private input, and they receive rewards for completing the computation task. Participants are assumed to be rational, meaning they strategically act to maximize their own utility. In addition, we

adopt a standard honest-majority assumption, namely that more than half of the participants behave honestly. This assumption ensures that the consensus-based verification of computation results and Shapley value submissions can be correctly enforced, as any falsified reports from a minority of participants cannot override the honest majority.
- **Smart Contract:** The smart contract are deployed to store task information, collect deposits and rewards, verify computational submissions, perform random audits, and automatically execute the final payment distribution.

3.2 Assumption

In this paper, we consider an honest client who publishes a multi-party computation task and compensates participants for computing the result. For the client, the goal is to get the correct result while minimizing the cost. The participants are unreliable and can engage in malicious behavior, such as submitting erroneous computation data or exiting prematurely. Note that in this paper, we do not distinguish between intentional and unintentional faults herein, as gathering reliable evidence is challenging. We assume that the participants are rational and selfish: each participant always acts in a way that maximizes its payoff, and is capable of thinking through all possible outcomes and choosing strategies which will result in the best possible outcome.

We assume that the smart contract is trusted and tamper-resistant, and that it correctly and faithfully executes all predefined rules. Given the security of the underlying cryptographic primitives, the smart contract is able to detect any malicious behavior by participants during the protocol execution. We further assume that producing an incorrect computation result incurs a lower cost than honest computation (e.g., by skipping the actual computation), which creates an incentive for participants to cheat. For analytical simplicity, we assume that a participant can generate an incorrect but plausible result at zero cost; although this is not free in practice, this assumption ensures that the derived lower bound on the required security deposit remains valid, as any positive cheating cost would only increase the loss incurred by dishonest participants. In addition, we assume the existence of a secure and trusted cryptocurrency that supports smart contracts, is universally accepted by all parties as a medium of exchange, and maintains a stable value throughout the lifetime of the contract. Finally, we assume that the underlying blockchain infrastructure is secure and that all smart contracts are executed correctly and without tampering.

4 Cryptographic Primitives

The proposed mechanism relies on the following cryptographic primitives to ensure security and verifiability.

4.1 Secure Multi-party Computation

Secure multi-party computation (MPC) is a cryptographic framework that enables multiple parties to jointly compute a function's results without revealing private inputs, thereby ensuring data privacy. Following the framework for MPC proposed by Zhang et al. [23], we define the formalization as follows:

Definition 1 (Secure Multi-Party Computation). *Given a computational problem t, a set of parties $P = P_1, P_2, \ldots, P_n$, where each party P_i has private inputs x_i, a secure multi-party computation protocol allows these parties to interactively compute $f(x_1, x_2, \ldots, x_n)$ without exposing their private inputs to one another.*

4.2 Hash Function

A hash function is a deterministic algorithm that maps an input of arbitrary length to a fixed-length hash value. It can be represented as $F : \{0,1\}^* \rightarrow \{0,1\}^n$ where n is the fixed output length. A secure hash function should satisfy the following properties:

- Arbitrary-length input: it accepts inputs of any length.
- Fixed-length output: it produces digests of a fixed length.
- Efficient computability: given any input x, the value $h(x)$ can be computed efficiently.
- One-wayness: given a hash value z, it is computationally infeasible to find any input x such that $h(x) = z$.
- Weak collision resistance: given an input x, it is computationally infeasible to find a distinct input $y(y \neq x)$ such that $h(y) = h(x)$.
- Strong collision resistance: for any efficient algorithm, the probability of finding two distinct inputs x and y such that $h(x) = h(y)$ is negligible.

5 Incentive Mechanism

This section presents the detailed design of the proposed incentive mechanism for secure multi-party computation. Our objective is to simultaneously deter malicious behavior and ensure a fair reward distribution that reflects participants' heterogeneous contributions. To this end, we first introduce the key variables and their relationships used throughout the mechanism. We then describe a non-cooperative game–based incentive mechanism that enforces honest computation through security deposits and random auditing. Building upon this foundation, we further incorporate a cooperative game–theoretic reward allocation scheme based on the Shapley value, which aligns individual incentives with actual contributions while remaining scalable through off-chain computation and on-chain verification.

5.1 Variables

Before introducing the specific incentive mechanisms, we first present the variables that will be mentioned later. Below are the variables we will use in the smart contracts. They are all non-negative.

- c: The true cost incurred by the participant for performing the computation honestly (e.g., computational power, time).
- w: The average reward paid by client C to each honest participant.
- w_0: The baseline reward guaranteed by the mechanism to each honest participant.
- d: The security deposit posted by the participant.
- p: The probability that the smart contract randomly audits participant P_i.
- R: The penalty duration (in rounds) for detected malicious behavior.

Based on the rationality assumptions of the participants and the basic requirements for incentive compatibility, the following relationships among the variables are assumed to hold throughout the mechanism design:

- $w_0 > c$: the participants do not accept under-paid jobs.
- $w \geq w_0$: In the final design, the reward is divided into two components: a baseline reward w_0, and an additional portion determined by each participant's contribution.

The variables w, w_0, and p can be set by the client. And variables R and d can be set by the smart contract. Meanwhile, the true cost of honest computation is determined by the specific computational task. The interdependencies among these variables, as well as the constraints required to ensure honest participation, will be discussed in detail in subsequent sections.

5.2 Non-cooperative Game Theory-Based Incentive Mechanism

The incentive mechanism based on non-cooperative dynamic games aims to prevent malicious behavior by participants in secure MPC. It incentivizes correct computation by requiring participants to post a bond. In secure MPC tasks, participants may choose to compute honestly or engage in malicious behavior, such as submitting erroneous computation data or exiting prematurely. The smart contract randomly samples participants' computation processes for verification. If a participant engages in malicious behavior and is detected, their deposit will be forfeited, and they will lose eligibility for reward distribution. Moreover, to further discourage repeated misbehavior, the detected participant will be prohibited from participating in subsequent computation tasks for the next R rounds. Otherwise, honest participants can retrieve their deposit and receive the task reward. By randomly auditing the computation processes of participants, the contract reduces the expected payoff for malicious behavior, thereby incentivizing computational participants to remain honest.

To make participants' computation process verifiable, each participant P_i uses a hash function. During the submission phase, P_i computes a hash value

$h_i = H(t_i)$, where t_i is the parameter representing its computation process. The smart contract implements a verification function V to audit participants. This function is used to verify the hash value h_i and computation process t_i submitted by participant P_i. This function computes $b = V(t_i, h_i)$, where $b = 1$ if and only if the computation process is correct, signifying an honest participant. The specifics of the smart contract are as follows:

- Step 1: The smart contract should be signed between a client (C) and n participants($P_1, P_2, ..., P_n$).
- Step 2: All participants P_i agree to perform a MPC $f(\boldsymbol{x}) = (y_1, y_2, \ldots, y_n)$, where $f(x)$ is chosen by C, and $\boldsymbol{x} = \{x_1, x_2, ..., x_n\}$ is privately held by P_i.
- Step 3: C and the participants agree on the deadlines $T_1 < T_2 < T_3$.
- Step 4: C agrees to pay w to each participant P_i for the correct and timely computation of $f(\boldsymbol{x})$. The total amount $n*w$ shall be transferred to the smart contract.
- Step 5: As a condition, each P_i must pay a deposit of amount d when signing the contract. The deposit will be held by the smart contract.
- Step 6: All participants P_i must pay the deposit before T_1. If any P_i fails to do so, the contract will terminate, and any deposit paid will be refunded.
- Step 7: P_i must upload the corresponding proof of the computational process parameter $h_i = H(t_i)$ to the smart contract before T_2.
- Step 8: Upon receiving computation results from all participants or when the deadline T_2 has passed, and until the payment time T_3, the smart contract will randomly select a number of participants P_i with probability p. The randomly selected participants are required to submit the computational process parameter t_i. Then smart contract will execute $b = V(t_i, h_i)$. If $b = 1$, P_i is deemed an honest participant. If $b = 0$, P_i is deemed a malicious participant.
- Step 9: When time T_3 is reached, the smart contract will automatically execute the payment process. It will first distribute the reward w and return the deposit d to each P_i not identified as a malicious participant. For participants detected as malicious, their deposit will be forfeited, and they will lose eligibility for reward distribution; additionally, they may be prohibited from participating in subsequent computation tasks for the next R rounds. And remaining funds will be returned to C.

The contract includes various deadlines ($T_1 < T_2 < T_3$). The purpose of these deadlines is to ensure timeliness and prevent funds from being locked if certain parties refuse to advance the process. The latter is particularly essential in smart contracts, as the balance in a contract is controlled by a program. The absence of such time-based state transitions could result in the permanent loss of access to locked assets.

5.3 Cooperative Game Theory-Based Incentive Mechanism

Previous subsection designed an incentive mechanism based on security deposits and random auditing to effectively deter malicious behavior in MPC. While this mechanism successfully discourages dishonest behavior, it employs a fixed reward distribution that fails to adequately capture participants' heterogeneous contributions. To further enhance both fairness and efficiency, and to better align individual rewards with actual contributions while addressing the free-rider problem, we introduce an enhanced reward distribution mechanism based on the Shapley value [16]. To reduce computational and on-chain overhead in large-scale settings, Shapley values are computed off-chain using a Monte Carlo approximation, while a smart contract–generated random seed deterministically fixes the sampling order, enabling consistent contribution evaluation and enforceable reward settlement.

The Shapley value is a solution concept in cooperative game theory that fairly distributes the total gains among participants based on their average marginal contributions. By replacing the original flat payment model, this approach aims to motivate participants not only to behave honestly but also to contribute high-quality data and computation to the collaborative task.

We begin by formalizing the calculation of the Shapley value. Consider a set of participants $N = \{P_1, P_2, \ldots, P_n\}$. Any non-empty subset $S \subseteq N$ is referred to as a coalition of participants. For each coalition S, a characteristic function $v(S)$ quantifies the total value of the computational result achieved by members of S. The Shapley value provides a principled way to assign a fair share of the total value to each participant, based on their marginal contribution to all possible coalitions. Formally, it is defined as:

$$\phi_i = \sum_{S \subseteq N \setminus \{P_i\}} \frac{|S|!(n - |S| - 1)!}{n!} (v(S \cup \{P_i\}) - v(S)) \tag{1}$$

where S represents any subset of $N \setminus \{P_i\}$, meaning it is any group of players that does not include participant P_i. $|S|$ denotes the cardinality of coalition S. The Shapley value satisfies several desirable properties that collectively ensure a fair allocation of rewards among rational participants.

The definition of the characteristic function v depends on the specific computational task and must accurately capture the value contributed by any subset of participants. In tasks assessing correctness, a binary function is frequently adopted, assigning $v(S) = 1$ or a correct output and 0 otherwise. For tasks with quantitative or continuous outcomes, an accuracy-based characteristic function is more appropriate; in such case, $v(S)$ can be defined as inversely proportional to the deviation between the subset's result and a reference.

As a concrete example, in a use case where secure MPC is used to aggregate distributed learning models, the model's prediction accuracy on a validation set can serve as the characteristic function v. Here, $v(S)$ is defined as the accuracy achieved by a model trained exclusively on the data held by the subset S of participants, evaluated on a standardized validation set. The Shapley value for a participant P_i is then calculated based on their marginal contribution to this accuracy across all possible subsets. Participants providing high-quality or complementary data will yield greater improvements in $v(S)$, and consequently, higher Shapley values. This formulation naturally incentivizes both data quality and data diversity, which are critical in collaborative learning environments.

While the Shapley value provides a principled and fair method for allocating rewards, its exact computation requires evaluating all 2^n coalitions, which becomes infeasible as the number of participants increases. Moreover, executing such computationally intensive operations directly on smart contracts would incur prohibitive gas costs and high latency due to the resource constraints of the blockchain. To ensure that the proposed incentive mechanism remains scalable and cost-effective, we adopt an off-chain computation strategy combined with an efficient Monte Carlo-based approximation algorithm [1]. In this approach, the complex calculation of Shapley values is offloaded to off-chain entities, thereby avoiding the high overhead of on-chain execution. This method has been widely used in cooperative game theory and provides a practical trade-off between accuracy and computational efficiency.

Instead of exhaustively enumerating all possible subsets, the algorithm samples m random permutations of the participants and computes each participant's marginal contribution within each permutation. The approximate Shapley value is obtained by averaging these marginal contributions over all sampled permutations. This reduces computational complexity from $O(2^n)$ to $O(mn)$, where m is the number of sampled permutations. In practice, a moderate value of m is sufficient to obtain stable and reliable approximations. Algorithm 1 summarizes the detailed procedure of the Monte Carlo–based Shapley value approximation. The output $\hat{\phi}_i$ is subsequently used by the smart contract for reward allocation.

Algorithm 1: Monte Carlo Approximation of Shapley Value

```
Input: Participant set N = {1, ..., n}, characteristic function v(·), number of
       samples m
Output: Approximate Shapley values φ̂_i for all i ∈ N
Initialize φ̂_i = 0 for all i ;
for k = 1 to m do
    Sample a random permutation π of players in N ;
    S ← ∅ ;
    for i in order of π do
        Compute marginal contribution:
            Δ_i = v(S ∪ {i}) − v(S) ;
        φ̂_i ← φ̂_i + Δ_i ;
        S ← S ∪ {i} ;
Normalize: φ̂_i ← φ̂_i/m for all i ;
return φ̂_i for all i ;
```

Although the Monte Carlo approximation significantly reduces computational complexity, standard random sampling leads to non-deterministic results across different nodes. To ensure the correctness and consistency of the contribution assessment, we propose a seed-driven deterministic consensus process.

The smart contract generates a verifiable random seed s_{rand}. This seed is broadcast to all participants to initialize their local pseudo-random number generators (PRNG). Consequently, all honest participants executing Algorithm 1 with the same seed s_{rand} and the same characteristic function $v(\cdot)$ will sample an identical sequence of permutations, thereby producing an identical vector of Shapley values $\hat{\boldsymbol{\phi}} = (\hat{\phi}_1, \hat{\phi}_2, \ldots, \hat{\phi}_n)$.

Instead of performing the calculation, the smart contract acts as an aggregator and verifier. Participants calculate the Shapley values off-chain and submit their results to the blockchain. The smart contract then aggregates these submissions and determines the final reward allocation based on the consensus of the results (e.g., the majority result). This redundancy-based verification ensures that as long as the majority of participants are rational and honest, the correct contribution values are enforced without executing the heavy Monte Carlo logic on-chain.

The efficiency property of the Shapley value states that the total contribution must meet the following condition:

$$\sum_{i \in N} \phi_i = v(N) \tag{2}$$

Consequently, each participant's proportional contribution to the collective outcome is given by $\frac{\phi_i}{v(N)}$. In order to ensure that the expected payoff for honest strategies is higher (the specific reasons will be discussed in detail later), the mechanism guarantees every honest participant a baseline reward w_0, with the remaining reward distributed according to the Shapley value. Thus, for each honest participant P_i, the final reward is calculated as:

$$w_i = w_0 + n \cdot (w - w_0) \cdot \frac{\hat{\phi}_i}{v(N)} \tag{3}$$

where $\hat{\phi}_i$ denotes the Monte Carlo approximation of the Shapley value computed off-chain.

The incentive mechanism based on the Shapley value must be integrated into the smart contract's payment process. This contract is an enhancement of the non-cooperative game-based incentive mechanism contract. The contract specifically improved the reward distribution mechanism. The specifics of the smart contract are as follows:

- Step 1-Step 8: The contents of these steps are identical to those in the previous contract.
- step 9: The smart contract publishes a global random seed s_{rand}. Each participant P_i downloads s_{rand} and executes the Monte Carlo Shapley value approximation (Algorithm 1) off-chain locally. This process yields a contribution vector $\hat{\boldsymbol{\phi}}^{(i)}$, representing P_i's calculation of everyone's contribution.
- step 10: Before the payment deadline T_3, all participants must upload their calculated results $\hat{\boldsymbol{\phi}}^{(i)}$ to the smart contract. The contract then performs a

consistency check by grouping identical submissions, identifies the vector $\hat{\phi}$ submitted by the majority as the valid consensus result.

- Step 11: At time T_3, the smart contract will automatically execute the payment process. It first refunds the security deposit d to all participants who have not been identified as malicious. For participants detected as malicious, their deposits will be forfeited. After that, the contract allocates the reward w_i to each participant P_i according to the incentive mechanism.

6 Game Theory Analysis and Security Analysis

This section analyzes the proposed incentive mechanism from both game-theoretic and security perspectives. We derive the conditions under which rational participants are incentivized to behave honestly and show that the mechanism achieves stable equilibria. We further examine the security properties of the protocol and demonstrate its robustness against strategic manipulation and malicious behavior under the stated assumptions.

6.1 Game Theory Analysis

We will first analyze the incentive mechanism based on non-cooperative game theory to determine the necessary parameter conditions. Following that, we will examine the cooperative game incentive mechanism based on the Shapley value, clarifying how this approach ensures participants remain honest and actively engage in computational tasks.

To analyze the non-cooperative game, we first construct a symmetric non-cooperative game model. We assume that all participants P_i are rational, aiming to maximize their own expected utility. In the game, since all n participants are symmetric in the mechanism, we can focus on analyzing the decisions of a single participant P_i, assuming the behavior of the other $n-1$ participants is given. Participant P_i is considered to have two pure strategies: to compute honestly (S_h) or to behave maliciously (S_m). The strategy S_h involves correctly performing the computation and submitting the required proofs, while S_m encompasses any malicious act that would be detected by a successful audit, with consequences unified as a penalty. The participant's payoff depends on their own strategy and the outcome of the smart contract's random audit.

Based on this setup, we define the expected payoff for participant P_i under each strategy. The expected payoff under each strategy are shown in Table 1.

When the participant P_i chooses an honest strategy S_h, his computation is always correct, whether they are audited or not. As a result, his deposit is not confiscated. The honest participants pay a cost c for computing. Therefore, the expected payoff for the honest participant $E(S_h) = w - c$.

The payoff for the malicious strategy S_m is more complex, as it depends on the audit outcome. If audited and caught (with probability p), the participant loses their deposit and any reward, resulting in a payoff of $A = -d$. Given that

Table 1. Expected Payoff Under Different Strategy

Strategy	Audited	Not Audited
Honest	$w - c$	$w - c$
Malicious	$-d - R \cdot (w - c)$	w

the participant is excluded from participation and cannot earn task benefits for the subsequent R rounds, they will incur a long-term loss of benefits amounting to $R \cdot (w - c)$. If not caught (with probability $1 - p$), they get their deposit back and may still receive the reward if the task succeeds, leading to a payoff of $B = w$. The expected payoff for the malicious participant is therefore $E(S_m) = p \cdot (-d) - p \cdot R \cdot (w - c) + (1 - p) \cdot w$.

The participant compares the expected payoff of honest and malicious strategies to determine the optimal strategy. In order to guide all participants toward honest computation, it must be satisfied that $E(S_h) > E(S_m)$. As a result, the following inequality must hold:

$$d > c \cdot R - (R + 1) \cdot w + \frac{c}{p} \tag{4}$$

The previous analysis focuses on a single participant's decision, assuming others' behavior is given. However, in a multi-participant setting, multiple equilibria might exist. The condition (4) supports the existence of a desirable "all-honest" Nash Equilibrium, where no single participant can gain by unilaterally deviating to malicious behavior.

Analyzing the above conditions, it can be observed that the key to guiding participants to choose an honest strategy lies in setting appropriate parameters: audit rate, reward, and deposits. The audit rate p and reward w are set at the client's discretion. Crucially, the deposit d is not a fixed or client-defined value; instead, it is automatically determined by the smart contract based on the other parameters to satisfy the condition for honest participation. The contract can be executed if and only if the deposit meets the requirement (4). Clients are responsible for the costs associated with the audit operations defined in the contract, which incentivizes them to prudently set a reasonable audit rate.

The mechanism integrates several design features that help reinforce the "all-honest" equilibrium. First, the requirement of an upfront deposit creates a sunk cost, encouraging participants to commit more firmly to the contract from the very beginning. Second, the client's act of locking the total reward in the contract in advance serves as a credible commitment to the task's viability. This enhances participants' confidence in the fair execution of the system and ensures that honest efforts will be duly rewarded, thereby increasing the attractiveness of the honest strategy. Third, malicious participants are banned from participating in tasks for the next R rounds, which directly reduces their long-term payoff. This exclusion mechanism raises the opportunity cost of dishonest behavior, further steering participants toward sustained honest participation.

From the perspective of dynamic game theory, the proposed incentive mechanism can be modeled as a repeated non-cooperative game. It constitutes a dynamic game of imperfect information. In each round, participants choose between two strategies: honest computation or malicious behavior. The outcome of one round influences future payoffs because detected malicious participants are penalized not only by losing their deposits and rewards but also by being excluded from the next R rounds. This intertemporal dependency transforms the static interaction into a dynamic game with history-dependent strategies. Rational participants maximize their long-term utility by comparing the discounted expected payoffs of honest and dishonest behaviors. Since the expected loss from being detected outweighs the short-term gains from cheating, the subgame perfect equilibrium of the repeated game leads participants to adopt honest computation as their optimal strategy. Therefore, the dynamic nature of the mechanism effectively sustains cooperation and deters persistent malicious behavior in secure MPC environments.

Then, we enhance the reward distribution mechanism within the existing incentive framework to assess and reward participants' contributions fairly, aligning with the principles of cooperative game theory. We analyze this mechanism using the concepts of cooperative game theory. The Shapley value is a solution concept in cooperative game theory that fairly distributes the total gains among participants based on their average marginal contributions across all possible coalitions. This method is widely applied due to its unique satisfaction of four key fairness axioms:

- Efficiency: The total value generated by the coalition is fully distributed among all players.
- Symmetry: Players who contribute equally to all coalitions receive the same allocation.
- Dummy Player: A player who adds no additional value to any coalition receives zero.
- Additivity: For two games combined, a player's allocation is the sum of their allocations in each game separately.

By the efficiency property of the Shapley value, the total contributions satisfy (2). As the reward is calculated as (3), we can find that

$$\sum_{i \in N} w_i = n \cdot w_0 + n \cdot (w - w_0) \cdot \frac{\sum_{i \in N} \hat{\phi}_i}{v(N)} \approx n \cdot w \tag{5}$$

In the Shapley value-based reward allocation mechanism, each honest participant is guaranteed a baseline reward w_0. Since the smart contract must set a single deposit value d prior to knowing exact contribution-dependent bonuses, it is prudent to use the minimum guaranteed per-round payment when deriving a conservative bound. Replacing w in (4) by the baseline w_0 (note $w \geq w_0$) produces a stricter requirement

$$d > c \cdot R - (R + 1) \cdot w_0 + \frac{c}{p}, \tag{6}$$

This mechanism treats symmetric players equally, ignores non-contributors, fully distributes the total value fully, and behaves consistently under the combination of games, making it a principled and unique fair allocation.

6.2 Security Analysis

To address MPC security issues, we propose a dynamic game theory-based incentive mechanism with cryptographic primitives, and we implement our mechanism by smart contracts. We analyze the security properties of the proposed mechanism and prove that the mechanism can achieve our security goals.

Proposition 1. *A participant cannot cause the contract to fall into a deadlock by refusing, delaying, or withdrawing from performance.*

Smart contracts and MPC protocols commonly depend on multiple parties to execute ordered steps within predefined time windows. By enforcing a sequence of deadlines ($T_1 < T_2 < T_3$), the contract preserves liveness and prevents funds or state from becoming permanently locked, ensuring the protocol can progress according to schedule even if certain parties fail to fulfill their obligations.

Proposition 2. *A participant cannot upload a forged parameter of the computation process that passes verification.*

By the collision-resistance of the hash function, it is infeasible for any participant to find a distinct parameter t' such that $H(t') = H(t)$. Consequently, if a participant selected for audit submits a forged computation parameter t', the smart contract will be able to detect the forgery during verification.

Proposition 3. *No single participant or minority colluding coalition can successfully enforce a falsified Shapley value vector and obtain undue rewards.*

By the majority consensus mechanism and the use of a verifiable random seed in the Shapley value computation process, it is computationally infeasible for a minority coalition to generate and submit a falsified Shapley value vector that aligns with the honest majority's calculation. Specifically, the smart contract generates and broadcasts a global random seed s_{rand} to all participants, ensuring that all honest participants executing the Monte Carlo approximation algorithm (Algorithm 1) with the same seed and characteristic function produce identical Shapley value vectors. During the submission phase, the contract performs a consistency check by grouping identical submissions and identifies the vector $\hat{\phi}$ submitted by the majority as the valid consensus result. Consequently, if a single participant or a minority coalition attempts to submit a falsified vector, it will not match the majority's output and will be rejected by the smart contract, thereby preventing the allocation of undue rewards and ensuring that only honest contributions are compensated.

7 Conclusions

This paper proposes a blockchain-based dynamic game-theoretic incentive mechanism for privacy-preserving computation, aiming to address the limitations of traditional MPC systems in motivating honest participation. The proposed framework integrates both non-cooperative and cooperative game theories to achieve rational stability and fairness simultaneously. Specifically, a deposit–audit mechanism is introduced to make honest participation a Nash equilibrium and deter malicious behavior through a deposit–audit mechanism. While this approach reduces reliance on expensive cryptographic assumptions and ensures rational stability, it alone cannot guarantee fair reward distribution. To address this, cooperative game theory is incorporated via a Shapley value–based reward scheme, aligning each participant's payoff with their actual contribution. Off-chain Monte Carlo approximation of Shapley values is enabled through a seed-driven deterministic consensus process, ensuring verifiability without opening opportunities for manipulation. All incentive and verification processes are automated via smart contracts, providing transparency, trustless execution, and a joint achievement of economic and cryptographic security.

Nevertheless, several challenges remain. The current model assumes an honest majority, which introduces security risks under sybil attacks or when adversaries coordinate large-scale manipulation of off-chain computation. In future work, we plan to explore integration with advanced consensus protocols and machine learning-based anomaly detection for reputation systems to further enhance both efficiency and security in real-world deployments.

Acknowledgments. This work is supported by National Key Research and Development Program of China (Grant No. 2023YFB2704000), Guangxi Key Research and Development Project (Guike AB25069120), Beijing Natural Science Foundation (Grant No. L251002, L254058), National Natural Science Foundation of China (Grant No. 62372040, 62572045, 62272040), Natural Science Foundation of Beijing, China (Grant No. 4254086), and Beijing Institute of Technology Research Fund Program for Young Scholars.

References

1. Castro, J., Gómez, D., Tejada, J.: Polynomial calculation of the Shapley value based on sampling. Comput. Oper. Res. **36**(5), 1726–1730 (2009). https://doi.org/10.1016/j.cor.2008.04.004. https://www.sciencedirect.com/science/article/pii/S0305054808000804. Selected papers presented at the Tenth International Symposium on Locational Decisions (ISOLDE X)
2. Chen, J., Yan, H., Liu, Z., Zhang, M., Xiong, H., Yu, S.: When federated learning meets privacy-preserving computation. ACM Comput. Surv. **56**(12), 1–36 (2024)
3. Dong, C., Wang, Y., Aldweesh, A., McCorry, P., Van Moorsel, A.: Betrayal, distrust, and rationality: smart counter-collusion contracts for verifiable cloud computing. In: Proceedings of the 2017 ACM SIGSAC Conference on Computer and Communications Security, pp. 211–227 (2017)

4. Facchinei, F., Kanzow, C.: Generalized Nash equilibrium problems. Ann. Oper. Res. **175**(1), 177–211 (2010)
5. Gamiz, I., Regueiro, C., Lage, O., Jacob, E., Astorga, J.: Challenges and future research directions in secure multi-party computation for resource-constrained devices and large-scale computations. Int. J. Inf. Secur. **24**(1), 27 (2025)
6. He, X., et al.: A Shapley value-based incentive mechanism in collaborative edge computing. In: 2021 IEEE Global Communications Conference (GLOBECOM), pp. 1–7. IEEE (2021)
7. He, Y., et al.: A game theory-based incentive mechanism for collaborative security of federated learning in energy blockchain environment. IEEE Internet Things J. **10**(24), 21294–21308 (2023)
8. Hewa Kaluannakkage, C.A., Buyya, R.: Incentive-based federated learning. arXiv e-prints pp. arXiv–2510 (2025)
9. Lashkari, B., Musilek, P.: A comprehensive review of blockchain consensus mechanisms. IEEE Access **9**, 43620–43652 (2021)
10. Li, T., Sethi, S.P.: A review of dynamic Stackelberg game models. Discrete Continuous Dyn. Syst.-Ser. B **22**(1) (2017)
11. Luo, G., et al.: EdgeCooper: network-aware cooperative lidar perception for enhanced vehicular awareness. IEEE J. Sel. Areas Commun. **42**(1), 207–222 (2024). https://doi.org/10.1109/JSAC.2023.3322764
12. Luo, G., et al.: Software-defined cooperative data sharing in edge computing assisted 5G-VANET. IEEE Trans. Mob. Comput. **20**(3), 1212–1229 (2021). https://doi.org/10.1109/TMC.2019.2953163
13. Murhekar, A., Yuan, Z., Ray Chaudhury, B., Li, B., Mehta, R.: Incentives in federated learning: equilibria, dynamics, and mechanisms for welfare maximization. In: Advances in Neural Information Processing Systems, vol. 36, pp. 17811–17831 (2023)
14. Oluwafemi, B.: Privacy-preserving computation (homomorphic encryption, MPC). J. Contemp. Educ. Res. **7**, 111–122 (2025)
15. Saha, S., Hota, A., Chattopadhyay, A.K., Nag, A., Nandi, S.: A multifaceted survey on privacy preservation of federated learning: progress, challenges, and opportunities. Artif. Intell. Rev. **57**(7), 184 (2024)
16. Shapley, L.S.: A value for N-person games. In: Contributions to the Theory of Games, vol. II, pp. 307–317. Princeton University Press (1953)
17. Sun, Q., et al.: ShapleyFL: robust federated learning based on Shapley value. In: Proceedings of the 29th ACM SIGKDD Conference on Knowledge Discovery and Data Mining, pp. 2096–2108 (2023)
18. Wang, C., Peeta, S.: Incentive mechanism for privacy-preserving collaborative routing using secure multi-party computation and blockchain. Sensors **24**(2), 542 (2024)
19. Xiaolin, L., et al.: POTA: a pipelined oblivious transfer acceleration architecture for secure multi-party computation. IACR Trans. Cryptographic Hardware Embedded Syst. **2025**(3), 262–292 (2025)
20. Xie, Q., et al.: Efficiency optimization techniques in privacy-preserving federated learning with homomorphic encryption: a brief survey. IEEE Internet Things J. **11**(14), 24569–24580 (2024)
21. Yang, Y.T., Zhang, T., Zhu, Q.: A game-theoretic analysis of auditing differentially private algorithms with epistemically disparate herd. In: International Conference on Decision and Game Theory for Security, pp. 349–368. Springer (2023)
22. Zhang, L., Li, C., Chen, L., Pan, B.: Predicting nodes' performance in peer-to-peer network based on game theory. Int. J. Inf. Syst. Manag. **17** (2023)

23. Zhang, S., Qu, G., Zhang, Z., Huang, M., Jin, H., Yang, L.: Efficient and secure multi-party computation protocol supporting deep learning. Cybersecurity **8**(1), 46 (2025)
24. Zhang, X., Fan, L., Wang, S., Li, W., Chen, K., Yang, Q.: A game-theoretic framework for privacy-preserving federated learning. ACM Trans. Intell. Syst. Technol. **15**(3), 1–35 (2024)

Author Index

C
Copeland, Adam 75

D
Dong, Tianran 163
Dong, Zeming 40

F
Fan, Qing 1

G
Guo, Yuejun 40

H
Hu, Manyue 1

J
Jia, Xiaoteng 142
Jia, Zhuliang 25

L
Li, Youqi 177
Lu, Rongxing 25

M
Mamun, Mohammad 25
Meng, Weizhi 75

P
Pan, Sicheng 177
Pieprzyk, Josef 1

R
Ray, Suprio 25

S
Saad, Ahmed Mohamed Saad Emam 119
Sun, Haoyu 163
Sun, Luyi 97
Sun, Shi-Feng 1

T
Tang, Jiayi 177
Tang, Qiang 40

W
Wang, Huaxiong 1
Wang, Licheng 177
Wang, Zenghui 59

Y
Yang, Bian 97
Yuan, Yanli 177

Z
Zhang, Songnian 142
Zhou, Xinyu 163
Zhu, Liehuang 1, 177
Zuo, Cong 1, 177

W. Li et al. (Eds.): EISA 2025, CCIS 2897, p. 197, 2026.
https://doi.org/10.1007/978-3-032-21177-4

The manufacturer's authorised representative in the EU is Springer Nature Customer Service Centre GmbH, Europaplatz 3, 69115 Heidelberg, Germany. If you have any concerns regarding our products, please contact ProductSafety@springernature.com

Printed and bound by CPI Group (UK) Ltd, Croydon, CR0 4YY

07/07/2026

02160913-0003